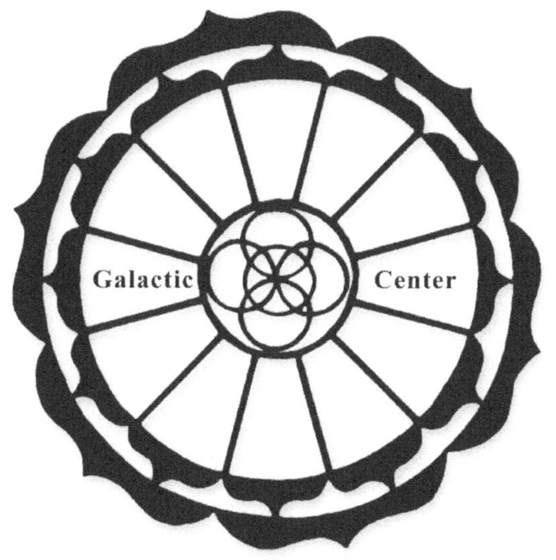

To read the stars is to read the messages of the Universe.

Joni Patry

Secrets of Prediction

World and Personal Cycles Using Vedic Astrology

Joni Patry

Editor: Roxana Muise and Enjoynew.com
Cover design and publishing services: http://enjoynew.com/en/
service@enjoynew.com

Photo credits:
A-bomb photo by Charles Levy, U.S. Army
JFK limousine photo by Walter Sisco
WTC south tower photo by Robert J. Fisch., Creative Commons Attribution-Share Alike, 2.0 Generic license

Published in Dallas, Texas by Galactic Center
http://www.Galacticcenter.org/
4333 Willow Grove Rd
Dallas, TX 75220
Printed in the United States of America
First Edition

ISBN-13: 978-0692413418
ISBN-10: 0692413413

I Dedicate this Book to My Family,

my husband Daniel and children, Christian, Preston, and Austin.

Thank you for all your reassurance, support and always believing in me.

Daniel, my life long partner, for your emotional encouragement.

Christian, for the many late nights of typing my columns and inspiration to never give up.

Preston, for your dedication and work recording my classes throughout the years.

Austin, for your amazing talent in filming and the production of my videos.

Table of Contents
Secrets of Prediction

Part I
Life of a Vedic Astrologer
Joni Patry

Part II
Prediction of World Events

Part III

How to Predict World Events

Part IV
How to Make Personal Predictions
The Birth Chart

Part V
The Kennedy Family
The Power of Prediction

Part I

The Life of a Vedic Astrologer Joni Patry

Chapter One

The Beginning

It was November 21, 1963. I was 8 years old watching our black and white television set as Jeane Dixon came on the evening news making a stark prediction. I can remember it as if it was yesterday, for it made a lasting impression. She stated clearly that if President Kennedy came to Dallas, Texas he would be assassinated.

This moved me deeply for I was born and raised in Dallas, and my mother adored President Kennedy.

When I went to school the next day, every classroom had television sets to watch the news while Kennedy visited Dallas. My mother had taken my two older sisters, Marsha and Carol out of school to greet the President at Dallas Love Field Airport. In old video clips you can see him walk off the plane and see my mother and sisters in the crowds greeting him.

But then the unthinkable happened as the crowds followed him to downtown Dallas. This whole event was close to home for me. Dr. Malcolm Perry, the doctor who tried to save President Kennedy lived across the street from your author on Willow Grove Rd.

I have to believe that this is very valuable information that can help us in many ways. I must say my fascination for prediction began at this time. I began reading books on parapsychology, metaphysics, psychics and astrology.

Many skeptics constantly state that astrologers and psychics never make real predictions before they happen, but only state things after the fact. In reality they are more concerned with disbelieving and debunking prophecy. I even read current skeptics who claim Jeane Dixon made a vague forecast, and that she never made the prediction about Kennedy; but I, myself saw her on the news desperately making this warning, hoping that Kennedy would change his mind.

Skeptics have never worked with prediction or experienced the gift of astrology. It can help in so many ways; it could possibly have saved President Kennedy if he had heeded the warning from Jeane Dixon.

From my life experience, astrology does actually work, and you will see the proof.

Of course it is fair to say there are a lot of bad psychics and astrologers out there, for there are no regulations, and no regulating body. Where there is easy money to be made all the charlatans and fakes come out of the woodwork. And those fakes give the true art of astrology a bad name.

Furthermore, there are many religions and beliefs that put astrology in a bad light. Nothing they are led to believe about astrology is based on facts. And unfortunately this has somehow consumed the minds of most people in America.

Miscommunications and ignorance about astrology has been passed down through the ages. It is believed that the religious leaders centuries ago didn't want the people to have power so they indicated to the masses that astrology was evil and satanic. Meanwhile the popes continued to use astrologers, and the Vatican still has the largest archive of astrology books. I am here to inform you that astrology has nothing to do with evil or the devil; nothing could be further than the truth. In fact most religious texts have references to the stars.

To be able to read and interpret the information in the stars gives wisdom and guidance. In the bible the three wise men follow a star that indicated the birth of Christ. It is a known fact that the three wise men were astrologers. They are called "Magi" which translates into "astrologer." The fact that they are called "Wise Men" insinuates that they were wise for following the stars. Astrology gives wisdom, and this has been my experience. Scientifically, astrology is the study of cycles.

Historically it is a well-known fact that many presidents, kings, and the rich and famous used astrologers. The men who built America built Washington DC in accordance to the stars. Stonehenge and the pyramids, both Egyptian and Mayan were built according to the stars. President Reagan and his wife Nancy used astrologer Joan Quigley. President Franklin D. Roosevelt, President Eisenhower, President Nixon all used Jeane Dixon. But I truly wished that President John F. Kennedy had heeded advice from Jeane Dixon. Adolph Hitler, Winston Churchill, Einstein, Carl G. Jung, Princess Diana, and Edgar Cayce to name a few, used astrologers.

It is a well-known fact that J.P. Morgan's astrologer Evangeline Adams told Morgan not to get on the Titanic. He listened, as he had the utmost respect for astrology. Another quote by Morgan is "Anyone can be a millionaire, but to become a billionaire, you need an astrologer." This is based on the fact that many people who work in the stock market use astrology. Donald Reagan, formerly Ronald Reagan's Chief of Staff explains, "It's common knowledge that a large percentage of Wall Street brokers use astrology."

Unbeknown to many, President Theodore Roosevelt kept his horoscope mounted on a chessboard in the oval office. When asked about it he would reply, "I always keep my weather eye on the opposition of my seventh house Moon to my first house Mars."

Chapter 2

You are an Astrologer?

There is nothing more frustrating than trying to convince skeptics that astrology works, or to religious fanatics that it is not of the devil.

It is like I am trying to undo centuries of damage and the ignorance that has been embedded in their minds. It is useless in many cases, because to get someone to understand what you are saying you have to speak to an open mind. I am speaking to closed minds that cannot hear what I am saying, and for some reason they don't want to hear. It is already a part of their impenetrable belief system. They have always heard astrology is silly nonsense but they really have no understanding of what it is based on. To religious fanatics it shakes the foundation that their lives are built on. But again they are unaware of what it is and are not open to listening to a different view.

I live in a conservative part of Texas and when people ask what I do, I sometimes cringe as I tell them, "I am an astrologer." The responses vary, but for the most part they look puzzled, usually asking me "Do you really believe in that?"

How do I respond to that? Do I try to explain myself to someone who already has me sized up as a quack, a weirdo or a flake?

It is usually pointless because they really don't care what I say once the cat is out of the bag about me. Then they generally lean away and find conversation with others. A few think they heard astronomer instead of astrologer and sometimes don't know the difference. Then there are those who jump in and ask "Do you believe in Jesus? Are you Christian?" This is the worse conversation because they believe you are a devil worshiper. And nothing you have to say has any validity, as they are completely closed off. Another response is actually a laugh out loud, for their views as a scientist are repulsed by the thought of something as ridiculous as believing in astrology. Their only understanding is based on the sun sign columns in the newspapers. And yes, they are so broad they cannot do any justice to real astrology. So I do understand where they are coming from but none of these usual suspects I meet give an open ear to listen to what astrology is actually all about. And then again astrology is so complex, it usually goes right over their heads.

Then I get those who think astrology is fun and just want to know about their sign, and when they will meet someone or win the lottery. Those types usually stick their hand out for me to read their palm. Here I go again trying to explain the unexplainable to a superficial audience. When I get into the reality of what astrology is and that their sign is really a different one than that with which they are familiar their eyes become glazed over and I totally lose their interest. They want me to tell them their whole life by just knowing their sign. They don't care about what astrology is, it is just about them, and they think that I can start having visions about their future.

When people come to my beginning classes on astrology they are excited to take this fun class that will tell them all about themselves, such as when they will meet someone to marry and find wealth and money. But when they realize they have to study and that astrology is an in-depth subject using math, they drop out of class.

It seems Astrology is a dying science with all the misrepresentation. I had a newscaster call to debunk astrology. He went into his spill that we are not really the signs we think we are so how can astrology have any validity? But when I explained that I do Vedic astrology, which takes into account the shift of the signs he hung up on me. He didn't expect me to be knowledgeable about this and couldn't make me look stupid by attempting to debunk astrology. I don't know why I put myself through this.

But as time goes on I no longer explain myself to people who don't want to learn and grow. I speak now to only those who want to know my vast knowledge of astrology. As my son Christian has repeatedly told me, "Mother, don't cast pearls to the swine." Perfectly said Christian! But it is still hard to feel misunderstood.

Chapter 3

Early Years

As a child my mother had books on astrology lying around the house. She had the same sun sign as I have, "Scorpio." So I began reading the books out of curiosity. I thought the books really spoke to me as to certain personality characteristics.

My mother and I were very psychic and had unexplainable events happen that lead us to believe in metaphysics. Before someone in the family died my mother would have an ominous dream of her father walking down the hall of our house dressed in a black robe. I had prophetic dreams as well but they became more vivid as I got older. Some believe physic gifts or talents are genetic.

In the late 1960s astrology became vogue through Jeane Dixon, Sidney Omar and Linda Goodman. Subjects like reincarnation were of fascination and the trend towards yoga and meditation became hip. Even the Beatles took a trip to India to learn more of meditation, karma, and spirituality. Most everyone knew his or her sun sign, and mind-altering drugs created a new generation seeking a world beyond the conservative status flow. I still get chills when I hear the song by the 5th Dimension, "The Dawning of the Age of Aquarius." Even Kenny Loggins from the rock group Loggins and Messina sang of his son's birth chart in the song "Danny's Song." I actually met his wife on a flight who told me she was an astrologer and had helped him with the lyrics.

When I was in 7th grade around age 13, I began seriously reading Linda Goodman's "Sun Signs." And mentally tracked the qualities of everyone I met through their sun sign. But then I began to understand that there was more to this than just a sun sign.

I came to realize that we have all the planets in signs not just the Sun and that these planets comprised a chart much like a life map. This was fascinating, and I set out to learn more on this fascinating subject. I bought my first real books on astrology before going off to college: The Basics of Astrology, a three book series on chart calculation and analysis. I struggled to learn on my own, but it was all too confusing.

Chapter 4

College

In 1974, I was off to college at the University of Texas, in Austin. Austin was a really hip place to be in the 1970s and the hippy movement was still in full swing. As I went to "the Castilian", my dorm in Austin I had my box of books that consisted of my precious gems: The Basics of Astrology, Ruth Montgomery, Jeane Dixon, Sidney Omar, Jess Stern and Edgar Cayce.

This was my main interest but absolutely no one shared my interest in the dorm. I was called a witch and devil worshiper. My interest really set me apart from all the students with whom I was trying to get along. I always felt different, and was never accepted because of this. But this was who I was and the arguments and discussions were endless and fruitless.

One day, driving down Guadalupe Street (I will never forget exactly where I was) they announced on the car radio: "Astrology classes are beginning next week". It gave a time, and location. I couldn't believe it! I was thrilled!

I was eagerly there on the beginning night, finally finding my clan who I could talk about astrology. I had so many questions and could finally get some answers. Finally someone spoke my language. While my dorm roommates were involved in college sororities I was attending astrology classes with a group of hippies! Attending this class, I had painted nails, a Farrah Fawcett hairdo, and wore a dress with matching purse and shoes. I definitely stuck out like a sore thumb with the natural hippie group -- vegetarianism, marijuana and carrot juice.But my teacher was incredibly brilliant. He gave us tests, and I learned real astrology from chart construction using logarithms, an ephemeris, and looked up time changes in the world. I stuck with him till I graduated and even flew back for classes once I began working for the airlines.

I began doing charts professionally, and teaching in the late 1970s.

Chapter 5

Working for the Airlines

For the first part of my college career I was a studio art major, but then I changed to psychology to support my fascination with parapsychology. The school of psychology was rather regimented and not so much a part of my interests. So I thought of taking a break after receiving my degree in psychology before going to graduate school to become a psychologist. The perfect job for this seemed to be a stewardess (now called a flight attendant). I thought I would do this for a couple of years, but as many who know about working for the airlines, you somehow get hooked and can't quit, for I am still employed there after 35 years.

I loved the aspect of flying and traveling. It was a job and paid the bills. It also allowed me to practice and study astrology for you have a lot of time off. This was not the usual 9-5 job. So I had my practice as an astrologer and also worked as a flight attendant. But usually when people ask what I do, my answer was flight attendant to avoid the usual confrontation.

As a flight attendant I would feel around for peoples' birth information, for nothing was more interesting than figuring out their signs. I got really good and could usually tell them their Sun Sign to their amazement. Then at times I would begin drawing charts out on napkins telling them their futures. I became well known amongst the flight attendants at the airlines as someone who could see the future.

Through out the years I felt my job with the airlines was a part time job and my astrology was my full time job.

While flying, I couldn't help but use my knowledge to help a few flight attendants along the way. And I have many stories.

While flying I sometimes tell other flight attendants that I am an astrologer. Most of the time, I keep this to myself for it goes two ways. One is they believe I am of the devil if they are the born again Christian type, or they bug me to tell them when they will meet a rich man. They may not realize I charge a fee for my information and don't usually give it out free. Therefore I am quiet unless I know them really well or I think they may actually enjoy my information.

I have read the charts of many flight attendants therefore like a counselor. I know much about them and their lives. One flight attendant came to me many years ago. She was very concerned about her husband's health. I looked at her chart and her husband's chart and told her there was nothing to worry about. He would live for many years to come and she said "but how much longer?" I asked, "Do you really want to know?" She demanded to know, so I thought because it was so far in the future this information would give her peace. So I looked it up, it was seven years in the future and gave her a date.

I forgot about the reading and many years later I ran into her at the airport and she told me her husband had died. I told her how sorry I was. Then she said you know that recording you made of our last reading, well I listened to it recently and you gave the exact date my husband died.

I didn't know what to say, but I know astrology works.

On another trip I was flying with a flight attendant that had a very hard and difficult year, she recently lost both of her parents and her husband just died of cancer. I was wondering what could be in her birth chart that could have caused so many bad events. So I asked her "Do you know what time you are born?" She did! We were waiting in the jet way for our plane and it was late. I pulled up her chart on my computer. I saw all the reasons for her difficulty but I saw something very unusual that was happening that day. This aspect happens once only every 12 years and was happening exactly that day. I told her you are going to meet someone TODAY! And this will be your husband and bring great happiness. She said I was nuts and that information scared her to death.

But the captain that day began speaking to her and he had lost his wife the year before in a car accident. The next morning they went for a walk on our layover. A year later I ran into her in the crew lounge, she said you are not going to believe this Joni, but I am getting married and I met him that day we were flying together and you told me I would meet someone that day. I didn't believe you but you were right.

Boarding a flight from Houston to Dallas, in the heart of Texas an unexpected experience was about to open my awareness. This was a special flight, for upon boarding the flight attendants were announcing that it was the very last flight for a captain that was retiring from the airlines. There was his entire family cheering him on. I know how special this is being a flight attendant for many years.

Walking down the aisle I hear my name called out. I look to a beautiful woman beaming with light and energy, and she was so excited to see me. She said, "Joni you may not remember me but you had such an impact on my life 20 years ago". She said I will never forget when we were flying together and I was in the darkest time of my life but you looked at my chart and you gave me such hope, and I never forgot it.

This came at me so suddenly I was taken back. She said I was going through a difficult divorce as a single mom and my house just burnt down and you told me I was about to meet the man of my dreams, and that he would have something to do with the stars.

She was there for her husband's last flight and he was an astronaut for NASA. Others got on the microphone with tears of appreciation about the captain and his accomplishments. So many were choked up with gratitude about the love they had for this very special man that was her husband. His life accomplishments were beyond belief and the sincerity and emotion made me cry too. Before the flight was over she gave me her published children's book signed with the sweetest note "Thank you for your wisdom and beautiful heart". This was a highlight of my trip.

Upon boarding a flight recently, I hear music over the intercom. I listen to hear wondering what this noise is, we haven't had music on our planes in over 30 years. I finally figured it out. It was the song "This is the Dawning of the Age of Aquarius!" One of my favorite captains of over 30 years seniority saw me walk on board and played it on his IPod over the intercom as a notification that he knew I was there. I ran into the cockpit and announced, "That song isn't for me, is it!"

Chapter 6

From Western to Vedic Astrology

While still in high school, I read the Autobiography of a Yogi by Paramahansa Yogananda. It opened the door to many new beliefs and possibilities. I became fascinated with India and their spirituality. It all made sense to me. There was something in that book that interested me but I didn't completely understand till much later. It had to do with Yogananda's guru who was an astrologer. I didn't know there was a difference from western astrology and the astrology of India. But later when I discovered this I made it a mission to learn this very in depth study.

I had seen these astrologers from India make very specific predictions unlike the general predictions made in Western astrology. I came to find out that the placements of the planets in western astrology were actually the placements used 2,000 years ago and that the true placements of where the planets actually are in the heavens are the sidereal placements used in Vedic astrology, the astrology of India.

I thought, how can you deny the fact that these are the real placements according to the astronomers? No wonder these Vedic astrologers could make such profound specific predictions when they are using the real zodiac. So no matter how hard it was, I was going to learn the astrology of India, that which has been passed down from the spiritual sages of India.

Opening my Center

In the early 1990s I opened a metaphysical center. My parents, particularly my mother wanted me to pursue my love of astrology, spirituality and metaphysics. So we purchased a small commercial building where I could have classes and workshops. At this time I was practicing western astrology. I taught weekly western astrology classes and brought speakers in from out of town for weekend workshops. My center was the Dallas Metaphysical Center.

But during the time I was trying to think of the name of my center I asked that it be revealed in a dream. That night I had a very specific dream to name my center the Galactic Center. When I told my husband of this dream he commented that the name was too strange and people would associate it with the show Star Trek. So I felt comfortable naming it the Dallas Metaphysical Center.

In the late 1990s I began bringing teachers to my center to teach Vedic astrology. I immersed myself completely in the study and came to realize the importance of the Galactic Center. As my studies began to completely revolve around Vedic astrology I felt the need to rename my center. I realized my dream was so very significant and that my center was to be named the Galactic Center.

You see, the Galactic Center is where consciousness emanates from the center of our Universe. And in the process of precession of the equinoxes the closer we are (earth) to the Galactic Center the more evolved mankind becomes. So the Galactic Center essentially is where the center of God consciousness resides.

As my knowledge of astrology grew with my Vedic astrology studies I began to become even more proficient with making predictions. I began making predictions monthly for the world on my website, which began in 1999.

Since then I have been asked to speak and write for websites around the world. I have a website in Japan and write for websites in India and Turkey. My articles have been shared around the world in almost every country.

When I was asked to speak in India I went to a very wise old astrologer who used the palm to draw out the astrological chart. From my palm he drew out correctly my astrological chart. He knew where the planets were and the signs. One very specific thing he told me was that I was to make world predictions. So when I returned home I took this into serious consideration and began writing and speaking on my predictions for the coming year 2014.

To get the word out of the validity of astrology and proving this with my world predictions I have videos now seen on YouTube. Reading some of the comments on YouTube the skepticism is again rampant. People have such strong opinions concerning astrology and they don't have a clue what it is. Why is it people have such strong opinions on something they know nothing about? I am sure the answer to this varies from person to person, but the fact is that they are judging information that is heresy, not facts.

The purpose of this book is to bring forth the importance of astrology and to inspire others to learn and read the language and message of the stars. The wisdom and healing it brings is essential to awaken the consciousness during this time.

Chapter 7

How Does it All Work?

It is unbelievable that something as abstract as astrology could possibly work. It just doesn't make sense that you can predict life through something so far away and seemingly unrelated to us as the planets. How do planets, stars and their movements affect us? How is this possible? Many make sense of this by claiming that it has to be gravity. Look at the Moon and its effects on the oceans and tides. But it is definitely more than gravity. I don't believe there is anyone evolved enough to completely understand the reason behind how astrology works. But I believe we are on the tip of the iceberg. The science of astrology is intricately involved in the web of connecting all that is in the Universe. Astrology involves physics, geometry and calculus. It is essentially based on mathematical formulas that define the mechanics of all that is. It is based on the involvement of understanding matter, space and movement. It includes the measurements of variables that are not seen or measurable with any physical means.

Because we have not currently advanced enough to have an understanding of how to measure that which is immeasurable, I guess astrology will remain an elusive thing that science cannot measure therefore they will call it a pseudo science, meaning quackery. But to discount that which we do not yet understand is ignorant. Remember Galileo was imprisoned for saying the Earth was round instead of flat, and that it revolved around the Sun instead of the Sun revolving around the Earth.

Scientists cannot measure or understand spontaneous healings, the power of love or even the rhyme or reason why the brain functions. They have no means to heal mental disorders or addictions. With all our technological advancements we still have no real cures for certain diseases for the real cause and issue steams from their psychological and emotional disposition. Where does this all come from? I don't have the answer, but I do know that it is all about energy.

Aside from all our assumptions and opinions there is a Divine Force that gives life to all that exists and lives. This Divine Force of life is a part of nature. Nature reacts through the force called cause and effect. It makes no exceptions and definitely has no opinion. This force is always in effect to bring balance. Storms, fires, earthquakes, and seasons are all the balancing forces of our planet or nature. Even disease is a way to balance the world. At times when the world gets out of balance through the emotional imbalance of people events occur that seem catastrophic but are actually a way and means to balance. It is not about our judgments or opinions but just the way of nature through which the reaction brings balance.

Nature and the stars work in divine order seen in the seasons with mathematical patterns. Astrology is the study of the energy of the planets and cycles. There is a better time to do things in accordance to the cycles. This is what the Farmer's Almanac is based on.

The phases of the Moon as well as the seasons are based on astrology. So astrology is an understanding of the cycles of the planets and how they can be used for every activity on earth. Everything is connected and has meaning. It is these laws of nature, science, and cycles that affect world events and individuals personally. Hence the saying "As Above so Below."

Yes it is still unimaginable that it works this way, but sometimes you have to trust that things work even if you cannot understand how or why. I want to take you into my world of astrology and the very real experiences I have had throughout my life using the astrology of prediction.

I have to say that no astrologer has ever been 100% accurate, but to be 80% accurate is the best there is. Let me explain why. Anytime I am wrong on any prediction people focus on it to discount astrology, while never giving credit to the 80% correct predictions.

Why? I have to believe this is because people do not want to believe our life is totally predestined and predictable. There is great fear in believing this way. And I have to say I agree. And this is the exact reason why nothing is etched in stone.

The reason why no astrologer is 100% accurate is because we have free will. We have choice and the ability to change our destiny. And this is exactly why I believe astrology can be used to direct our lives for the better.

It is important to heed the timing that is best for certain activities. The ancients used astrology with reverence as a tool for guidance and balance in life. But now that the world has become so out of balance where ignorance is commonplace, people have turned away from the most ancient science of all, astrology. Astrology gives us insight into the unknown and can actually give understanding to the mechanisms that direct the Universe.

We are meant to understand and know the powers that direct our Universe. This will dissolve all fear, for knowledge gives wisdom and eliminates the unknown and fear, just as the light dissolves the darkness.

Patterns in the Sky

The aspects of the planets have the most important effect on grand world predictions. The aspects are the formations the planets form to each other in the heavens. When looking at the patterns the planets that form in the sky there is no birth chart, only the planets. To see the effects of world events astrologers base their predictions on the aspects of the planets to each other. This is simply the formations or degrees that the planets form to each other as they move in the heavens. This is gauged from the longitude, latitude and declination distances of the planets from one another.

We view the planets from the reference point of the ecliptic, which is the apparent path of the Sun across the sky.

The aspects are certain degrees the planets form between each other in their orbits around the sun. These aspects are geometrical and the same as the musical scales, for some are harmonious and some are dissonant. As in all cycles or life experiences in the flow of energy there are periods of obstacles before the easy flow that goes further into a time of unrest. This is seen in the ebb and flow of the tides or the cyclic ups and downs.

In the process of birth there is a critical period of constriction and limitation, as the baby has outgrown its environment and needs to go through a difficult period before a new beginning. This is the birthing process. Throughout life, cycles flow in this manner. There is a time of obstacles before a break through flowing into ease and comfort.

Global events occur as the motions of the planets evolve, but in an individual's birth chart the planets are fixed from the time and place of birth.

Another factor to be considered in prediction is the specific portion of the sky the planets occupy. Certain areas of the sky involve specific fixed stars. The stars constitute the meanings of the signs relevant to certain portions of the zodiac.

For example the constellation of Leo is made of stars that relate to the constellation of the Lion. The fixed star Regulus has the qualities most associated to the qualities attributed to the sign Leo: leadership, kings, and loyalty. When the planets are transiting the sky where these stars sit, it can produce an event relative to the energy depicted by the star.

Likewise when someone has a star conjunct a natal planet it can predict a certain destiny for the individual. In Vedic astrology these portions of the zodiac are further refined to smaller portions that have even more meaning. There are 27 divisions of 13 degrees and 20 minutes. These are called the nakshatras. They are relative to the stars in each nakshatra.

The stars are like the backdrop of the 12 signs of the zodiac. It is viewed as the zodiacal band that surrounds the earth. There are 12 divisions of this zodiacal circular band, each 30 degrees making up the 360 circle of this zodiacal ring. As the planets move through the signs from our vantage point on earth they are moving across this zodiacal band. This is how we have certain planets in signs. They are moving across this band in and out of certain areas we know as the signs and the nakshatras. As these planets move they are forming aspects to one another causing friction, and then ease and flow. They are constantly forming these angular arrangements that cause events on planet Earth, globally and personally.

The meanings of the planets and the areas they rule over have to be learned and the energy of the aspects must be understood. This is essential to making predictions with astrology.

Part II

Prediction of World Events

Chapter 1

Precession of the Equinoxes Cycles within Cycles

There are cycles within cycles. From this we will begin with the largest cycles down to the smallest cycles to understand the process of evolution and prediction through astrology.

Precession is based on the focal point of the zodiac from Earth. This point continues to move due to the continual wobble of the Earth.

The biggest determinate of the evolution of mankind involves the big cycle of Precession. This is a 24,000-26,000 year cycle that indicates the conscious awareness and progression of mankind. This cycle involves the signs and constellations in the cycle of our planet earth as it is referenced from the Galactic Center. The closer our planet is to the Galactic Center the higher the awareness or consciousness.

This cycle like all cycles has a circular pattern. The first half is growing toward the halfway mark and the second half is reverting back to the starting point. In the growing half cycle Earth is moving towards the Galactic Center. When at the halfway point Earth is closest to the Galactic Center. This first half cycle is half the time of the entire cycle of precession (about 26,000 years) so it is around 12,000-13,000 years in the process of moving towards the Galactic Center. Once it reaches its closest point then there is another 13,000 years where it reverts back to the point that is furthest from the Galactic Center. Like the cycle of the Moon the waxing phase moves towards the fullness of the Full Moon then a waning phase moves to the darkness, the New Moon. The Galactic Center is situated around 3 degrees Sagittarius. This is symbolic that we are moving towards fullness of light or enlightenment and reverting back to darkness.

The beginning reference point is where the zodiac begins and this is ever changing through the grand cycle of precession. This point as it evolves is moving 1 degree backward in the zodiac every 72 years. To complete the cycle through all 12 signs of 30 degrees (360 degrees) and as mentioned before takes 24,000-26,000 years.

In Western astrology the beginning reference point of the zodiac is 0 degrees Aries and does not change. But in reality the zodiac of stars is changing due to precession.

The sidereal placements of planets in relation to the changing zodiac are the actual locations of planets astronomically. Vedic astrology uses these true positions. Western astrology uses the Tropical system based on the seasons in relation to the Sun and Vedic astrology uses the sidereal system based on the stars. This is why in Vedic astrology (sidereal) the positions of the planets are different from the positions in western astrology (tropical). The difference in planetary positions at this time is 23 degrees. This difference in the zodiacs is called the ayanamsha. Therefore, the sidereal planetary positions are 23 degrees backwards in the zodiac from the tropical positions. For example if a planet is 15 degrees Scorpio in the tropical zodiac then it is 22 degrees Libra in the sidereal system. This is because the sidereal system takes into account precession of the equinoxes.

The point of lowest consciousness on earth is when we were furthest from the Galactic Center, two thousand years ago. This point in the zodiac is 0 degrees Aries. This was a dark barbaric time in humanity. Aries is the sign that can relate to violence and war.

During this era of darkness and lack of hope came the revolution of the birth of Christ and Christianity. This was the beginning of the age of Pisces as precession moved from 0 degrees Aries into Pisces beginning with 29 degrees and continues to move in backward motion through the signs 1 degree every 72 years. So from 2,000 years precession has taken us from 29 Pisces to the point we are today which comes to approximately 6 degrees of Pisces. This means we are in the increasing cycle of precession moving towards the highest point of consciousness. From the darkest point 2,000 years ago, this means we have about 11,000 years to go towards the highest peak of this precessional cycle coming towards the Galactic Center. Once we have reached this point then begins the waning phase back to the dark point away from the Galactic Center taking another 13,000-14,000 years.

The signs and constellations relative to the starting point of the zodiac determine the ages we are in and reveal an enormous amount concerning humanity. The starting point of the zodiac is the focus of where humanity is in terms of the experiences.

As precession of the equinoxes continues it will slowly move from the early degrees of Pisces into the sign of Aquarius. Remember precession moves backwards through the zodiac so when the beginning point is finally in Aquarius it will enter the last degree 29 degrees Aquarius and continue through the sign till it reaches 0 degrees. The beginning of the zodiac is currently 6 degrees of Pisces. It will take us about 432 years before we enter the Age of Aquarius, 6 degrees X 72 years = 432.

Each age lasts approximately 2,160 years, as the beginning reference point moves through a 30-degree sign. Every 72 years the zodiac moves 1 degree, therefore covers an entire sign of 30 degrees in 2,160 years. The ages are in accordance with the signs.

The age of Pisces may be about the birth of Christianity. For it was at the beginning of the age of Pisces that Jesus Christ was born. From that dark point in time Christianity began. Out of the darkness came a philosophy of spirituality to enlighten the people with a belief in eternal life through the savior Jesus Christ to save them from darkness or eternal damnation. From that point all the churches were built and today religion is a major part of the world. The fish is the symbol for Pisces and also for Christianity. Massive magnificent churches were built in respect to attain salvation. Pisces is the sign of faith and belief and this is the major component of religion, but the darker side of religion has to do with sense of denial of the gifts of prosperity with the belief that suffering is essential with renunciation of this world. Mass corruption has occurred through the greed of many in control of organized religions. The original message of Christianity became distorted with the story of Jesus' suffering. The victim consciousness and suffering has stayed with people throughout the age of Pisces and will continue till another new age of consciousness emerges.

The saying for Pisces is "I believe" and that is the most important aspect of the age of Pisces to believe in that which we cannot see. It is a time of faith in the Divine. The coming age of Aquarius will be different since the saying for Aquarius is "I know". This will be an age of very advanced technology. This technology will connect humanity to a new way of thinking and open the mind in areas never thought of or believed. The effects of this age are already being felt right now as we are approaching Aquarius. Technology, air travel, computers, and the internet are the effects of the coming Age of Aquarius. Pisces concerns religious beliefs and religious dogma still controls the world. The Age of Aquarius will bring the unity of thought concerning religion. This will bring a time of true spirituality not man made religion.

It is important to realize as a world of duality there will always be a positive and negative side of humanity and as the ages evolve the negative and positive side of the signs will prevail. This duality is seen through our planet's essence of the Sun and Moon, male and female, father and mother or night and day. Therefore good and evil will always exist and we can choose through free will the positive or negative in our lives no matter which age we live.

Chapter 2

Prediction of World Events Uranus, Neptune and Pluto

The transiting planets are assessed to make predictions for events around the world. The big trends will involve the slower moving planets. The outer planets Uranus, Neptune and Pluto will influence the collective unconscious. This means the emotions of the masses of people will be influenced and react to the pressures and indications of the planets. These planets' aspects to each other give the big picture of what is occurring globally. They will bring the emotional climate of mankind and the development of humanity through rebellion, creative ideas, fear or disease.

The Collective Unconscious: Uranus, Neptune and Pluto

When making world predictions the planets to be analyzed are the 3 outer planets. These planets govern the collective consciousness of the masses of the people. They are not considered personal planets, but their influence can alter the energies of the personal planets when combined with the personal planets both in the sky as transits, or in a person's birth chart.

They are generational because these planets move so slow that certain generations of people have them in the same sign giving certain groups of people their special characteristics.

The ancients did not use the outer planets because they could not see them. But with the discovery of telescopes we discovered each of them. With each discovery the essence of what the planet represented became prominent in society. It is through hindsight that we can clearly see what each planet represented and what they brought into our awareness during the time of their discovery.

Generational Change

The planets that dictate generational change globally are the three outer planets: Uranus, Neptune, and Pluto. They specifically influence mass consciousness and are transpersonal. Their planetary patterns in the heavens reveal the political, financial and societal climate in the world.

The three outer planets actually determine specific eras with their combinations and patterns. It is their relationships to each other that predict movements and eras in history.

It is important to understand the symbology of the outer planets to apply their meanings for all world affairs. They are constantly forming different patterns, unique like fingerprints. There are definite similarities with patterns of planets in the past. Therefore, we can draw from the events that occurred before to help us understand certain planetary configurations.

Through hindsight we have come to understand what the planetary energies brought into our being and awareness.

Uranus

Uranus was discovered in 1781. Around the onset of the industrial revolution, inventions were discovered to make work and trade possible on a global scale. Use of electricity and inventions like the cotton gin were beginning. All this opened the world to mass communications.

Rules: Change, eccentricity, rebellion, erratic behavior, sudden and unexpected happenings, shock, earthquakes, lightning, electricity, computers, inventions, airplanes, astrology.

Neptune

Neptune was discovered around 1846. At that time, photography was beginning, symbolic of Neptune's creation of illusions that seem real, as in photos or films. This was the onset of screen movies that would connect the world with collective trends and messages. Neptune is about ecstasy, either the "high" received through spiritual revelations or the "high" received through drugs and alcohol. It is connected with intoxication, art, music and dancing. It rules the illusions of the world, spirituality and psychic powers.

Rules: Illusions, deception, confusion, denial, drugs, alcohol, fantasies, fog, dreams, romance, glamour, spirituality, higher consciousness, devotion, cults, oceans, liquids, oil and gas, sensitivity, psychic.

Pluto

Pluto was discovered in 1930. At that time, the Depression was in full motion. Tyrants of underworld quality controlled the masses. Mafia leaders, gangsters and dictators like Hitler and Stalin were rampant. The discovery of atomic energy caused mass destruction and threats of total human annihilation from massive weapons of war.

Rules: Explosiveness, power, control, manipulation, surrender, transformation, underworld, mafia, secrets, obsessions, compulsions, revenge, big money, sex, atomic energy, big government, corruption, birth, death, healing.

The big picture cycles involve the outer planets as they aspect each other. There were many world events that were caused by the hard aspects of these outer planets. And of course generations are born out of these times as well.

With this information, many cycles from the past can be studied to understand the future and, therefore, make political and economic global predictions.

The rate of speed of each planet determines when they will form major aspects to each other.

Chapter 3

Planetary Cycles

The amount of time a planet spends in a sign will give an idea how to gauge the speed of a planet in terms of making predictions.

Moon: 2½ days, takes 28 days to transit all 12 signs

Sun: 1 month, takes 1 year to transit all the 12 sign

Mercury: 1 month, takes 1 year to transit all the 12 signs

Venus: 1 month, takes 1 year to transit all the 12 signs

Mars: 2 months, and takes 2 years to transit all 12 signs

Jupiter: 1 year, and takes 12 years to transit all 12 signs

Saturn: 2½ years, takes 30 years to transit all 12 signs

Uranus: 7 years, and takes 84 years to transit through all 12 signs

Neptune: approximately 14 years, and takes about 165 years to transit all 12 signs

Pluto: 12-30 years (Pluto has an elliptical orbit; when furthest from the Sun, it can stay in a sign for 30 years.) and takes 245 years to transit all 12 signs.

Cycles of each planet indicate a turning point in a person's life.

Within the cycle that a planet takes to complete a full revolution through all the 12 signs there are periods of crises. This is during the hard aspects. The outer planets are important in these periods of crises.

The hard aspects involve the quarter cycles of each planet, dividing the entire cycle into four. The hard aspects are 0-90 degrees (square), 90-180 degrees (opposition), 180-270 degrees (square) 270-360 degrees back to the conjunction. So it takes 4 cycles 90 degrees (square) apart. Each of these cycles of 90 degrees are a point of action and crisis always producing a change.

This can be viewed like the waxing and waning the phases of the Moon. The waxing square is the quarter moon that is increasing in light, then the full Moon is the opposition and the waning square is the quarter Moon decreasing in light returning to the new Moon, the conjunction. All cycles are circular in this way.

Jupiter takes 12 years to complete a full cycle; it is 4 times within this cycle that these periods of crisis will occur. Every 3 years Jupiter will form a square from its starting position. At age 60 Jupiter will have completed 5 revolutions through the zodiac.

Saturn is the most noticeable as it takes 28-30 years to make a complete revolution, and at each 7 years there is a crisis point in life from birth till Saturn returns to its starting point. Therefore there is a big change every 7 years of our lives: at age 7, 14, 21, 28, 35, 42, 49, 56, 63, and so on.

Uranus has a cycle that comes as a breaking point or a breakthrough. Uranus takes about 84 years to complete a cycle therefore every 21 years there is a crisis, ages 21, 42, 63 and 84

Neptune and Pluto take over 168 years to make a complete revolution but make a square around age 42.

It is interesting to note that when someone turns age 60 Saturn and Jupiter both return to the starting position in a chart. This can indicate a new beginning and change in attitude. There are many cycles that occur round the same years indicating a time of change and transformation in certain periods of life.

Chapter 4

Applying the Planetary Cycles Together

Combining the cycles of the planets is what brings the manifestation of world events. These are the cycles that will be analyzed throughout past events and can be the means to make future predictions. This involves two planets in movement and the time it takes for them to form hard aspects to each other.

Number of Years for Conjunction

Neptune/Pluto: 492 years

Uranus/Pluto: 127 years (average)

Uranus/Neptune: 171 years

Saturn/Pluto: 33 years

Saturn/Neptune: 36 years

Saturn/Uranus: 45 years

Jupiter/Pluto: 13 years

Jupiter/Neptune: 13 years

Jupiter/Uranus: 14 years

Jupiter/Saturn: 20 years

Hard aspects between the three outer planets Uranus, Neptune and Pluto define the astrological era and reveal information concerning that time in history. The hard aspects bring difficulties to the forefront producing big events and transformational changes.

Outer Planets to Outer Planets: Uranus, Neptune and Pluto

Pluto and Neptune are in hard aspect about every 124 years, Waxing square, opposition, and waning square taking about 492 years to complete.

Uranus and Pluto are in hard aspect around 35 years, taking an average of 127 years to complete.

Uranus and Neptune are in hard aspect around every 43 years, taking 171 years to complete.

From the slowest moving planets to the faster moving planets we are looking at the big picture of world events to personal events. This means the aspects of the outer planets to one another predict the trends of world events. Within this framework we are looking at Pluto to Neptune, and Pluto to Uranus as the outer most transits that affect global trends.

Neptune and Pluto

Neptune and Pluto form a hard aspect around every 124 years.

Around the turn of the century in the 1890s Neptune and Pluto were conjunct in Taurus, initiating the beginning of a spiritualist movement. Madame H.P. Blavatsky, the founder of modern Theosophy, Henry David Thoreau, and Ralph Waldo Emerson were instrumental in activating the spiritual movements. Many were communicating with spirits, séances were commonly practiced throughout America. This is the result of Pluto's power and transformation combined with the spiritualizing power of Neptune.

Neptune and Uranus

Neptune and Uranus form a hard aspect around every 43 years.

Neptune and Uranus last conjoined in 1995. Around this time technology really began to grow at top speed. Cell phones and computer technology became the way of the future. Neptune pertains to outer space and Uranus relates to inventions and the future. As these two planets transited together technology advanced. This year was very difficult triggering the onset of extreme terrorism in America beginning with the

Oklahoma City Bombing. This was the effect of unforeseen explosive events. The Neptune Uranus conjunction is one of the denominators in this horrific event. Neptune can pertain to deception, and delusions, which can activate fundamental beliefs and cults. Uranus rules sudden unexpected events around rebellion and radical change. The combination of Uranus with Neptune brings explosive events concerning extreme beliefs that set forth sudden disruption around acts of terrorism.

Uranus and Pluto

Uranus and Pluto form a hard aspect about every 35 years.

The signs play a part in the planetary picture of the time. The planetary patterns and aspects are the most predictive element in astrology. They were opposed at the turn of the century in 1901: Pluto was in Taurus and Uranus was in Scorpio. Then they formed a waning square in the 1930s, Uranus was in Pisces and Pluto was in Gemini. Then they formed a conjunction in the 1960s in Leo bringing us to the waxing square of 2011-2015 with Uranus in Pisces and Pluto in Sagittarius.

There is a huge turning point in history each time there is a hard aspect with these planets of transformation and change.

Pluto rules the powers that control the world, the financial markets and monopolies. In the past and even today, this power is seen in dictatorships and even mafias.

Uranus is connected through retaliation of dictators throughout the world. Freedom comes with a price.

Control and power of the churches are brought to justice, as the priests and corruption of the churches are held accountable. The Associated Press estimated the settlements of sex abuse cases from 1950 to 2007 totaled more than $2 billion. Accountability puts the figure at more than $3 billion in 2012. Uranus square Pluto indicates a break down of powers that control the world, and this was evident from 2011-2015 during the Uranus-Pluto square.

Chapter 5

Saturn and Jupiter to the Outer Planets

Saturn to Outer Planets

Saturn is the planet that will bring large breakdowns, death and endings. Combined with the outer planets, it produces extremes in world events.

Saturn and Pluto are in hard aspects around every 9 years taking approximately 33 years to complete their cycle.

Saturn and Pluto aspects bring disasters. They are in hard (conjunction, square and opposition) aspects about every 9 years. The last square was in 2010, which had many natural disasters – an earthquake in Haiti that was one of the deadliest on record, a massive earthquake in Chile, volcanic eruptions in Iceland, and man-made destruction with the oil spill in the Gulf of Mexico. Saturn and Pluto were in opposition nine years prior in 2001 when the 9/11 terrorist attacks occurred. The square nine years before, 1992-1993, was the first world trade center bombing.

Saturn and Neptune are in hard aspects around 9.25 years taking 36 years to complete their cycle.

Saturn and Neptune together indicate a point of awaking to reality. Neptune represents illusion or delusions, and when combined with Saturn the planet of realizing what is real there is an awakening. They were conjunct in 1952 and again 1989. Interestingly enough Neptune rules fog and not able to see things clearly as in delusions. But in 1952 a "killer fog" descended on London. This was a thick industrial smoke that covered the city causing more than 4,000 deaths. And in 1989 one of the worse oil spills in history occurred when the Exxon Valdez, spilled over 240,000 barrels of oil, polluting the ocean. Neptune rules both fog and oil. But the outcome with Saturn resulted in new laws and regulations to clean up the environment.

Saturn and Uranus are in hard aspects about every 12 years taking nearly 45 years to complete their cycle.

Saturn is quite the opposite of Uranus. Saturn is structure and organization while Uranus is revolution and freedom. Saturn rules the old and the past while Uranus rules the future and the new. Saturn and Uranus were conjunct in 1942 and 1988. These two energies together will be conflicting, explosive, and destructive but bring needed change. During 1942 World War II was at a peak. There was great destruction occurring all over the world. Both planets together produce destruction. In 1988 A Pan Am Boeing 747 exploded over Lockerbie, Scotland from a terrorist bomb. This was a major turning point for attacks with airlines. Uranus rules air travel and airlines.

Jupiter to Outer Planets

Jupiter brings expansion and freedom. Combined with the outer planets it can bring extreme events. Depending on the nature of the sign and planet it can make events more expansive or bigger for good or bad.

Jupiter and Pluto are in hard aspect every 3 years taking 13 years to complete their cycle.

Jupiter and Pluto alignments coincide with large-scale events that tend to overpower. The danger with Jupiter-Pluto aspects is that they tend to correlate with great success and windfalls or extreme downfalls. They were in conjunction in 2007 -- a time when the markets were teetering on disaster. 2008 was a financial fall that brought ruin to many people around the world. The result was negative due to the configuration of Jupiter and Pluto close to Rahu and the time of eclipses.

Jupiter and Neptune are in hard aspects every 3.2 years taking 13 years to complete their cycle.

Neptune rules the oceans and waters and when conjoined with Jupiter brings floods and severe weather globally. They were conjunct in 2009 and there were major floods and tsunamis around the world. Record floods were recorded in the Philippines, Istanbul and the US.

Jupiter and Uranus are in hard aspects every 3.5 years taking 14 years to complete their cycle.

Uranus brings sudden unexpected events and with Jupiter there can be sudden windfalls. Both planets indicate freedom therefore the conjunction can represent a time of freedom and expansion. But as

Uranus is the planet for discovery and inventions it is no surprise that in 1969 the first man landed on the moon and Jupiter and Uranus were exactly conjoined in Virgo.

Jupiter conjoined Uranus in the sign of Pisces in the year of 1928. To confirm that this is a time of major medical discoveries: Alexander Fleming discovered penicillin in 1928 and changed the world of modern medicine by introducing the age of antibiotics and his discovery of penicillin continues to save millions of lives.

Chapter 6

Rahu and Ketu: North and South Nodes of the Moon

The north node of the moon is called Rahu and the south node of the moon is called Ketu. Rahu is where the Moon crosses the ecliptic (path of the Sun) ascending and Ketu is where the Moon crosses the ecliptic descending. They are always exactly opposite in the zodiac, so together they are called the nodal axis.

So Rahu and Ketu are the points where the Sun and Moon cross paths, thus they determine where the eclipses occur for that year. The signs in which they occur indicate where change will occur for that year.

****These points in the heavens are one of the most critical and most powerful indicators for prediction in world affairs.***

Rahu magnifies the planets it conjoins. These planets and what they represent become critical for that year.

Rahu and Ketu make a complete revolution through the zodiac about 18 and half years. Therefore every 18 and half years there is a huge turning point in life, as one leaves home and goes off to college around this age. This is the biggest turning point in life. Each 18 and half years there is another big change, 18, 37, 55, 74

Rahu rules fanaticism, obsessive and compulsive behavior, extremes, fear, addictions, drugs, alcohol, fame, power, worldly success, outer turmoil, and gives sudden and unexpected results and windfalls. Rahu rules our desires in the material illusionary world.

In mundane astrology (world events) Rahu rules technology, computers, nuclear energy, collective trends, epidemics, disease, poisons, foreign lands and foreigners, aliens, dark skin, medicine and air travel.

Rahu is said to have the qualities of Saturn, and Ketu the qualities of Mars.

Ketu is the opposite in energy to Rahu. Rahu gives gains and exaggerates while Ketu brings loss, and denies or dissolves. But one thing never to forget about Ketu is its quality of intense burning desire that comes from a sense of lack, or that something is missing. As Rahu is outer turmoil Ketu is inner turmoil. This is what gives Ketu the energy of Mars. It can be very fiery as it deals with burning desires. Mars is a planet that will indicate fanaticism and is an indicator of terrorism or terrorists.

It is said that as our material desires, Rahu brings us into this world and Ketu will take us out of this world for it is a powerful indicator for death.

Ketu rules inner turmoil, loss, negation, lack of confidence, self-doubt, fantasies, confusion, indecision, illusions, drug addiction and alcoholism, psychic influences, fire, injury, death, spiritual insight, liberation, perception, wisdom, psychic disorders, radiation, diseases, cancer, surgery, and medical malpractice.

In mundane astrology (world events) Ketu represents fire, war, turmoil, terrorists, terrorism, fear, destruction, weapons, unexpected events, secrets, hidden agendas, great losses, and death.

Rahu and Ketu conjunct Saturn, Jupiter, Uranus, Neptune and Pluto

Jupiter conjunct Rahu

Jupiter takes 12 years to cycle through the zodiac and Rahu takes 18 1/2 (transiting backwards). They conjoin every 3-4 years. Rahu can eclipse or wipe out the energy of Jupiter. This combination has major effects on the economy. The sign they are in can determine if it magnifies the economy for the better or worse. In 2008 when Jupiter crossed Rahu in Jupiter's weakest sign Capricorn the economy had a major fall.

Saturn conjunct Rahu

Saturn takes 30 years to cycle through the zodiac and Rahu takes 18 ½ (Rahu travels backwards in the zodiac). They conjoin every 11 years, but the signs they converge in are crucial in their effects.

Each time Saturn and Rahu form a conjunction every eleven years the following events occur: warfare, revolutions, rebellions, end of monopolies or dictatorships, civil rights and prejudices, natural disasters, and nuclear energy involving attacks.

Uranus conjunct Rahu:

Uranus takes 84 years to cycle through the zodiac and Rahu takes 18 ½ years to transit backwards through the zodiac. They conjoin every 16 years. The last time they were conjunct was in 2007. This is a time of inventions and progression in technology. The IPhone was announced this year. Rahu will magnify Uranus bringing forth inventions and change. It will also activate the potential for more intense earthquakes. One of the worse earthquakes in 35 years hit Peru.

Neptune/Rahu

Take 16 years to form a conjunction. The last time they were conjunct was 2008.

Rahu always magnifies the planets it is conjunct. In this case Neptune as the planet of deception and denial the year of 2008 was a devastating year for the economy. Many suffered the economic downfall while millions of dollars were unaccounted for in the banks. Neptune can deal with thief and thieves and many mega wealthy individuals got away with trillions of dollars. The economy suffered with the hidden agendas still left uncovered. Trillions of dollars in secret federal loans made to the big banks during the 2008 financial crisis, a process that helped them rake in billions of dollars in undisclosed profits. The Federal Reserve spent $7.7 trillion in bank bailouts!

Pluto/Rahu

Currently take 16 years to come to a conjunction. The last time they were conjunct was 2010.

Pluto rules massive powers that control the world and the conjunction with Rahu brought to the surface controlling powers. The control and powers of the Catholic Church was brought to the surface with the sexual corruption of many priests. A huge revelation of power and corruption occurred when British Petroleum's gigantic oil leak exposed their corruption and power.

This was also a big year of massive earthquakes as a massive earthquake of magnitude 7.0 hit Haiti killing almost 250k people, injuring 300k and more than one million people were made homeless. The earthquake that hit Chili was more powerful but less destructive.

Saturn/Ketu

Saturn and Ketu conjoin every 11 years.

Saturn and Ketu were together in 2007-2008. This was a depressive year in the economy. The economic down turn brought great depression and destruction to the world. There were many variables occurring during this time but this was a major player in the end result of this devastating time.

Jupiter/Ketu conjoin every 3-4 years

Jupiter with Ketu can bring gains and losses. The sign they are in is very important as to the effects. But mostly this can represent losses in the area they represent. Ketu many times indicates terrorist and Jupiter can expand this potential.

Uranus and Ketu conjoins every 16 years.

The last conjunction was year 1999. This was a year of massive expansion in the stock market where the bubble of the housing markets and the dot com bubble were about to explode. The writing was on the wall. This was a very volatile time. As Uranus rules technology this indicated the huge loss around the dot.com industry.

Neptune and Ketu conjoins every 16 years.

The last conjunction was the year 2000. This year was explosive with great loss. As both Uranus and Neptune came together with Ketu there was a worldwide depression. This involved the deception and illusion (Neptune) of the world of technology (Uranus).

Pluto and Ketu conjoins every 16 years.

The last conjunction was year 2001-2002. This was one of the worse times globally for terrorism. Pluto was with Ketu and Mars. Ketu rules terrorist and fear. The world has never been the same from this time forward.

Chapter 7

Saturn and Jupiter the Social Planets

Jupiter and Saturn determine the economy and the social climate of the world. It takes 20 years to circle through the zodiac and form a conjunction, and 10 years following their conjunction they form an opposition. Their hard aspects bring crises and change in the economy.

These points are to be tracked in the economic cycles globally, the 20-year cycle of Jupiter's and Saturn's conjunction, and the half-way point between this 20 years where they oppose each 10 years after the conjunction. Then about a year and a half following the conjunction or opposition of Jupiter and Saturn, both Jupiter and Saturn will cross over the nodal axis.

1) Jupiter conjunct Saturn 20 years

2) Jupiter opposed Saturn 10 years after the conjunction

3) Within the conjunction and opposition of Jupiter and Saturn their crossing over the nodes of the moon (Rahu and Ketu) create the shifts.

It is cycles within cycles of Rahu/Ketu and Jupiter/Saturn that produce the many changing tides within the framework of our society and lives. It is not only just the patterns and cycles that these planets form, but it is also important to understand what signs these planets occupy, for the signs can make the energy positive or negative. This adds another layer to this complex web of life.

But there is a synergy and a pattern that can be recognized and used for the understanding and betterment of our lives.

The vast scheme of the social, economic and mass emotional climate in the world involves the cycles of Saturn and Jupiter with Rahu and Ketu.

There are cycles within cycles that determine the trends of each year. The most important cycle that concerns all of life's experiences is the nodal axis of the moon, composed of Rahu and Ketu. The axis of fate and destiny for Rahu brings us into life and deals with all things in the material world, and Ketu pertains to the spiritual world and determines our spiritual development and our exit from this world.

Within the nodal axis the other planets that determine the emotional trends globally are the social planets Jupiter and Saturn. These cycles of Rahu/Ketu and Jupiter/Saturn will work together to determine the cyclic patterns of events on planet Earth. Both Rahu and Ketu are diametrically opposite in meanings and results, and Saturn and Jupiter are opposites as well in meaning. Rahu is the material world and Ketu is the spiritual world, and Jupiter is growth and expansion while Saturn is contraction and limitation.

With this understanding, Rahu is much like Jupiter, it expands and increases things; and Ketu is like Saturn for it is about withdrawal, loss and contraction.

Again it is imperative to look to the cycles of Jupiter and Saturn as they conjunct every 20 years, and oppose 10 years after the conjunction. These 10-year increments are just as important as the 20-year conjunction.

Rahu and Ketu, constitute a revolving axis of two points that travel backwards through the zodiac. These two points are always exactly opposite. These points travel through the entire zodiac of 12 signs in 18 and a half years. So they reach their halfway point in about nine years. They remain in a sign for one and a half years, or 18 months. The halfway point of Rahu and Ketu is almost the same as the half cycle of Jupiter and Saturn when they form an opposition.

The big picture will be revealed with these 20-year and 10-year segments, but to really observe the smaller trends for the global economy involves the breakdown of these cycles, which are:

- 9 years is the half cycle of Rahu/Ketu
- 3-4 years: Jupiter will conjoin one of the Nodes (Rahu or Ketu)
- 6 years: Saturn will conjunct one of the nodes (Rahu or Ketu). At these intersections there will be a rise or a fall.

Chapter 8

Aspects in World Prediction

The next step in prediction is to understand the aspects, which are measured by the degrees between the planets. In the previous sections we covered the major aspects called hard aspects, which are the quarter cycles within the transits of each planet as it transits through the entire 360-degree zodiac. The outer planets reflect the big picture of world events. Next, the application of these planetary cycles to each other as they form hard aspects cause events. But there are other important aspects that are important to cause events in the prediction of world events.

When looking at a world prediction there is no beginning reference point as to a birth so the houses cannot be used. Therefore the transits of the planets and their cycles are what are observed in understanding world events, trends and cycles. The planets aspects to each other are the most important variables to be considered. The signs the planets are in, flavor the events as well.

In looking at the aspects between the planets, certain ranges of degrees are meaningful. There are 360 degrees in the entire zodiac. Each sign and house is 30 degrees. Each of the 12 signs is 30 degrees, 12 x 30 =360 degree circle of the zodiac. The basic aspects used are 0, 30, 60, 90, 120, 150 and 180 degrees. This means the planets spaced close to these degrees of separation to each other, form an aspect. Aspects connect the planets in specific ways. Some are beneficial and some are challenging. The planets (based on their meanings) actually send the energy for positive or negative results. There are benefic planets and malefic planets.

The way I advocate to read aspects is simply to measure the distance of the number of signs from each other. For example, if two planets form the aspect of 150 degrees from each other, then it will be 6 signs counting from the 1st planet to the 2nd planet, and 8 signs counting back around to the first planet, always counting forward in a counter-clockwise direction. The aspects do have names with Western astrology, but they can be seen by the number of signs they are apart from one another. The 150 degree aspect is called a quincunx or a 6/8 relationship. The degrees of the planets are important, and the more exact aspects are the more powerful. For example the conjunction of two planets that are closer in degree is more powerful then a conjunction that is 10 degrees apart. But they are still conjunct by or in aspect by being in the same sign.

Aspects

Conjunction: 0 degrees (1/1) Intensity, activation, big events,

Semi Sextile: 30 degrees (2/12) Receiving and giving, or acquiring and losing, gains and losses

Sextile: 60 degrees (3/11) Opportunities, ease, friendly, unites

Square: 90 degrees; (4/10) action, crisis, hard, difficult, obstacles

Trine: 120 degrees: (5/9) ease and comfort, release, breakthrough, and luck

Quincunx/ Shastastaka:150 degrees; (6/8) Complications, accidents, endings, death

Opposition: 180 degrees: (7/7) conflict, balance, and reorientation

Important Aspects to Consider in Prediction

Certain aspects seem to be more intense and produce events due to the conflicting influence of energy. Also, a combination of these aspects form powerful patterns when in aspect simultaneously. These are the specific patters that will produce very powerful events in world prediction.

Shastastaka/ Quincunx (6/8)

Shastastaka, the 6/8 relationship, is known as an unfortunate relationship in Vedic astrology, and is better known as the quincunx in western astrology. It has to do with life changing events. It has the energy of the combination of the 6th and 8th house. The 6th house can produce accidents, but also the need to improve or make one's life better, while the 8th house indicates major change or transformations. The extreme result is death. It is prominent in health matters and illness, financial reversals or residence changes. I have seen it involved in sudden death or an opportunity to wake up and turn one's life around. The nature of the planets involved will produce the exact effects.

The Yod

There is a more complex planetary configuration that involves three planets; two planets form a 6/8 relationship to one planet, while the two planets forming the 6/8 relationship are 3/11 from each other. This configuration forms a Y and is referred to in western astrology as the yod, "Finger of God", hand of destiny, or the slingshot. It is one of the most important configurations in a chart. It will explain many important matters not explained with traditional aspects.

It is triggered by a transit that activates a planet involved in this configuration. If a transiting planet crosses one of the two planets that are in 3/11 the effect will not be as stimulating as when a transiting planet crosses the 3rd planet that is 6/8 from the other two planets. It will activate two 6/8 relationships to the two planets in 3/11 relationship (sextile). This third planet is called the action point. Furthermore, the point exactly opposite the action point which will be the midpoint between the two planets in 3/11 relationship is a trigger as well. It is the reaction point. This will be the result or indicate the problem that is the result of the trigger point. If the yod consists of natural benefic planets there will be benefits from the shake up. If it involves natural malefics it indicates shake-ups that could involve death or events that change a life forever in an instant.

Rules for Forming the Yod

Two planets are 3 signs away and one planet is 6/8 from each of the two planets, forming a Y configuration.

The third planet that is in 6/8 relationship to the other two planets is called the **action point**.

There is a midpoint between the two planets that are 3 signs away from each other that is in opposition to the action point is called the **reaction point**, indicating the cause.

Natural benefics will generally be beneficial and natural malefics will generally be detrimental.

*Remember that the orb of the transiting planet to the natal planet is very important. Look for exact degree hits, or a three-degree orb as the most powerful. But transits are still making an aspect to the entire sign. As a transiting planet applies to an aspect, (meaning before the exact hit) it is more powerful than when it is separating (or moving away from the exact hit).

T-Square

The T-Square is when two planets form a 4/10 relationship with a 3rd planet in opposition to one of the planets in a natal chart. Two of the planets are 90 degrees from one another and two of the planets are 180 degrees from one another. A transiting planet will activate this configuration by conjoining one of these planets. It will oppose (7/7) one planet and square (4/10) the other planet. This will activate an event concerning the houses involved and the nature of the planets as well as the houses they rule. A transiting planet can create this configuration when two natal planets are square each other (4/10) and a transiting planet will come to the point of opposition to one of the planets 4/10 or square to each other, thus creating a **T-square** configuration with the transiting planet as the third planet.

Grand Cross

The **Grand Cross** is when four planets are in a 4/10 relationship from each other, occupying four signs, from each other. There are two planets opposing each other and four planets squaring each other. Four planets are 90 degrees from each other with two planets 180 degrees from each other. The planets will all be the same quality, either cardinal (movable), fixed (sthira) or mutable (dual). This is an extremely volatile and event oriented chart. There is always a crisis going on. It is triggered by other transiting planets crossing over this configuration formed in the heavens or the natal planets in a birth chart.

*If there is a **T-square**, a transiting planet will fill this fourth sensitive point to complete a grand cross configuration. This will trigger a very important event.

Watch the transiting lunar nodes, Rahu and Ketu: as their midpoint conjoins a natal planet an event will be produced. This planet will be 90 degrees from each node or 4/10 relationship. This forms T-square.

When making predictions, the lunar nodes, Rahu/Ketu are what produce eclipses and therefore, are always involved in major changes.

Grand Trine

The grand trine is when three planets form a trine (120 degrees) from each other. They are all in the same element. It may be a grand fire, earth, air or water trine.

Vedic Aspects

In considering the most important aspects with planetary patterns the full Vedic aspects are to be considered

These aspects are always counted in forward direction

These aspects are considered full aspects, meaning they are 100% in power, and so produce powerful effects. These will be considered in prediction.

All Planets aspect in full 100 % aspect with conjunction and opposition (0 degrees and 180 degrees)

Mars: aspects 100 % full aspect: 4 and 8 signs from where it is located (90 degrees and 210 degrees)

Saturn: aspects 100% full aspect: 3 and 10 signs from where it is located (60 degrees and 270 degrees)

Jupiter: aspects 100% full aspect: 5 and 9 from where it is located (120 degrees and 240 degrees)

Rahu and Ketu aspects 100 % full aspect 5 and 9 from where they are located (120 degrees and 240 degrees)

Chapter 9

Eclipses

Eclipses are the result of the Sun, Moon, and Rahu/Ketu aligning. A solar eclipse occurs when the new moon aligns with Rahu and Ketu. A new Moon is when the Sun and Moon are conjunct. There is a new Moon every month, but only when the nodes come into the specified degree orb to the Sun and Moon can an eclipse occur. This happens six months apart. One eclipse is with Rahu and the other is conjunct Ketu. Two weeks before or following a solar eclipse there can be a lunar eclipse. The lunar eclipse is when the Full moon is conjunct Rahu or Ketu. A full moon is when the Sun and Moon are in opposition. The eclipse seasons happen twice a year, six months apart.

The exact degree in which the Sun and Moon conjoin in eclipse should be watched for at least a year. This degree in the zodiac becomes like a land mine. Each year there are two specific degrees to be marked and watched. These are the degrees of the two solar eclipses that occur in a year. When another transiting planet crosses that mark an event occurs. If the eclipse degree falls within three degrees of a planet it will influence the indications of that planet for that year as well. Because an eclipse wipes out the light of the Sun or Moon, some astrologers believe it will wipe out or strongly effect negatively what the planet represents. Eclipses create unpredictable events in the year. They radically change things. During a six-week period of the eclipse season major events occur globally. This entails two weeks before, two weeks during the solar and lunar eclipse and two weeks after the eclipse. It is well noted that during these times there are more earthquakes, tsunamis and volcanic eruptions. Interestingly, transiting Mars crossed over the previous solar eclipse degree on September 11th 2001. This was the day of the most terrible terrorist attack in history.

When slower moving planets are close to Rahu or Ketu they will be involved with the eclipses for that year. The planet is "eclipsed." This means their energy is wiped out. The planet and the energies they represent become a major focus for that year. Generally it is a strong indication for losses concerning the areas that the planet rules.

Chapter 10

Planets Karakas (Indicators) in World Events

The planets are indicators of certain things in life and in the world. Karaka means the indicator or ruler of a specific thing. In world prediction certain planets all by themselves will be an indicator of something when making world predictions. Such as Ketu can be a karaka of terrorists.

The outer planets Uranus, Neptune and Pluto have been discussed in the big picture of world events. Next, the social planets Saturn and Jupiter come together in the social climate of the world. The biggest determination of change is Rahu and Ketu. Because they indicate where the eclipses are occurring, they produce huge changes and transformations according to their signs and planets that they conjoin.

Planetary Karakas

Sun: World Leaders, CEOs, Presidents, Authority figures, Bosses, Gold

Moon: The Public, Mass emotional swings, Women, Fame

Mercury: Mass Communications, Mass transit or travel (cars, buses, trains, ships, airplanes) Television, Internet, Radio, shipping, Import/Export, Sales, Education, Youth

Venus: The Arts, Fashion and Clothing, Film, Vehicles, Beauty, Creative endeavors, Luxuries

Mars: War, Anger, Weapons, Guns, Knives, Energy, Blood, Conflict, Real Estate, Sports

Jupiter: Wealth, Money, Prosperity, Opportunities, Expansion, Freedom, Children

Saturn: Restrictions, endings, Death, Old Age, Elderly, Wisdom, Land, Animals and Live Stock

Rahu: Epidemics, Disease, Pandemics, Poisons, Drugs, Addictions, Obsessions, Power, Extremes, and Accidents

Ketu: Terrorists, Death, Other Worlds, Violence, Accidents, Spirituality

Uranus: Rebellion, Revolution, Mass changes, Sudden occurrences, Electricity and Lightening, Machinery, Inventions, Airplanes, Computers, Social uprisings, Earthquakes, Astrology

Neptune: Water, Floods, Tsunamis, Earthquakes, Mysticism, Spirituality, Ghost, Deception, Illusions, Fraud, Film, Oil, Gas, Magic, Outer Space

Pluto: Power, Money and Government controls, Manipulation, Dictators, Atomic Energy, Volcanic Eruptions, Mafia Organizations, Corrupt Power

Planets as Personal Karakas

Planets can indicate the people in our lives and certain occurrences.

Sun: Father, Bosses, Authority, Self Esteem, Spirit, Life Force, Physical Energy, Physical Health, Heart

Moon: Mother, Emotions and Feelings, Safety and Protection, Security, Home, Family, Food, Cooking

Mercury: Siblings, all communications, speaking, writing, teaching, how we think or cognitive processing, neighbors, aunts and uncles

Venus: Wife in a Male's chart, Creative endeavors, artistic pursuits, beauty, relationships

Mars: Siblings (particularly younger), anger, conflict, energy, athletic, Physical energy level, Intelligence, Sexual attraction, Men is a woman's chart

Jupiter: Children, Husband in a female's chart, Wealth, money, prosperity, teachers or gurus, growths, expansion, freedom

Saturn: Elderly people, grand parents, uncles, death, endings, blockages, restrictions, discipline, organization, structure, set backs, delays, land, cattle, pets, wisdom, old age, and Reality

Rahu: Obsessions, Addictions, Desires, Foreigners and Foreign Lands, Attachments, Drugs, Powerful people, Materialistic pursuits and gains

Ketu: Outcasts in society, psychic powers, other worldly pursuits, detachment from the world, death

Uranus: Radical and unexpected changes, Rebelliousness, Eclectic, unusual interests, ingenious, odd and unusual, scientist, Nervousness

Neptune: Deception, Deceit, Fraud, Lies, Illusions, Cheating, spells, ghosts, spirits, mystics

Pluto: Power and manipulation, Controlling, Betrayal, Explosive, Controlling forces, Magnetism and charisma

Chapter 11

Faster Moving Planets: Mars, Venus, Mercury, Sun and Moon

There are cycles within cycles, and the faster moving planets are what determines the exact day events actually occur.

The faster moving planets Sun, Moon, Mercury, Venus and Mars are the triggers. When they form an aspect to the outer planets, social planets and the nodes of the moon, the events are set into motion. These planets predict the exact time within the bigger context of aspects that an event happens.

When there is a configuration of the slower moving planets these patterns are in effect for a long time. For example if there is a T- square forming with the slower moving planets Uranus, Pluto and Saturn, this aspect can be in effect for months. To time an event that comes out of this aspect will be when the faster moving planets come into aspect with the long-standing pattern. It may be when transiting Mars hits the point where it squares these planets. Or it may be when a planet fills in the position where it creates a grand cross.

Mars is instrumental in triggering events. Mars as a planet of energy and force is involved in many major events. It can instigate anger, conflict, and war. Mars' movement is slower and more impactful than are Venus and Mercury.

Therefore, the slower a planet is moving the more effect it has on world events. It is making a stance focusing their energy. It is like it wants us to pay attention to what it saying to us. This is why the outer planets are so impactful; their movement is slow and deliberate.

Because the faster moving planets transit through the zodiac very quickly they are constantly forming aspects. Mercury and Venus transit through the entire zodiac every year. So this comes down to when the faster moving planets begin to slow down in their cycles and turn retrograde or direct that their effects begin to take effect in a powerful way. The faster moving planets most important events occur around the degrees throughout the year where they make their stations. This is when they become stronger and make reference points in the zodiac.

Because the Sun and Moon do not go retrograde their effects are made with the eclipses. The dates and degrees of the solar and lunar eclipses are points to take note of within the year. In addition, the dates of the transiting planets as they cross over these degrees are also noted. They also create events.

Chapter 12

Retrograde Planets

Movement of planets marks timing of events; there are phases in their cycles that planets are moving faster and slower. When a planet is about to turn retrograde, it is moving slowly and marks a time when affairs ruled by the planet will seem to slow down. When Jupiter slows down and goes retrograde, the economy slows down. Generally, this is a time of reorganizing before forward progress. The cycles are like the ebb and flow of the tides. There is a time to move forward and a time to pull back.

Retrograde planets appear to travel in reverse through the zodiac from our perspective, this involves the speed and relationship of the planets to Earth as we orbit the Sun. As they align with Earth in their orbits, retrograde planets appear to be traveling backwards from our vantage point.

When a planet turns retrograde, it slows and appears to stop before it actually travels backwards (stationary retrograde) in the zodiac and, when a planet turns direct (stationary direct), it again slows and appears to stop before reversing its transit to forward movement. The period when it changes direction is called a station. The degrees in the zodiac where a planet stations become powerful as these degrees are emphasized in the zodiac. The faster moving planets — Mercury, Venus, and Mars — change the emotions of the masses when they turn retrograde. This affects trends, financial markets, and major events involving the planet's indications.

When these faster moving planets slow to go retrograde and travel with the outer slow-moving planets, they trigger the timing of important world events.

For Mercury and Venus, a line up can happen when the planet is between the Earth and the Sun (an inferior conjunction) or when the planet is on the other side of the Sun from the Earth (a superior conjunction). At the inferior conjunction, Mercury or Venus will always be retrograde. With the superior conjunction, the planet is traveling in forward motion behind the Sun from Earth's viewpoint; and so it will be direct. It will be at its farthest point from the Earth at the superior conjunction and the closest point to the Earth in the inferior conjunction.

The outer planets, Mars through Pluto, form an opposition to the Sun when they line up and go retrograde. These planets that travel outside the Earth's orbit, beginning with Mars, are considered more social as they influence worldly affairs or the collective consciousness. Because Mercury and Venus orbit with the Sun they can never be in opposition to the Sun.

Since the slower a planet moves, the deeper is its impact. These stationary times and the zodiac degrees involved are extremely powerful. Individuals who are born with a planet stationary will exhibit the planet in its most powerful state. This planet and whatever it rules will be magnified enormously in their life.

The retrograde process symbolizes a time for retreat, reflection and review. In a birth chart the energy of the retrograde planet is sometimes delayed till later in life. Because a planet that is retrograde is at its closest point to the earth, it will seem larger in the sky. Therefore, symbolically the intense effects of a retrograde planet stand out and demand to be addressed. As it does not function like a forward-moving planet, it can seem a bit eccentric, out of control and likely to cause problems.

The planet in its forward, faster motion specifies the time in life to move forward and start new projects. But when a planet slows down and turns retrograde, it is time to slow down and review. Like the ebb and flow of the tides of the ocean there is a time to push forward and a time to pull back. Our lives must heed the cycles for understanding and development, instead of forcing things against nature.

Mercury is retrograde three to four times a year for approximately 20 days. Venus is retrograde the least of any of the planets; it retrogrades every 18 months for 42 days. Mars will retrograde every 24-26 months for 60-80 days. Jupiter retrogrades every 9 months for 4 months at a time. Saturn retrogrades every 8 months for 4-5 months. The outer planets Uranus, Neptune and Pluto turn retrograde every 7 months and are retrograde for 5 months out of the year.

But the length of time the faster moving planets remain in a sign is most important. Because of the forward and backward motion while in the retrograde process planets remain in a sign much longer and the sign is what indicates the many events occurring during this process. In the retrograde process Mercury remains in a sign for about 2 months, Venus about 4 months, and Mars about 7 months.

The Sun and the Moon never go retrograde. Rahu and Ketu travel backwards – therefore they are always retrograde but seem to station around the times of the eclipses, intensifying their effects. They remain in the same degree for about 3 months then move faster making up the time they spend in a sign, which is 18 months. They move approximately 1 ½ degree a month on the average.

Applying all these steps to actual world events will exemplify how the planetary cycles reveal the trends and the actual prediction of these major events in the world.

These are the cycles within cycles, and the combination of many aspects occurring at one time produce these world events.

Planets (Symbols) and Meanings

Symbol	Planet	Meaning
☉	Sun	CEOs, Presidents, Bosses, Power, Father, Gold
☽	Moon	Public, Fame, Mother, Silver, Water
☿	Mercury	Communications, Media, Advertising, Trade, Sales, Travel
♀	Venus	Luxuries such as Cars, Boats, Airplanes, Opulent wealth
♂	Mars	Real Estate, Engineers, Intelligence, Siblings
♃	Jupiter	Luck, Fortune, Freedom, Money, Teaching, Philanthropy, Travel
♄	Saturn	Land, Cattle, Trusts, Government
♅	Uranus	Change, Electricity, Airplanes, Computers
♆	Neptune	Oil, Water, Oceans, Prescription and Illegal Drugs, Alcohol, Films, Movies, Photography
♇	Pluto	Big business, Monopolies, Mafia, Control and Power
☊	Rahu	Magnifies the planets it aspects, especially a conjunction.
☋	Ketu	Depletes the Planet it Aspects, especially the conjunction, Psychic Intuitive Powers (used in business)

Signs (Symbols)

♈	Aries
♉	Taurus
♊	Gemini
♋	Cancer
♌	Leo
♍	Virgo
♎	Libra
♏	Scorpio
♐	Sagittarius
♑	Capricorn
♒	Aquarius
♓	Pisces

The Nakshatras

	Nakshatra		Degrees
1	Ashwini	"the horse woman"	00:00 ♈ to 13:20 ♈
2	Bharani	"the bearer - of new life"	13:20 ♈ to 26:40 ♈
3	Krittika	"the one who cuts"	26:40 ♈ to 10:00 ♉
4	Rohini	"the red one"	10:00 ♉ to 23:20 ♉
5	Mrigashira	"head of a deer"	23:20 ♉ to 06:40 ♊
6	Ardra	"the moist one"	06:40 ♊ to 20:00 ♊
7	Purnavasu	"return of the light"	20:00 ♊ to 03:20 ♋
8	Pushya	"to nourish"	03:20 ♋ to 16:40 ♋
9	Ashlesha	"the embracer"	16:40 ♋ to 30:00 ♋
10	Magha	"the great one"	00:00 ♌ to 13:20 ♌
11	Purva Phalguni	"the former reddish one"	13:20 ♌ to 26:40 ♌
12	Uttara Phalguni	"the later reddish one"	26:40 ♌ to 10:00 ♍
13	Hasta	"the hand"	10:00 ♍ to 23:20 ♍
14	Chitra	"the bright one"	23:20 ♍ to 06:40 ♎
15	Swati	"the sword or independence"	06:40 ♎ to 20:00 ♎
16	Vishakha	"the forked shaped"	20:00 ♎ to 03:20 ♏
17	Anuradha	"the discipline of the divine spark"	03:20 ♏ to 16:40 ♏
18	Jyeshta	"the eldest"	16:40 ♏ to 00:00 ♐
19	Mula	"the root"	00:00 ♐ to 13:20 ♐
20	Purva Ashadha	"early victory"	13:20 ♐ to 26:40 ♐
21	Uttara Ashadha	"latter victory"	26:40 ♐ to 10:00 ♑
22	Shravana	"the ear"	10:00 ♑ to 23:20 ♑
23	Dhanishta	"the richest one"	23:20 ♑ to 06:40 ♒
24	Shatabishak	"the hundred healers"	06:40 ♒ to 20:00 ♒
25	P: Bhadrapada	"the former happy feet"	20:00 ♒ to 03:20 ♓
26	U: Bhadrapada	"the latter happy feet"	03:20 ♓ to 16:40 ♓
27	Revati	"the wealthiest one"	16:40 ♓ to 30:00 ♓

Sequence of Cycles for Use in Prediction:

Outer Planets Aspects and Patterns

Saturn and Jupiter Aspects

Rahu, Ketu, and Eclipses

Transits of faster Moving Planets

Retrograde Cycles in Prediction

Vedic astrology uses the square charts wherein the planets move clockwise instead of the counter clockwise movement of the western circular charts.

In this book the south Indian style charts are used where the signs are fixed, meaning the signs are always in the same places, the houses move according to the ascendant (first house). The houses will not be discussed in this section because the planets aspects are to be the focus in world prediction.

Remember these are the sidereal placements of the planets used in Vedic astrology meaning they are 23 degrees behind the western positions in the zodiac, due to the precession of the equinoxes.

Part III

How to Predict World Events

War and Destruction

World War II 1939
Bombing of Pearl Harbor 1941
Bombing of Hiroshima 1945
Tiananmen Square Massacre 1989

Global Disease

Outbreak of Pandemic 1918-1919
Aids 1981

Economic Crashes

Stock Market Crash 2008, 1987, 1929

Earthquakes

Earthquake in San Francisco 1906
Earthquake in Japan 2011

Assassinations

John F. Kennedy, 1963
Martin Luther King Junior 1968
Robert Kennedy 1968

Airline Crashes and Terrorist Attacks

American Airlines Flight 11 2001
Malaysian flight 370 disappearance 2014
Malaysian flight 17 2014
Attack on America September 11th 2001

Chapter 1

War and Destruction

World War II

This chart is an evolving snap shot in time, as we know this war and violence was brewing for some time before the declaration day of World War II. The slowest moving aspect is the Uranus and Pluto waning square. This war was building as Uranus formed the square causing the effects set in motion at the time of this event chart.

But it is Saturn that set off these world events. Saturn is square Pluto while conjoining Ketu. It is also approaching Uranus. This was the official day of the start of World War II, one of the worse times globally in history. Saturn's aspect to Pluto causes terrible explosive events, and with Uranus leads to death and endings. The combination of Saturn with Ketu indicates great loss and destruction. Saturn is eclipsed by the nodes (Rahu and Ketu). This is a very bad omen in a chart. And at this time faster moving Mars sets off this combination of ill-fated events as it aspects Saturn, Ketu, Uranus and opposes Pluto. Actually, this is a grand cross with Rahu/Ketu/Saturn/Uranus, Pluto and Mars. This is a good example of the combination of planets as the slower moving planets and their combinations create world events.

5th h. 23	6th h. 29	7th h. 27	8th h. 29
☽ 15:50 UBh ♃℞ 13:57 UBh ♓	☋ 07:19 Ash ♄℞ 07:57 Ash ♅℞ 28:56 Kri ♈	♉	♊
4th h. 29 ♒	World War II Fri 09-01-1939 12:00:00 Washington, District of Columbia USA		9th h. 23 ♇ 09:04 Pus ☿ 28:06 Asl ♋
3rd h. 35 ♂ 01:25 USh ♑	Timezone: 5 DST: 0 Latitude: 38N53'42 Longitude: 77W02'11 Ayanamsha : -23:01:02 Lahiri		10th h. 29 ♀ 14:11 PPh ☉ 15:19 PPh ♆ 29:29 UPh ♌
♐ 2nd h. 28	Asc 01:17 Vis ♏ 1st h. 32	☊ 07:19 Swa ♎ 12th h. 24	♍ 11th h. 29

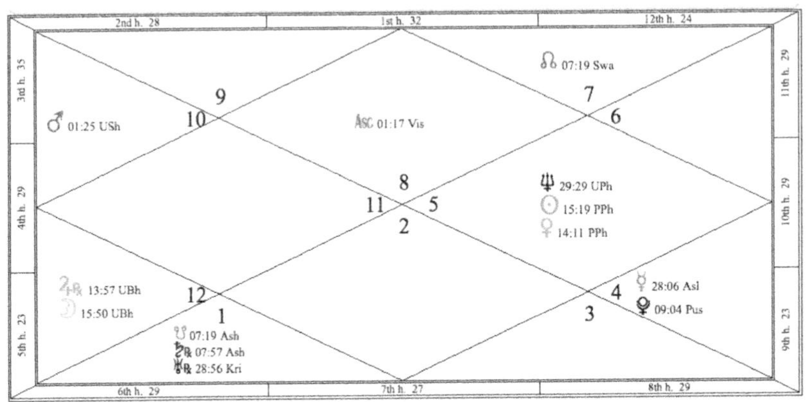
2nd h. 28
1st h. 32
12th h. 24
3rd h. 35
11th h. 29
4th h. 29
10th h. 29
5th h. 23
9th h. 23
6th h. 29
7th h. 27
8th h. 29
01:25 USh
Asc 01:17 Vis
07:19 Swa
29:29 UPh
15:19 PPh
14:11 PPh
13:57 UBh
15:50 UBh
07:19 Ash
07:57 Ash
28:56 Kri
28:06 Asl
09:04 Pus

Attack on Pearl Harbor

The attack on Pearl Harbor was a surprise military strike conducted by the Imperial Japanese Navy against the United States naval base at Pearl Harbor, Hawaii, on the morning of December 7, 1941. The attack led to the United States' entry into World War II.

At the onset of the war Saturn and Uranus were approaching a conjunction. This conjunction involves the breakdown of old patterns. But in this case Uranus was activated by Saturn and Jupiter. Furthermore, Rahu and Ketu are activating this combination as Jupiter is at the midpoint of Rahu and Ketu. This creates a T-square and the transiting Sun activates this as to the exact day this event occurred.

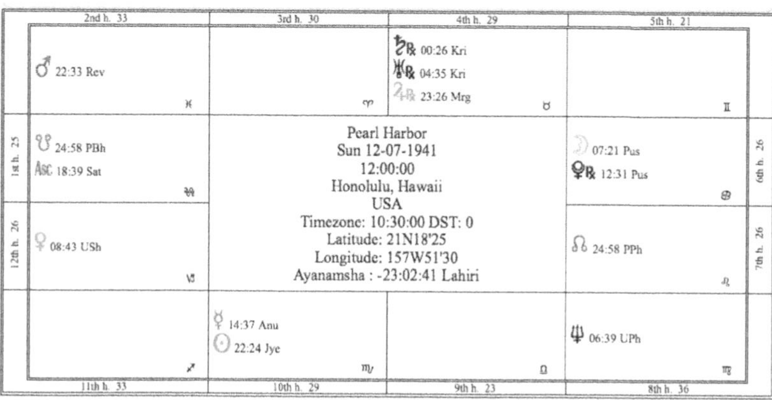

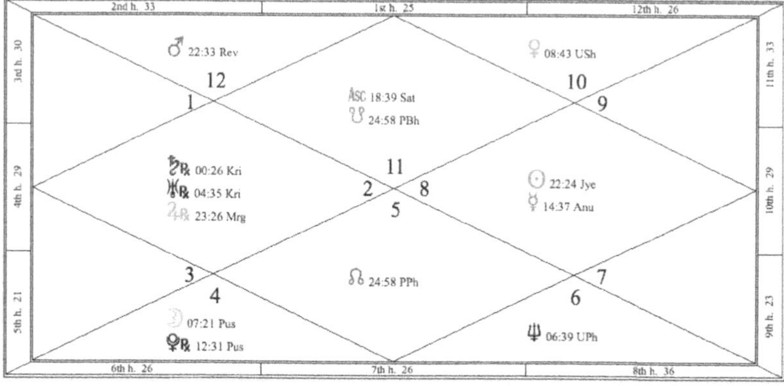

The Bombing of Hiroshima

On August 6, 1945, during World War II (1939-45), an American B-29 bomber dropped the world's first deployed atomic bomb over the Japanese city of Hiroshima. The explosion wiped out 90 percent of the city and immediately killed 80,000 people; tens of thousands more would later die of radiation exposure. Three days later, a second B-29 dropped another A-bomb on Nagasaki, killing an estimated 40,000 people. Japan's Emperor Hirohito announced his country's unconditional surrender in World War II in a radio address on August 15, citing the devastating power of "a new and most cruel bomb." Mercury turns retrograde this day indicating a reversal of events. This day changed everything worldwide.

The end result of this massively destructive war came through the most destructive explosive event possible. This was a turning point globally. Saturn seems to be instrumental in all massively destructive events. As Saturn moved into Gemini it is combined with Rahu and Jupiter forming a waxing square. Jupiter conjoins Neptune, the planet of unforeseen events. Saturn is eclipsed (conjunct) by the north lunar node (Rahu), which indicates a time of massive changes. Remember, as Saturn conjoins one of the nodes every 11 years there is a destructive event that changes humanity.

But the most significant aspect to be noted during this time is the aspect of Mars as the triggering aspect in this event. Mars is approaching a conjunction to Uranus. This is a combination of sudden unexpected war, Uranus being unexpected explosive events and Mars as the karaka of violence, war and weapons.

But there is a very specific key to learn here. This involves the additional note of the quincunx aspect forming the Yod. Yods are called the finger of God because they are always involved in transforming events through destruction and death that brings transformation. This quality comes from the aspect of the 6/8 relationship denoting qualities of accidents and enemies around death and transformation. In this chart Mars and Uranus are sextile Pluto/Sun and they are quincunx Ketu. This combination of Mars, Uranus and Pluto is lethal, indicating explosive events, and Ketu is the trigger in this yod.

The triggering force within this day is the Moon as the second hand of the clock in timing. It is in Gemini activating Saturn and Rahu, and almost in exact conjunction with Saturn. Both Venus and Rahu are in the nakshatra Ardra. This nakshatra seems to be prevalent in most events that affect the masses with extreme sadness globally. This Nakshatra's symbol is a teardrop and the ruling deity Rudra represents the howling winds. This nakshatra represents the many tears shed by all of humanity.

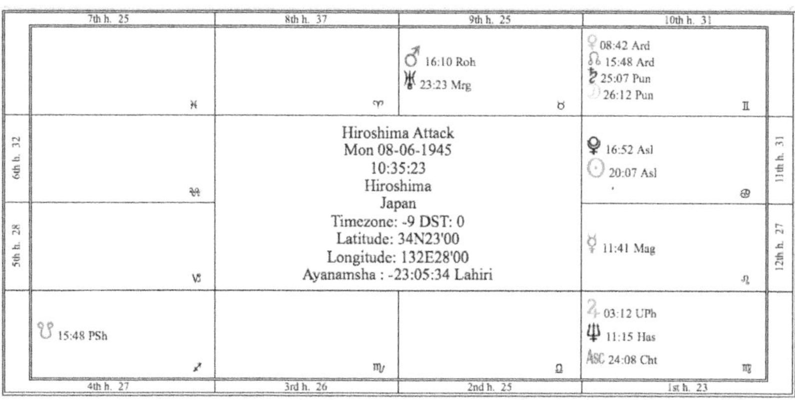

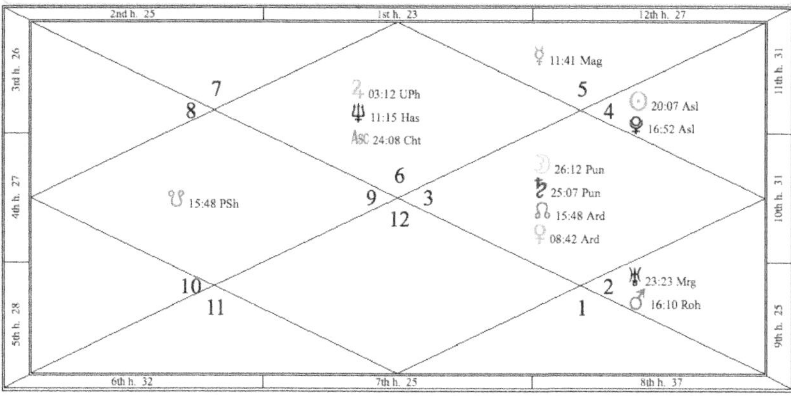

Tiananmen Square Massacre

The Tiananmen Square protests of 1989, student-led popular demonstrations in the heart of Beijing that received broad support from city residents, exposed deep splits within China's political leadership.

The protests were forcibly suppressed by hard-line leaders who ordered the military to enforce martial law in the country's capital. The crackdown, initiated on June 3–4 became known as the Tiananmen Square Massacre or the June 4 Massacre. Troops with assault rifles and tanks inflicted casualties on unarmed civilians trying to block the military's advance towards Tiananmen Square, which student demonstrators had occupied for seven weeks. The death toll was in the thousands.

The reason why this event is important is it involves the essence of the power of the Yod to create the change that eventually frees and transforms the world but through death and destruction.

In 1989 Uranus and Neptune are conjunct beginning a transformational revolution. The combination of Saturn conjoined in this combination represents the lifting of delusion.

Saturn is the planet of reality and Neptune is delusions so this was an awakening as the students rebelled against a dictatorship government. The opposition of Mars to Saturn, Neptune and Uranus triggered the violence.

The yod is created with Sun/Jupiter quincunx Pluto, and Pluto sextiles Uranus, Neptune and Saturn. The Sun was the faster moving planet that triggered the day as it forms the perfect Yod on this day with Pluto and Saturn. Here the power of the transformational qualities of a Yod can be seen.

8th h. 43	9th h. 29	10th h. 24	11th h. 24
♓	♈	☿℞ 04:29 Kri ☉ 19:46 Roh ♃ 23:34 Mrg ☽ 23:44 Mrg ♉	♀ 05:33 Mrg ♂ 28:32 Pun ♊
7th h. 30 ☊ 05:07 Dha ♒	Tiananmen Square Massacre Sun 06-04-1989 12:00:00 Tiananmen Square, Beijing China Timezone: -8 DST: 1 Latitude: 39N54'00 Longitude: 116E23'00 Ayanamsha : -23:42:42 Lahiri		12th h. 27 ♋
6th h. 27 ♑			1st h. 24 ☋ 05:07 Mag Asc 07:33 Mag ♌
♄℞ 18:52 PSh ♆℞ 18:01 PSh ♅℞ 10:27 Mul ♐	♏	♇℞ 19:16 Swa ♎	♍
5th h. 24	4th h. 22	3rd h. 36	2nd h. 27

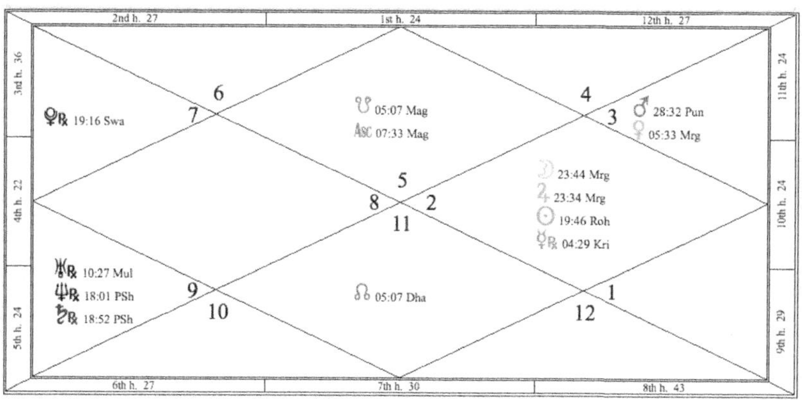

Chapter 2

Global Disease

Pandemic Mars Virgo
Mon 02-04-1918
12:00:00
Dallas, Texas
USA
Timezone: 6 DST: 0
Latitude: 32N46'59
Longitude: 96W48'24
Ayanamsha : -22:43:06 Lahiri

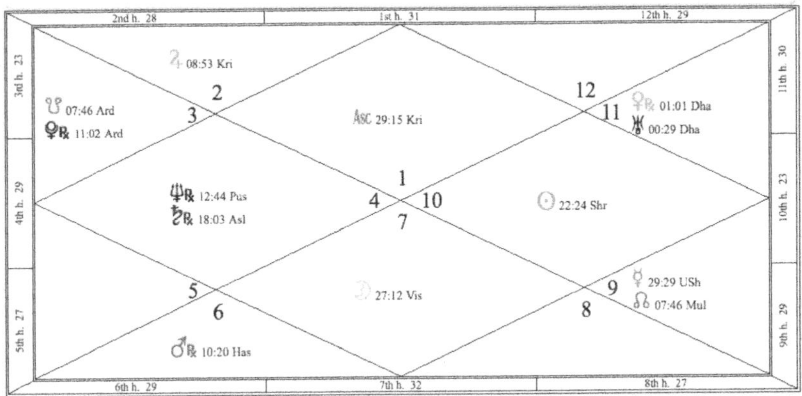

The Pandemic of 1918

The global flu outbreak of 1918 killed 50 million people worldwide, ranking as one of the deadliest epidemics in history. This deadly "Spanish flu" claimed more lives than World War I, which ended the same year the pandemic struck.

Since there is no specific date that this started we will analyze the cycles of the outer planets as to what is behind such a world pandemic. Now we are looking for aspects that constitute the indications of disease and death.

The disease was sited as beginning around the end of 1917. For the next few years the cycles of outer planets are strongly indicating a time for of definite problems. Uranus and Neptune are in opposition while Saturn is conjoining Neptune. This indicates an awakening to hidden forces and in this case it could mean disease. Neptune is indicative of disease. Along side Pluto is Ketu, the indicator of loss in the nakshatra Ardra.

Aids Epidemic 1980s

April 24, 1980, San Francisco resident Ken Horne, the first AIDS case in the United States to be recognized at the time, is reported to the Center for Disease Control. And October 31, French-Canadian flight attendant Gaëtan Dugas pays his first known visit to New York City bathhouses. He would later be deemed "Patient Zero" for his apparent connection to many early cases of AIDS in the United States. Rick Wellikoff, a Brooklyn schoolteacher, dies of AIDS in New York City. He is the 4th US citizen known to die from the disease.

A gay tipster overheard his physician mention that some gay men were being treated in intensive-care units in New York City for a strange pneumonia. It was around 1982 that Aids created a mass epidemic that created mass fear around the world. Fear took the world by a storm, for no body understood what it was or how you got it. Today this epidemic has killed more people around the world than any kind of catastrophe. 36 million people have died from aids since the first cases were reported in 1981.

9th h. 29	10th h. 26	11th h. 34	12th h. 30
♓	♈	♉	☊ 28:21 Pun ♊
8th h. 21: ☉ 09:16 Sat ♒	Aids Sun 02-21-1982 15:12:32 Washington, District of Columbia USA		1st h. 30: Asc 08:26 Pus ♋
7th h. 19: ☽ 15:10 Shr ☿ 12:55 Shr ♀ 02:01 USh ♑	Timezone: 5 DST: 0 Latitude: 38N53'42 Longitude: 77W02'11 Ayanamsha : -23:36:13 Lahiri		2nd h. 24: ♌
☋ 28:21 USh ♆ 03:05 Mul ♐	♅ 10:54 Anu ♏	♇℞ 03:10 Cht ♃ 16:43 Swa ♎	♂℞ 25:34 Cht ♄℞ 28:14 Cht ♍
6th h. 29	5th h. 35	4th h. 28	3rd h. 32

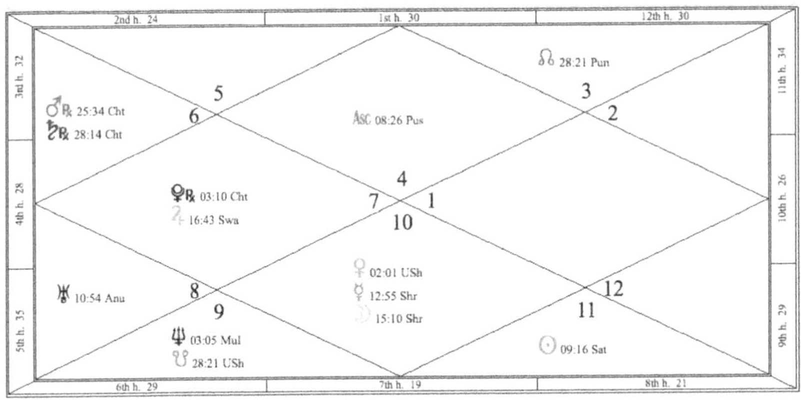

This is the chart of the day that Mars turned retrograde in Virgo. This is significant because Mars was retrograde in Virgo during the time of Pandemic of 1918. The period of time that Mars goes retrograde every two years indicates a sensitive spot in the zodiac. Transiting Mars travels through 12 signs of the zodiac every two years. Every two years when Mars turns retrograde it moves up a sign from its previous retrograde. So it takes Mars around 16-17 years to come back to the same sign where it was retrograde before. It is significant that Mars marks its spot as it retrogrades in Virgo the sign of health, healing and disease. At the time Mars went retrograde in Virgo in 1982 it was transiting along with Saturn. When Mars is retrograde it stays in a sign for around seven months. During Mars transit in Virgo it was with malefic Saturn. Mars and Saturn do not get along, and the negative effects of this retrograde are intensified enormously. Saturn and Mars are transiting at the midpoint of Rahu and Ketu. Rahu and Ketu are indicators of disease, epidemics and pandemics.

Also During this time Ketu was with Neptune another indicator of loss through disease. Jupiter and Pluto were together for the 13-year conjunction. Jupiter and Pluto together magnify things all the more.

The similarity to both charts that have the most destructive disease potential lies in the Mars retrograde in Virgo plus Mars is in both cases at the midpoint of Rahu and Ketu. Since Rahu and Ketu rule pandemics and epidemics in each chart, there was a destructive outer planet transiting with Ketu. In the 1918 Pandemic it was Pluto traveling with Ketu, and this disease killed so many quickly from all ages. But Aids was a mystery and progressed for so much longer killing many more over a longer duration. It is still not completely under control in some areas of the world. This is the power that Neptune has, as it is the planet that casts an illusion and a spell on people, and is definitely involved in death.

It is interesting to note that at the time of this writing 2014 we just finished the retrograde cycle of Mars in Virgo and based on these previous indicators I predicted an outbreak of a debilitating disease to hit the world. At this time the Ebola disease is killing many in Africa and the spread of the disease is feared throughout the world. It is deadly, with a fatality rate now of 60-80 percent with no cure in sight. There are now cases that have spread to the United States.

Chapter 3

Economic Crashes

Three Stock Market Crashes Analyzed

The cycles to be analyzed are three previous stock market crashes: 1929, 1987 and 2008. The similarities and understanding of these previous cycles can help predict future trends.

One commonality of these dates is that they all occurred around the month of October. From October 13th to November 13th, the Sun is in Libra each year. The sun represents leadership, power and life and is debilitated in Libra, meaning it is at its weakest point in the zodiac during this time of year.

October 29, 1929 was called Black Tuesday for it was the most devastating stock market crash of all time, and started the Great Depression. Pluto was square Uranus during this time. There is a global and generational effect when two outer planets aspect each other. It represents an event that destroys the powers that control the world. Pluto represents power and control. Uranus is the planet of sudden change and awakenings. If world leaders do not adapt to the changing times the people rebel. As these two planets form a hard aspect there is a sudden collapse of power that rules the world. Pluto square Uranus brought the Great Depression and the stock market crash of 1929.

Uranus and Pluto are square 2011- 2015. The powers that rule the world from an old paradigm that no longer supports the changing times are being destroyed and must clear the way for a new transformation. The old dictatorships are breaking down for a new generation. This involves a new financial paradigm. The old ways of dealing with money, business, stocks and banks are transforming.

Saturn's and Jupiter's most inharmonious aspect is the quincunx, 150 and 210 degrees. This aspect occurs before and after too much expansion, it balances extremes in the markets. They form a conjunction every 20 years. Following the conjunction they form an opposition 10 years later. The quincunx occurs before and after the opposition, which is the aspect of imbalance in the economy. There were Jupiter/Saturn quincunxes occurring in 1929, 1987 and 2008.

October 1929, Jupiter was retrograde at 22 degrees of Taurus and had just stationed. Jupiter was stationed at 22 degrees in October 2012. Jupiter is the planet that produces wealth and money. Jupiter is not very strong in the sign of Taurus, but it pertains to the banking industry and money. When a planet is retrograde its effects become more noticeable as it is closer to the earth.

The planet that becomes a fulcrum of Jupiter's energy while in Taurus is Venus, because Venus rules Taurus. This is called the dispositor. Therefore, Venus is the moderator of occurring events. On October 29, 1929 Venus was in the debilitation sign Virgo.

In 1929 Saturn was square Uranus. Saturn forms a hard aspect with Uranus every 45 years. The hard aspects are conjunction, square and opposition. This always indicates a volatile time globally. There are social uprisings around the world when outer planets aspect Saturn. Saturn represents the old and Uranus the new, and when they clash the old must dissolve to make way for new innovations that change the world. This involves extreme events that are upsetting. Saturn and Uranus were in opposition in 2008. This was a very turbulent time in American history for it was the eve of the presidential elections and the stock market crashed. The world has been in a very difficult place since that time. It has been compared to the time of the great depression.

In October 1929, Mars and Ketu were in Libra, and Rahu in Aries, which makes Venus and Mars the dispositors of the Moon's nodes.

Declination of a planet is another variable that should be considered by astrologers. When we consider the placement of a planet in zodiacal degrees we are measuring its position in longitude along the ecliptic, which describes the apparent path of the Sun. But a planet's placement should be viewed from declination and latitude as well. Declination is the distance of a planet either north or south of the celestial equator, which is the earth's equator extended out into space. Latitude is the distance of a planet either north or south of the ecliptic. When planets are aligned by declination both north, or both south they are parallel; and when they are aligned one north and the other south they are contra-parallel. Planets that are conjunct and parallel or contra-parallel have much more powerful effects than planets that are simply conjunct.

Planets aligned in declination on October 29, 1929 were Saturn contra-parallel Pluto, and Jupiter was parallel Pluto. As both Saturn and

Jupiter determine the social climate of the world both aligned by declination to Pluto represents world crisis. Pluto brings transformation and endings to anything non-productive. It breaks down old patterns for new beginnings. This can be catastrophic and devastating change.

In October 1987, the most significant aspect was Neptune conjunct Uranus. Together these two planets cause confusion and sudden upsets. Uranus causes a sudden awakening and Neptune pertains to denial and confusion. But together they can cause a spiritual awakening. This was the beginning of a revolution that changed the world in 1989, the break down of the Berlin Wall and the Tiananmen Square Massacre. But on October 19, 1987 Neptune was at the midpoint (square) of Rahu and Ketu, indicating something was brewing beneath the surface unknown to the public. This involved panic in the stock market and the world economy.

Pluto was aligned by declination with Rahu and Ketu in October of 1987 and again in October 2012 indicating an explosive year with events that will create massive change. The world is transforming just as before when the Berlin Wall came down. Many walls that have separated the world must dissolve.

Another significant correlation is that Mars was conjunct Ketu in October 1929 and 1987. In 1929, Mars was aligned by declination with Rahu and Ketu as well. In October 2008, Mars was at the midpoint (square) of Rahu and Ketu.

Certain points and degrees that were activated at these critical financial extremes were the specific degrees of 22 and 23. In October 1929, Jupiter was 22 degrees of Taurus and Mars 23 degrees of Libra. October 19, 1987 Saturn was 23 degrees of Scorpio. October 10, 2008 Saturn was 22 degrees of Leo and Rahu was 22 degrees of Capricorn and Ketu was 22 degrees Cancer.

In 2008, the crash in October was before a very emotional election where America became polarized by many issues aside from the economy. There was a sudden rise in oil prices right before the elections, and the crash of the stock market occurred in the midst of a political uproar.

The chart used for the stock market in America, is the opening of the New York Stock Exchange. It opened May 17, 1792, 10:10 am New York, New York. The charts to be examined with this date are the three major stock market crashes, October 1st 1929, October 19, 1987, and October 06, 2008.

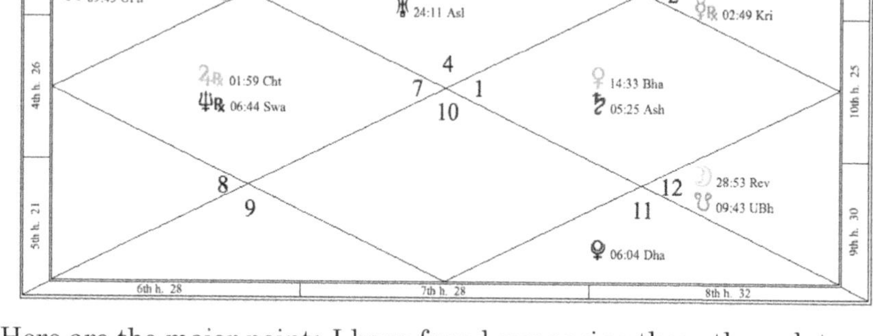

Here are the major points I have found comparing these three dates.

1) The first commonality is they all happened in October.

2) Jupiter was always in the sign before or after Rahu.

3) The next important variable is that Saturn and Jupiter were in the phase going from the quincunx to a trine, or a trine to a quincunx. That means from 150 degrees to 120, or 120 to 210. The 150 and 210 degrees of separation are the quincunx aspects. In Vedic astrology it is a 6/8 or 8/6 relationship. The trine is the 120 degree aspect in between the 6/8 relationship of these 2 planets that specifically relates to the economy.

4) Therefore, Saturn and Jupiter are imperative in analyzing the economy. In each of these charts Saturn is trine or quincunx Rahu, while Jupiter is in the sign next to Rahu.

5) The next variable is the result of Jupiter being 30 degrees from Rahu. Jupiter is always close to the eclipse degrees. The two eclipse degrees are to be watched within that year relative to the transits of Jupiter and Saturn. It is when Saturn and Jupiter are quincunx, and Jupiter is in the sign following before or after Rahu.

- The essence of predicting the economy is using the relationship of Saturn and Jupiter with Rahu and Ketu. Rahu and Ketu determine the area where the eclipses occur.

Most Importantly,

6) Eclipses are in effect for one year before or after their occurrences. The most significant effect in all 3 charts is that Jupiter is conjunct Rahu during the time of an eclipse occurring within a year of the event. This means Jupiter is eclipsed the year of a stock market crash. Eclipses are known to be associated with fated events!

Jupiter and Rahu come together every 7 years. But there is not a stock market crash every 7 years, therefore there must be the other variables in effect as well. This means that the transits of Jupiter and Saturn must be in a trine/quincunx aspect. Looking ahead Jupiter will conjunct Rahu in 2016 in Leo, but Saturn is in Scorpio (90 degrees). In 2023 Jupiter and Rahu will conjoin in Aries but Saturn is in Aquarius (60 degrees). The year 2030 looks the most treacherous with Jupiter and Rahu in Scorpio and Saturn in Taurus (opposition).

The first chart to be analyzed is the Oct 1st 1929 stock market crash.

2nd h. 27	3rd h. 30	4th h. 27	5th h. 29
♅℞ 16:34 UBh ♓	☊ 19:39 Bha ♈	♃ 23:30 Mrg ♉	♇ 26:40 Pun ♊
1st h. 32: Asc 11:43 Sat ♒	Stock Market Crash Tue 10-01-1929 16:15:43 New York, New York USA		6th h. 41: ♋
12th h. 23: ♑	Timezone: 5 DST: 0 Latitude: 40N42'51 Longitude: 74W00'22 Ayanamsha : -22:52:21 Lahiri		7th h. 22: ♆ 09:35 Mag ♀ 14:39 PPh ♌
♄ 01:56 Mul ♐	♏	♂ 03:59 Cht ☋ 19:39 Swa ♎	☽ 01:59 UPh ☉ 15:19 Has ☿℞ 28:13 Cht ♍
11th h. 28	10th h. 30	9th h. 26	8th h. 22

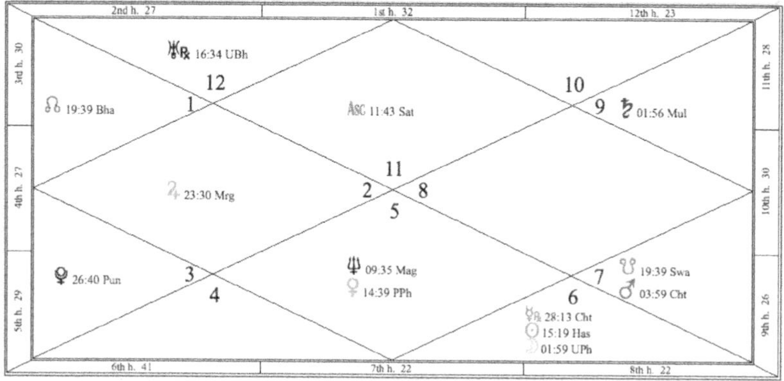

- Saturn and Jupiter are quincunx with Jupiter 30 degrees following Rahu.
- Solar eclipse May 9, 1929 at 24 degrees Aries. Rahu 28 Aries
- Solar eclipse November 1, 1929 at 15 degrees Libra, Ketu 19 Libra
- NYSE natal Venus 14 degrees Aries was aspected by the solar Eclipse 15 degrees Libra.
- Jupiter is 23 degrees Taurus a sensitive degree: sensitive degree seen in major events in the USA chart, Sensitive degree is 23 degrees Scorpio or Taurus.

October 19, 1987

4th h. 32	5th h. 20	6th h. 27	7th h. 31
☊ 08:37 UBh ♓	♃℞ 00:50 Ash ♈	♉	♊
3rd h. 33 ♒	Stock Market crash 2 Mon 10-19-1987 12:16:15 New York, New York USA Timezone: 5 DST: 1 Latitude: 40N42'51 Longitude: 74W00'22 Ayanamsha : -23:41:11 Lahiri		8th h. 29 ♋
2nd h. 27 ♑			☽ 26:10 PPh ♌ 9th h. 33
♆ 11:49 Mul Asc 02:28 Mul ♐	♄ 23:42 Jye ♅ 29:59 Jye ♏	☉ 02:03 Cht ♇ 15:38 Swa ♀ 17:17 Swa ☿℞ 18:56 Swa ♎	☋ 08:37 UPh ♂ 13:18 Has ♍
1st h. 26	12th h. 20	11th h. 28	10th h. 31

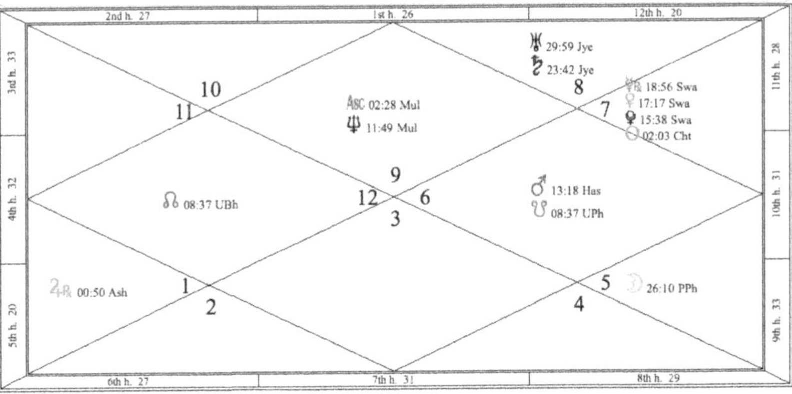

- Saturn and Jupiter are trine by sign and degrees 5/9 relationship with Jupiter, within 30 degrees following Rahu.
- Solar Eclipse September 22, 1987 at 5 degrees Virgo, Ketu 8 Virgo
- Solar Eclipse March 29,1987 at 14 degrees Pisces, Rahu 17 Pisces.
- Transiting Rahu and Ketu 8 degrees Pisces/Virgo is conjunct natal Rahu/Ketu in the NYSE chart at 9 degrees Pisces/Virgo.
- Saturn is 23 degrees Scorpio a sensitive degree: opposed the sensitive degree seen in major events in the USA chart, Sensitive degree is 23 degrees Scorpio or Taurus.

October 06 2008

6th h. 26 ♓	7th h. 23 ♈	8th h. 30 ♉	9th h. 30 ♊
5th h. 27 ♒ ♅℞ 25:47 PBh	Stock Market Crash 3 Mon 10-06-2008 09:43:50 New York, New York USA		10th h. 36 ♋ ☋ 22:45 Asl
4th h. 27 ♑ ♆℞ 27:40 Dha ☊ 22:45 Shr	Timezone: 5 DST: 1 Latitude: 40N42'51 Longitude: 74W00'22 Ayanamsha : -23:58:57 Lahiri		11th h. 32 ♌ ♄ 21:55 PPh
3rd h. 24 ♐ ♃ 19:48 PSh ☽ 10:54 Mul ♇ 04:42 Mul	2nd h. 28 ♏	1st h. 33 ♎ ♂ 07:37 Swa ♀ 21:11 Vis Asc 21:19 Vis	12th h. 21 ♍ ☉ 19:41 Has ☿℞ 20:20 Has

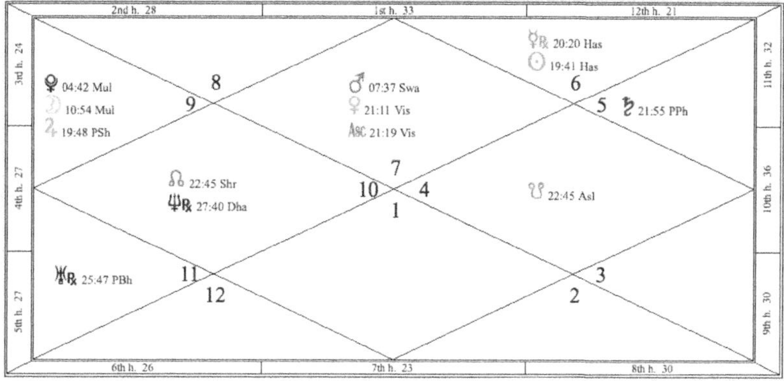

- Saturn and Jupiter are trine with Jupiter 30 degrees before Rahu
- Solar Eclipse August 1, 2008 at15 degrees Cancer, Ketu 24 Cancer
- Solar Eclipse January 26, 2009 at12 degrees Capricorn, Rahu 15 Capricorn
- Saturn is 22 degrees Leo Square (90 degrees) the sensitive degree: opposed the sensitive degree seen in major events in the USA chart, Sensitive degree is 23 degrees Scorpio or Taurus.
- Saturn and Uranus were in opposition causing this year to have sudden unexpected changes that damaged the economy. Saturn is conjunct natal Mars while Uranus opposes it in the NYSE chart.

Chapter 4
Earthquakes

The two earthquakes to be analyzed are the San Francisco earthquake of 1906 and the more recent earthquake that devastated Japan in 2011.

The San Francisco Earthquake 1906

The earthquake of 1906 struck San Francisco and the coast of Northern California at 5:12 a.m. on Wednesday, April 18, 1906. Devastating fires broke out in the city that lasted for several days. As a result of the quake and fires, about 3,000 people died and over 80% of San Francisco was destroyed.

The earthquake and resulting fires are remembered as one of the worst natural disasters in the history of the United States alongside the Galveston Hurricane of 1900 and Hurricane Katrina in 2005. The death toll from the earthquake and resulting fires resulted in the greatest loss of life from a natural disaster in California's history.

1st h. 32	2nd h. 24	3rd h. 28	4th h. 25
Asc 25:49 Rev ☿℞ 15:00 UBh ♓	☉ 05:02 Ash ♀ 20:46 Bha ♈	♂ 00:21 Kri ♃ 14:25 Roh ♇ 28:30 Mrg ♉	♆ 15:18 Ard ♊
12th h. 32: ♄ 18:51 Sat ☽ 07:28 Sat ♒	San Francisco Earthquake Wed 04-18-1906 05:12:00 San Francisco, California USA	Timezone: 8 DST: 0 Latitude: 37N46'30 Longitude: 122W25'10 Ayanamsha : -22:32:42 Lahiri	5th h. 26: ☊ 26:00 Asl ♋
11th h. 30: ☋ 26:00 Dha ♑			6th h. 29: ♌
♅℞ 15:56 PSh ♐	♏	♎	♍
10th h. 39	9th h. 28	8th h. 23	7th h. 21

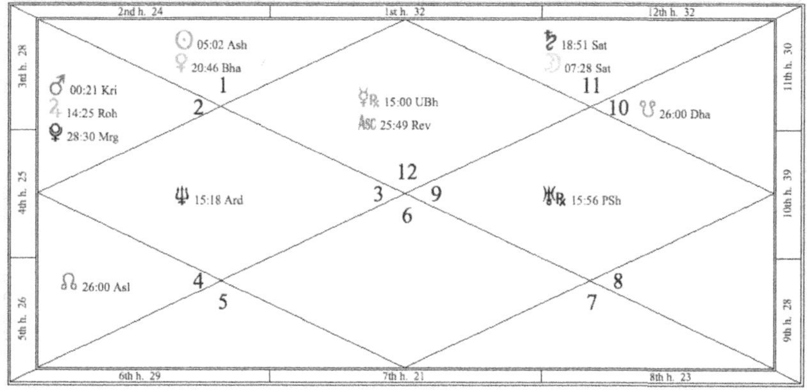

The chart on this day has the signatures noted specifically in earthquakes, one is Neptune exactly opposed Uranus. Mercury is the trigger that activated this tragedy. There needs to be a faster moving planet in hard aspect to activate the long-standing transits. Here Mercury comes to the exact midpoint of Neptune and Uranus – all at 15 degrees.

Saturn and Pluto are in a waning square, and Jupiter is combined with Pluto and Mars all in Taurus. This deadly combination may have been the reason for all the fires that destroyed the city. Mars (fire) with Pluto is dangerous plus Jupiter multiplies the effects.

Earthquake in Japan 2011

The Earthquake that hit Japan March 11, 2011 was a real monster of a quake. It was the most powerful earthquake ever recorded to have hit Japan, and the fifth most powerful earthquake in the world since modern record keeping began in 1900. The earthquake triggered powerful tsunami waves. The earthquake moved Honshu (the main island of Japan) 2.4 m (8 ft) east and shifted the Earth on its axis by estimates of between 10 cm (4 in) and 25 cm (10 in).

A Japanese report confirmed 15,887 deaths, 6,150 injured, and 2,612 people missing across twenty prefectures, as well as 127,290 buildings totally collapsed, with a further 272,788 buildings 'half collapsed', and another 747,989 buildings partially damaged. The earthquake and tsunami also caused extensive and severe structural damage in northeastern Japan, including heavy damage to roads and railways as well as fires in many areas, and a dam collapse. Japanese Prime Minister

Naoto Kan said, "In the 65 years after the end of World War II, this is the toughest and the most difficult crisis for Japan. Around 4.4 million households in northeastern Japan were left without electricity and 1.5 million without water.

The tsunami caused nuclear accidents, primarily the level 7 meltdowns at three reactors in the Fukushima Daiichi Nuclear Power Plant; and the damaged Nuclear planets are still putting out dangerous toxins.

I have to say this is one of the major predictions I made before this event occurred. I write monthly for a Japanese website; and I made the prediction that a dangerous earthquake would hit Japan the month before it happened. I did get thank you notes from readers who changed their plans on account of my prediction.

This chart shows Uranus and Saturn in an opposition both squared by Pluto. This combination of Uranus, Pluto and Saturn was prevalent during the 1960s social uprisings that brought about the many assassinations. These were extremely turbulent times. This T-square with Saturn, Uranus and Pluto takes around five years in the making and caused devastation during their aspects. The T-square continued from 2010-2015. There have been many extreme social uprisings during this time all around the world. Fighting and wars keep occurring in Egypt, Libya, Turkey, Israel, Middle East, Russia, and the Ukraine.

And as of this writing in 2014 I predict even more devastation to come from this powerful and explosive planetary combination.

The triggering force among this forming T square is Rahu and Ketu for the earthquake indicator planet Uranus is exactly at the midpoint of Rahu and Ketu. Rahu with Pluto causes many deaths as a result.

Jupiter and Saturn are also in opposition with Jupiter multiplying the effects of Uranus by being in the same sign.

As we sift through all the charts of huge change and destruction in the world the really hard part is to be able to predict where an event will occur even though we see the propensity for these catastrophes.

The answer is to apply all these event charts to a natal chart of a country. Here is where it can get tricky for we are unsure as to the accuracy of the birth charts as to when a country actually formed. The time of day is usually next to impossible, but we have some charts and they appear to work very well.

In this case I have the birth chart for Japan as it reformed after World War II. With this birth chart for Japan I was able to predict the day of this massive Earthquake.

Overlaying the transits of that day into the birth chart for Japan The most significant event was that transiting Mars hit the midpoint of natal Rahu and Ketu. Transiting Rahu and Ketu are powerfully charged by the fact that transiting Uranus is at the midpoint of the transiting lunar nodes (Rahu/Ketu). Transiting Ketu was exactly in 6/8 relationship (quincunx) with natal Mars causing the extreme reaction of this most devastating earthquake.

The other variable that set off this earthquake involves transiting Neptune as it squares natal Mars of Japan's chart. Mars is the ruler of the ascendant affecting this chart on a deeply personal level. Furthermore Neptune is in the 4th house of the home or land. (Houses are discussed in Part IV) Mars is to be watched as to future effects with Japan.

	9th h. 28	10th h. 22	11th h. 30	12th h. 21	
	♃ 16:06 UBh ☿ 08:47 UBh ♅ 05:56 UBh ♓	♈	☽ 06:06 Kri ♉	☋ 04:36 Mrg ♊	
8th h. 25	☉ 26:17 PBh ♂ 18:45 Sat ♆ 05:10 Dha ♒	Japan Earth Quake Fri 03-11-2011 14:46:00 Natori, Miyagi Japan		Asc 22:24 Asl ♋	1st h. 33
7th h. 27	♀ 16:48 Shr ♑	Timezone: -9 DST: 0 Latitude: 38N10'00 Longitude: 140E53'00 Ayanamsha : -24:01:06 Lahiri		♌	2nd h. 27
	♇ 13:15 Mul ☊ 04:36 Mul ♐	♏	♎	♄℞ 21:37 Has ♍	
	6th h. 38	5th h. 32	4th h. 28	3rd h. 26	

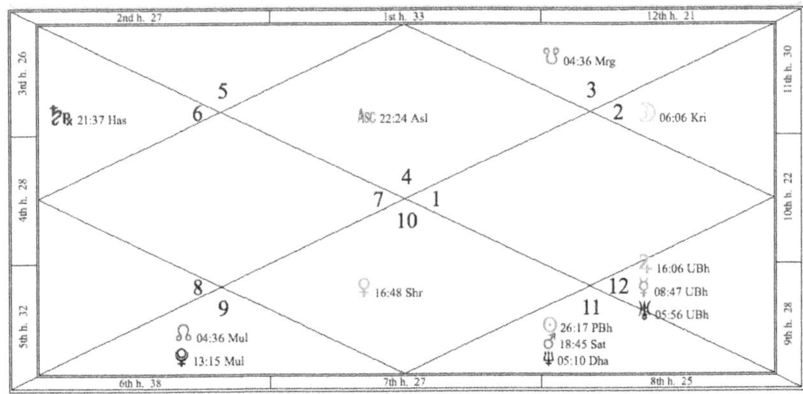

So the specific action of this chart involved the earthquake denominators both Uranus and Neptune through their transits, and Mars by its natal position and transit.

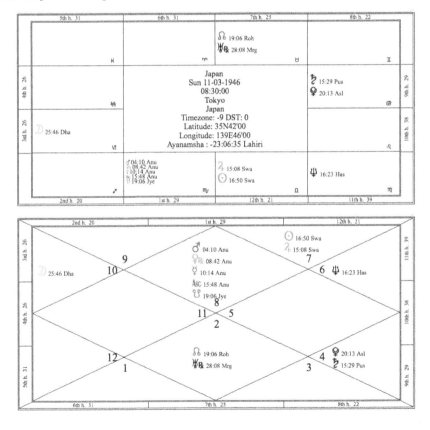

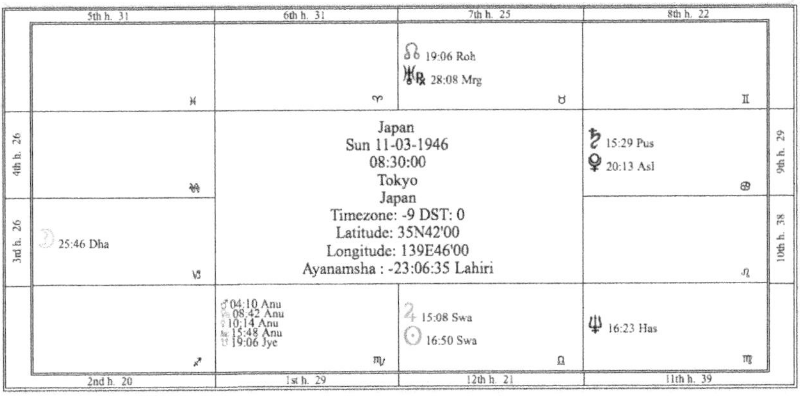

5th h. 31 | 6th h. 31 | 7th h. 25 | 8th h. 22

☊ 19:06 Roh
♅R 28:08 Mrg

Japan
Sun 11-03-1946
08:30:00
Tokyo
Japan
Timezone: -9 DST: 0
Latitude: 35N42'00
Longitude: 139E46'00
Ayanamsha : -23:06:35 Lahiri

4th h. 26 | 9th h. 29
♄ 15:29 Pus
♇ 20:13 Asl

3rd h. 26 | 10th h. 38
☽ 25:46 Dha

♂ 04:10 Anu
♀R 08:42 Anu
☿ 10:14 Anu
Asc 15:48 Anu
☋ 19:06 Jye

♃ 15:08 Swa
☉ 16:50 Swa

♆ 16:23 Has

2nd h. 20 | 1st h. 29 | 12th h. 21 | 11th h. 39

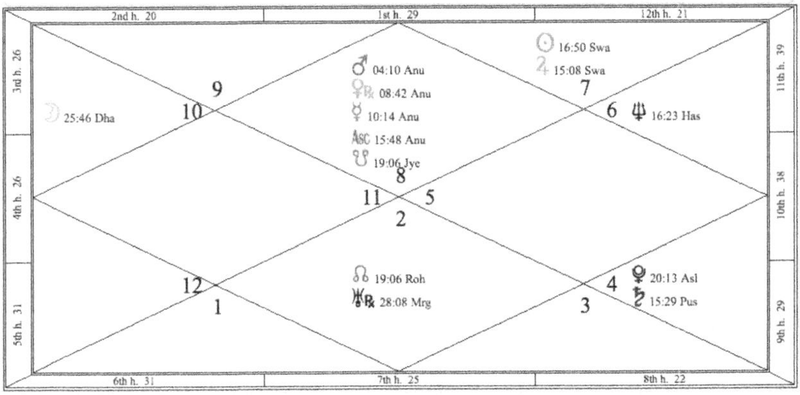

2nd h. 20 | 1st h. 29 | 12th h. 21
3rd h. 26 | 11th h. 39
☉ 16:50 Swa
♃ 15:08 Swa
♂ 04:10 Anu
♀R 08:42 Anu
☿ 10:14 Anu
ASC 15:48 Anu
☋ 19:06 Jye
☽ 25:46 Dha
♆ 16:23 Has
4th h. 26 | 10th h. 38
☊ 19:06 Roh
♅R 28:08 Mrg
♇ 20:13 Asl
♄ 15:29 Pus
5th h. 31 | 9th h. 29
6th h. 31 | 7th h. 25 | 8th h. 22

Chapter 5
Assassinations

1960s Assassinations

During times of World leader assassinations, there is generally social unrest around the world. This means there will be major indications apparent in the planetary configurations with the outer planets to each other. Remember it is the outer planets that give the indications of world events for they reflect the mass consciousness. Here we will look at the trends occurring in the world around the assassinations of Presidents and world leaders; and their personal charts will be analyzed in the next section.

What was happening in the 1960s that there was so much turbulence and many assassinations? The social uprisings concerning civil rights and protests against wars and assassinations dominated these times.

Assassination of President John Fitzgerald Kennedy

The assassination of President Kennedy was a huge event that was a part of the extremes that continued throughout the 1960s.

During these times there was great fear associated with the Cuban Missile crisis and the Viet Nam war. Cuba had missiles aimed at the US, and many young men were violently killed in Viet Nam. The government sent troops into colleges and Universities, and killed students over sit-ins (refusing to go to class) as protest over the war. Meanwhile, the racial tension throughout America was like the civil war in the south between blacks and whites. All the while there were the assassinations of President Kennedy, Robert (Bobby) Kennedy and Martin Luther King Jr., a black civil rights leader.

During the time of President Kennedy's assassination the outer most planetary aspect was the major conjunction of Uranus and Pluto. This set the tone for extreme events: Pluto represents powers that rule the world and dictators, and Uranus represents radical rebellion and revolution. Uranus and Pluto represent sudden explosive events that brought down the powers that ruled the world. This is exactly what was happening during these times. This reflects the big picture of the events that occurred.

To bring the picture down to a more specific time the aspects of Saturn to the outer planets signifies the years this event occurred as Saturn was square Neptune. Saturn is the old hierarchy and Neptune is the illusion and secrets behind what happened during these times. The mystery around who killed President Kennedy has never been solved. This reflects the qualities of Neptune, as you will never know the answer. Neptune can pertain to secrets around death. It is prevalent in death charts, and not understanding how or why a death occurred.

Neptune also rules drugs and alcohol. The 1960s were steeped in fascination and obsession with alcohol and drug use. Cigarettes and alcohol were simply a part of life. Drugs were a part of the hippy culture, as the use of marijuana, LSD, heroine, amphetamines and barbiturates dominated the lives of many movie stars, the counter culture and the rock and roll scene. Many died as a result. Around the time of President Kennedy's assassination movie star Marilyn Monroe died mysteriously, she had associations with the Kennedys and many believed she was murdered as a result. She was consumed with the drug use of the 1960s, using amphetamines and barbiturates. Many movies stars died from drug abuse including Judy Garland and even Elvis Presley. Harvard college professors Timothy Leary and Richard Albert conducted LSD experiments. Even movie star Cary Grant was administered LSD regularly as a treatment from his psychiatrist. Even President Kennedy was administered an energy tonic by his doctor that contained Amphetamines. The extreme dangers of these drugs were not yet understood during these times.

On the day of President Kennedy's assassination Pluto and Uranus are conjunct, and both are quincunx Saturn, which squares Neptune. There is a Yod formed with Jupiter and Saturn in sextile and both are quincunx Uranus and Pluto. This is the true formation that grounds this event. The trigger of faster moving planets involves Mars as it squares Uranus and Pluto. And for precision that day, faster moving planet Mercury is a trigger with an exact square to Uranus. One more interesting factor concerns the nodes of the Moon, for they are indicators of fateful events. Mars is sextile Saturn and both are quincunx Rahu, creating another

Yod. All these planets denote death and violence and remember the Yod is called the Finger of God as it indicates life-changing events.

Interestingly for many years during these times Pluto and Neptune continued in a sextile aspect, which generally is an easy aspect for opportunities. It is thought to be an aspect much like the trine indicating luck and opportunities. But as these two planets stay in this aspect for so many years during all the 1960s calamities they are the foundation for possible Yods to be formed alternately as planets move into the position of a quincunx from both these planets creating a Yod off and on while they stay in sextile.

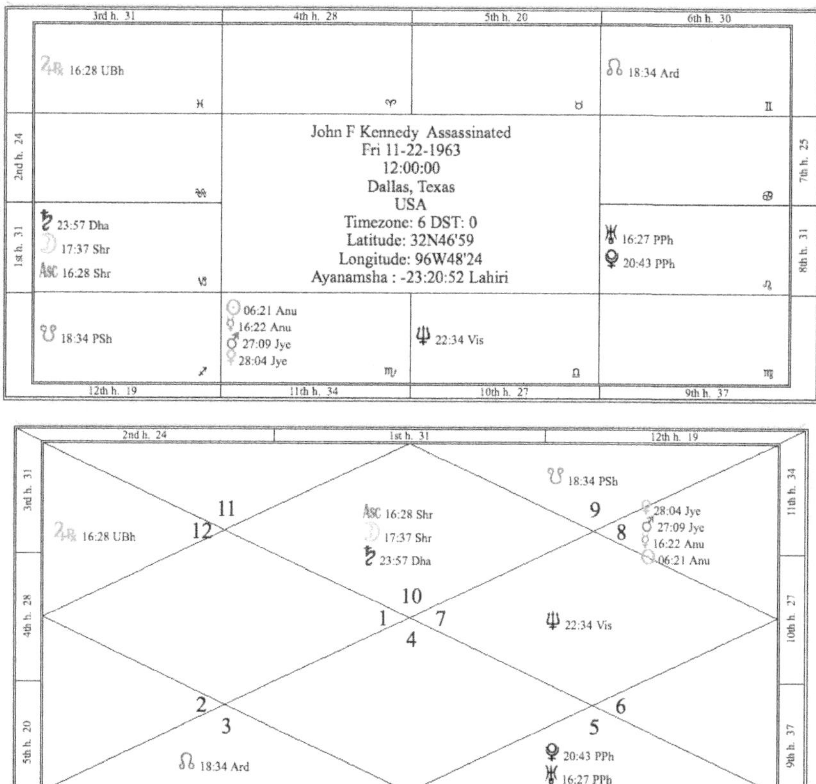

In 1968 there were the two assassinations: Robert (Bobby) Kennedy and Martin Luther King Jr. They sent the world into crises as though there was another civil war going on in America. During this time the Pluto and Uranus conjunction was still in effect, as they are less than 4 degrees orb.

Martin Luther King Jr. Assassination

During this assassination Neptune is sextile Uranus and Pluto; and the triggering force of this Yod involves Mars, as it is quincunx Neptune, Uranus and Pluto (wide orb).

Building on to the many treacherous aspects for this day, transiting Saturn was conjunct Rahu. This aspect occurs every 11 years producing volatile events. Saturn was quincunx Rahu at the time President Kennedy was assassinated.

But on this day of Martin Luther King Jr's death Saturn was exactly conjunct the Sun. The Sun as the faster moving planet in this case was the trigger for this event. The Sun does represent world leaders.

Last but not least notice Jupiter and Neptune from an exact square alluding to the mystery and secrets behind this evil act. Jupiter in the same sign as Pluto adds to the intensity, which increases till the next assassination involving Bobby Kennedy.

<table>
<tr><td>7th h. 21
☊ 25:18 Rev
♄ 21:56 Rev
☉ 21:51 Rev
☿ 03:07 PBh
♀ 01:46 PBh
♓</td><td>8th h. 24
♂ 12:28 Ash
♈</td><td>9th h. 27
♉</td><td>10th h. 30
☽ 09:00 Ard
♊</td></tr>
<tr><td>6th h. 26
♒</td><td colspan="2" rowspan="2">Martin Luther King Jr Assassination
Thu 04-04-1968
18:01:00
Memphis, Tennessee
USA
Timezone: 6 DST: 0
Latitude: 35N08'58
Longitude: 90W02'56
Ayanamsha : -23:24:43 Lahiri</td><td>11th h. 34
♋</td></tr>
<tr><td>5th h. 40
♑</td><td>12th h. 27
♃℞ 02:51 Mag
♇℞ 27:30 UPh
♌</td></tr>
<tr><td>4th h. 31
♐</td><td>3rd h. 32
♆℞ 02:44 Vis
♏</td><td>2nd h. 24
♎</td><td>1st h. 21
♅℞ 02:59 UPh
ASC 17:53 Has
☋ 25:18 Cht
♍</td></tr>
</table>

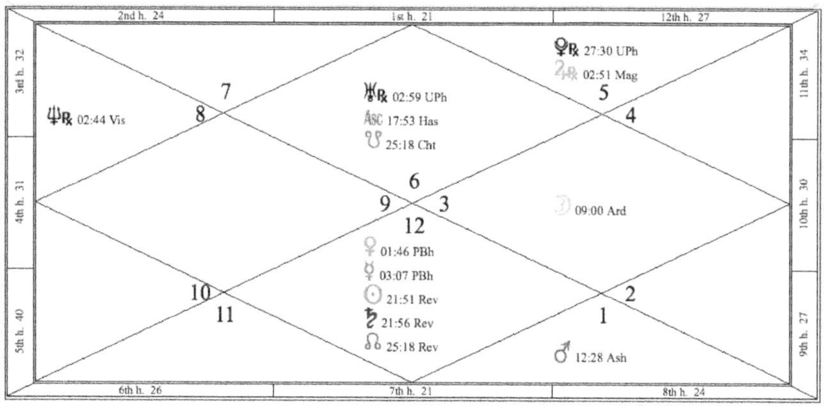
2nd h. 24
1st h. 21
12th h. 27
3rd h. 32
4th h. 31
5th h. 40
11th h. 34
10th h. 30
9th h. 27
6th h. 26
7th h. 21
8th h. 24
7
8
5
4
6
9
3
12
10
11
1
2
♇℞ 27:30 UPh
♃℞ 02:51 Mag
♅℞ 02:59 UPh
Asc 17:53 Has
☋ 25:18 Cht
♆℞ 02:44 Vis
☽ 09:00 Ard
♀ 01:46 PBh
☿ 03:07 PBh
☉ 21:51 Rev
♄ 21:56 Rev
☊ 25:18 Rev
♂ 12:28 Ash

Robert (Bobby) Kennedy Assassination

Bobby Kennedy was assassinated while he was campaigning as the Democratic nominee for President in California.

Looking at this event chart the major aspects that make up the combinations that are the cause of this event are there but not seen as readily for they are within a few degrees but out of sign, so look closely, because remember it is the formation of the patterns that constitutes world events.

On this day Saturn is still conjunct Rahu, which is the indicator for the tragic events of this year. But note the exact sextile between Uranus and Neptune are forming a quincunx with Saturn even though they may be out of sign. Also Pluto is not that far from Uranus affecting this Yod between Saturn and Rahu and Neptune and Uranus. With this Neptune and Uranus there is definitely a mystery, and secrets and corruption behind this vile scandal.

But what really pegs the violence in this event is Mars as it squares Pluto; and Saturn and Rahu are quincunx Pluto. These are really nasty planets in harsh aspects during this time.

The faster moving planet that triggers the day is the Moon as it conjoins Uranus and is in the same sign as Ketu.

Additionally, when planets turn retrograde they make a point of transition and change concerning the energy of the planet stationing. On this day both Pluto and Uranus stationed, both turning direct from retrograde. This combination means radical changes concerning these volatile times.

One more note concerning all three assassination charts is that each of these charts has the nakshatra Ardra prevalent. During the assassination of President Kennedy Ketu was in Ardra, Martin Luther King Jr. the Moon was in Ardra, and Bobby Kennedy Mercury was in Ardra. This nakshatra has shown up in all charts that involve tragedy and tears.

3rd h. 39	4th h. 25	5th h. 24	6th h. 34
♄ 28:59 Rev ☊ 23:32 Rev ♓	♈	♀ 17:08 Roh ☉ 21:15 Roh ♂ 25:48 Mrg ♉	☿ 08:34 Ard ♊
2nd h. 30 ♒	Robert Kennedy Assassinated Wed 06-05-1968 00:16:00 Los Angeles, California USA		7th h. 26 ♋
1st h. 30 Asc 29:02 Dha ♑	Timezone: 8 DST: 1 Latitude: 34N03'08 Longitude: 118W14'37 Ayanamsha : -23:24:53 Lahiri		8th h. 23 ♃ 05:14 Mag ♇ 26:45 UPh ♌
♐	♆R 01:12 Vis ♏	♎	♅ 01:39 UPh ☽ 05:07 UPh ☋ 23:32 Cht ♍
12th h. 23	11th h. 34	10th h. 30	9th h. 19

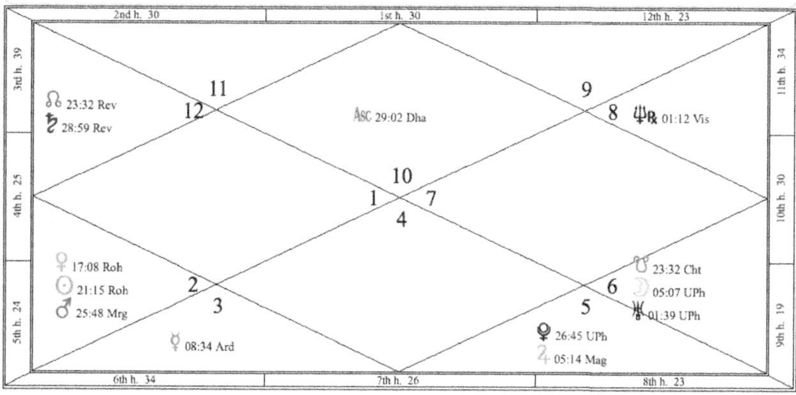

Chapter 6

Airline Crashes and Terrorist Attacks

Whenever there is an airline crash the world wakes up and takes notice, because almost everyone is familiar with traveling on airplanes. Even though airplane crashes are extremely rare considering the percentages of take-offs and landings around the world. We all know it is safer than driving a car, but still the horror of dying in a plane crash is something that terrifies everyone.

The three airline crashes to be analyzed here are American Airlines Flight 11 that was crashed into the World Trade Center and the more recent Malaysian Flights, Malaysian Flight 370 that disappeared and flight 17 that was brought down by a missile.

Two of those planes, American Airlines Flight 11 and United Airlines Flight 175, were crashed into the North and South towers, respectively, of the World Trade Center complex in New York City.

A third plane, American Airlines Flight 77, was crashed into the Pentagon (the headquarters of the United States Department of Defense), leading to a partial collapse in its western side. The fourth plane, United Airlines Flight 93, was targeted at Washington, D.C. but crashed into a field near Shanksville, Pennsylvania, after its passengers tried to overcome the hijackers. In total, almost 3,000 people died in the attacks, including the 227 civilians and 19 hijackers aboard the four planes. It was also the deadliest incident for firefighters and for law enforcement officers in the history of the United States, with 343 and 72 killed.

American Airlines Flight 11

American Airlines flight 11 has the chart that is used for the Attack on America for the airplane was used as one of the weapons that took down one of the twin towers of the World Trade Center.

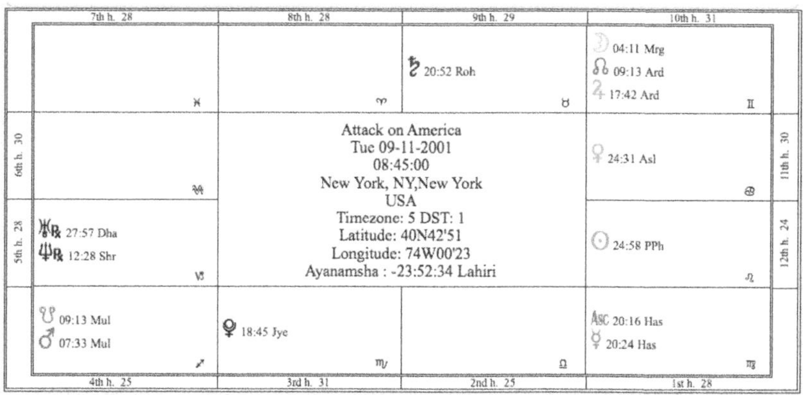

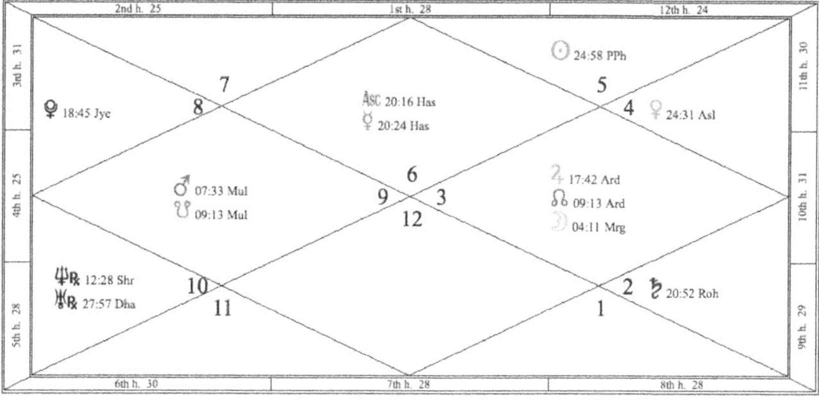

The horrific event of September 11th 2001 changed the world forever. We now live in a world consumed with acts of terrorism. And flying on airliners will never be the same, for security is now so stringent that we are constantly reminded of the dangers that 9/11 set into motion.

In this chart the outer most planets involved are Uranus and Neptune in the same sign. They were exactly conjunct in February 1993 when the first attempt to destroy the World Trade Center occurred. The attack, on February 26, 1993, killed six people in New York City and injured 1,000. A truck bomb exploded in the parking garage of the North Tower at 12:18

p.m. This was a Tuesday and September 11th 2001 was also a Tuesday. This is important because Tuesday is ruled by Mars, and many events of this nature do occur on Mars' days (Tuesday).

Even the Pan Am Flight that exploded over Lockerbie, Scotland, December 21, 1988 had the Combination of Neptune with Uranus but in this case even Saturn was involved in the conjunction. All three planets set the stage for a dangerous event, and the Sun nailed the day for they were conjunct the Sun.

But my point is the big picture aspect that was the indicator of violent events was this powerful conjunction of Uranus and Neptune. As they transit together in the same sign they influence world events. Both these planet as sighted before, pertain to death. Uranus indicates sudden unexpected events pertaining to assault and rebellion and Neptune points to the hidden secrets, as this plan was secretly devised. This combination is deadly.

The other compounding aspect of this treacherous time is the hard aspect, Saturn opposing Pluto. They are an indicator of the breakdown of the old world reign. Controlling powers are about to be brought down. But the most significant transit that tells when specifically this event is to occur is Mars conjunct Ketu. Mars is the planet that pertains to violence but Ketu is the point of terrorism. In this chart Mars and Ketu are within 2 degrees of an exact conjunction. But to specify the exact day of this event, the Moon came into aspect as the trigger. Here the Moon came into Gemini conjoining with Rahu and Jupiter, opposing the dangerous aspect of Mars conjunct Ketu. And as noted many times before, the involvement of Jupiter in aspects such as this means Jupiter can makes the events bigger. Jupiter multiplies the effects of an event.

Another interesting fact is that both Rahu and Jupiter are in the nakshatra Ardra, which is of course the indicator of tragic events.

To really understand where events will happen in the world, the charts of the individual countries must be analyzed. In this case we will apply the transit chart of September 11th to the birth chart of the USA.

4th h. 34	5th h. 43	6th h. 30	7th h. 21
♓	♈	♅ 18:12 Roh ♉	♂ 00:41 Mrg ♀ 12:27 Ard ♃ 15:13 Ard ☉ 22:39 Pun ♊
3rd h. 25 ☽ 07:14 Sat ♒	USA Thu 07-04-1776 18:30:00 Philadelphia, Pennsylvania USA		8th h. 28 ☿℞ 03:26 Pus ☊ 16:51 Asl ♋
2nd h. 25 ☋ 16:51 Shr ♇℞ 10:44 Shr ♑	Timezone: 5 DST: 0 Latitude: 39N57'08 Longitude: 75W09'51 Ayanamsha : -20:43:59 Lahiri		9th h. 16 ♌
Asc 08:50 Mul ♐	♏	♎	♆ 01:41 UPh ♄ 24:04 Cht ♍
1st h. 34	12th h. 28	11th h. 25	10th h. 28

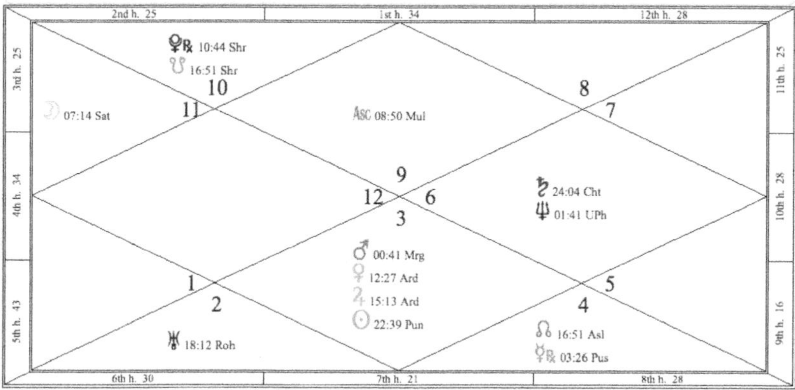

Applying the transits to this chart, transiting Mars and Ketu were conjunct the ascendant of the USA chart. The ascendant is the most personal degree of a chart; and both Mars and Ketu represent terrorism.

To recap, the defining points of the transiting outer planets hard aspect set the framework of the events that are happening, add the involvement of Jupiter and Saturn in connection to the outer planets, and for the exact timing within these longer-range aspects there must be the triggers of faster moving planets usually always involving Mars. But to specify further there will be the faster moving plants that indicate the exact days these event occur using Sun, Mercury, Venus and the Moon. So the main features that predict world events concern the aspects that these planets are forming. Therefore we analyze the cycles within cycles and the patterns combined in the sky. From this main standpoint it doesn't matter if you are looking at the sidereal placements of the planets used in

Vedic or the tropical placements used in Western astrology because the aspects are still the same. This is how we understand cycles and how to predict world events.

The more current tragedies around the more recent Malaysian Flights exemplify the aspect of terrorism.

The year of 2014 concerns a time that has the extraordinary aspect of the on-going square between Pluto and Uranus. This powerful aspect represents a time of revolution and transformation. As throughout the 1960s Uranus conjunct Pluto were the aspect of social revolutions and major transformations. Therefore this current Uranus/Pluto aspect depicts a time of revolution and change and many treacherous events are due to happen during these times.

Malaysian Flight 370

The disappearance of Malaysian flight 370 occurred March 8th 2014. To this day, there is still no trace of the airplane. I can explain this by looking at the placement of Neptune in this chart. If you want to understand the secrets and mysteries of an event, Neptune is the planet to be investigated. The Windhaven is the most public degree of the chart and the Nadir or IC is always exactly opposite this point. The Nadir is the deepest, darkest point in a chart. At the time this flight departed Kuala Lumpur, Neptune was exactly on the Nadir of the chart. As Neptune rules death and mystery it is also the planet ruling the seas and ocean, so I predict it is lost in the deepest part of the ocean. This probably means that as in most Neptune aspects (pertaining to the Kennedys) the truth is never known. This is generally because of some kind of hidden agendas.

5th h. 30	6th h. 29	7th h. 28	8th h. 27
♅ 16:58 Rev ♓	☋ 05:11 Ash ♈	☽ 13:14 Roh ♉	♃ 16:23 Ard ♊
4th h. 24: ☉ 22:58 PBh, ♆ 11:26 Sat ♒	Malaysian Flight 370 Sat 03-08-2014 00:41:00 Kuala Lumpor, Kuala Lumpur Malaysia	Timezone: -8 DST: 0 Latitude: 03N10'00 Longitude: 101E42'00 Ayanamsha : -24:03:28 Lahiri	9th h. 24: ♋
3rd h. 26: ☿ 26:31 Dha, ♀ 07:28 USh ♑			10th h. 31: ♌
♇ 19:08 PSh ♐	Asc 13:44 Anu ♏	♂℞ 03:14 Cht ☊ 05:11 Cht ♄℞ 29:14 Vis ♎	♍
2nd h. 27	1st h. 36	12th h. 27	11th h. 28

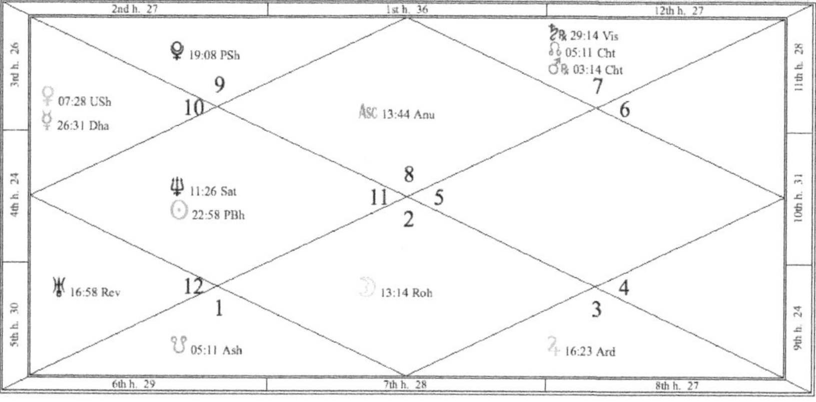

The next variable to be added to this planetary picture is Jupiter as it exactly squares Uranus and opposes Pluto. This T-square activates the large scale and long reaching events that surround this mystery. This is definitely a time of major tragedy for Jupiter is in Ardra.

The defining aspect that nails the event is transiting Mars with Rahu. Mars is critical during this time for it stationed turning retrograde. When Mars turns retrograde the portion of the zodiac and sign where it turns retrograde becomes sensitive to dangerous events. Saturn was stationing retrograde as well this week. The combination of Mars, Rahu and Saturn in the 12th house of this chart is an indication of loss around any event beginning at this time. As Mars is tied up with the nodes both Rahu and Ketu, so the indications here are related in some way to terrorism.

Malaysian Flight 17

Malaysia Airlines Flight 17 was a scheduled from Amsterdam to Kuala Lumpur and was shot down on July 17, 2014, killing all 283 passengers and 15 crew on board. The Boeing 777-200ER airliner lost contact near Hrabove about 50 km from the Ukraine–Russia border and crashed near Torez, 40 km (25 mi) from the border. The crash occurred in the conflict zone of the ongoing Donbass insurgency, in an area controlled by the Donbass People's Militia.

The aircraft is believed to have been downed by a Buk surface-to-air missile fired from the territory controlled by pro-Russia separatists.

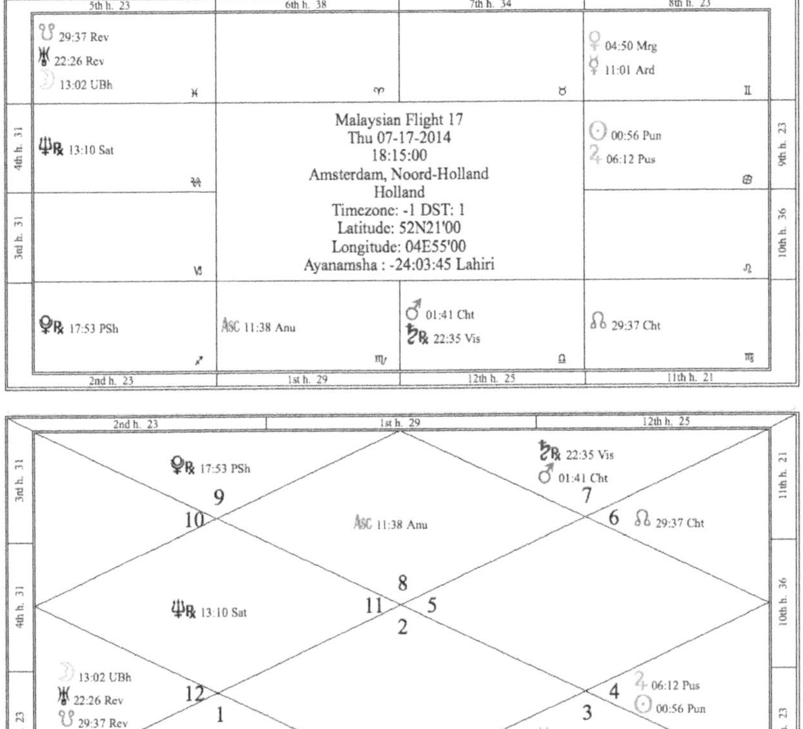

The chart for Malaysian Flight 17 is very similar to Malaysian Flight 370 because they are still under the influence of the Pluto and Uranus square that has plagued these times as an era of radical social uprisings and transformation. And Saturn and Mars are together again in the 12th house in Libra.

Interestingly Mars has returned to the same degree where it had turned retrograde, and when planets cross over the sensitive degrees marked in the retrograde stations an event occurs.

Another note of the power of stationing planets is the fact that Uranus stationed at 22 degrees Pisces and Saturn stationed at 22 degrees Libra forming an exact quincunx, Saturn turning direct and Uranus turning retrograde on this very day. The previous station of Saturn occurred during the time of last Malaysian tragedy. It was at 29 degrees of Libra and at this time Ketu is exactly quincunx this degree at 29 degrees Pisces. So when planets cross the degrees of planetary stations events occur in accordance with the indications of the planets involved. Saturn represents endings and death and Ketu loss and can indicate terrorism.

Mercury the planet that rules transit and travel is in the tragic nakshatra Ardra.

Saturn while it has been Libra for the last two years has been in full aspect (3rd aspect) to Pluto creating major breakdowns within governments during this time period.

But what puts the icing on the cake with this traumatic prediction is the Moon as it conjoins both Uranus and Ketu. This is the trigger that sets this prediction off. Last but not least the Moon is quincunx Saturn and Mars, they are in 6/8 relationship.

In the analysis of the cycles of world events we know there is a deeper aspect of astrology that ties all these events to us personally. In this study we have focused on the aspects concerning the outer planets down to the faster moving planets; but now with the analysis of each individual we are looking to achieve prediction, for everyone has a different birth chart and reality. In this next section taking what we have learned from world events we are now ready to understand and apply the mechanics of how to make very specific predictions for individual people using Vedic astrology.

Part IV

How to Make Personal Predictions The Birth Chart

Chapter 1

How the Birth Chart is Set Up

Chart Styles

There are two different styles of charts used in Vedic astrology, neither of which is like the circular charts used in Western astrology. They both ultimately give the same results. They originated from different regions in India.

The first to be explained is the North Indian Style of chart. This one is house based, meaning the houses are fixed and never change. There is a diamond in the middle of a rectangular chart. This diamond is divided into four equal corners and each corner represents one of the angles (Kendras) of a chart. (See diagram below). The top of the diamond is the first house. Then going counterclockwise, the left corner is the 4th house, the bottom is the 7th house, and the right corner is the 10th house. The houses between just follow around the chart counterclockwise.

It is the signs that change according to the ascendant (lagna), the sign in the first house. The signs are numbered in the order of the natural zodiac. Aries is 1, Taurus 2, Gemini 3, Cancer 4, Leo 5, Virgo 6, Libra 7, Scorpio 8, Sagittarius 9, Capricorn 10, Aquarius 11, and Pisces 12. So if the ascendant sign (lagna) is Cancer, the top box in the diamond will have number 4 in it, stating that Cancer (4th sign) is the first house. Then the 2nd house will have 5 on it for Leo, and continue on around to the last house of 3 for Gemini, the 3rd sign in the twelfth house.

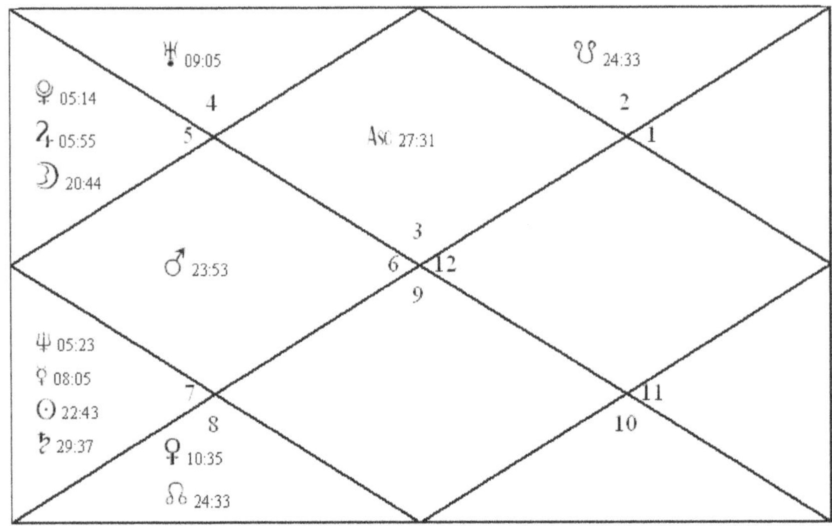

The *South Indian Style* charts are twelve individual squares within a larger rectangle that follow in a clockwise direction. The signs are fixed, and remain the same for all charts. For example, when looking at the chart (see diagram), the top right-hand individual square is always Gemini. What changes here are the houses. The first house will be marked according to what sign is the ascendant sign (lagna). It may have a line through it or be marked ASC. This indicates where the first house is and the signs that follow (clockwise) will be the 2nd house through to the twelfth house. In the example chart below, the first house is Cancer because ASC is there. That means that the Gemini house is the twelfth house going clockwise in this example. The signs and numbers of the houses may not appear on the chart, for one should know the signs are constant and the mark of the ASC starts the first house and you count from that point.

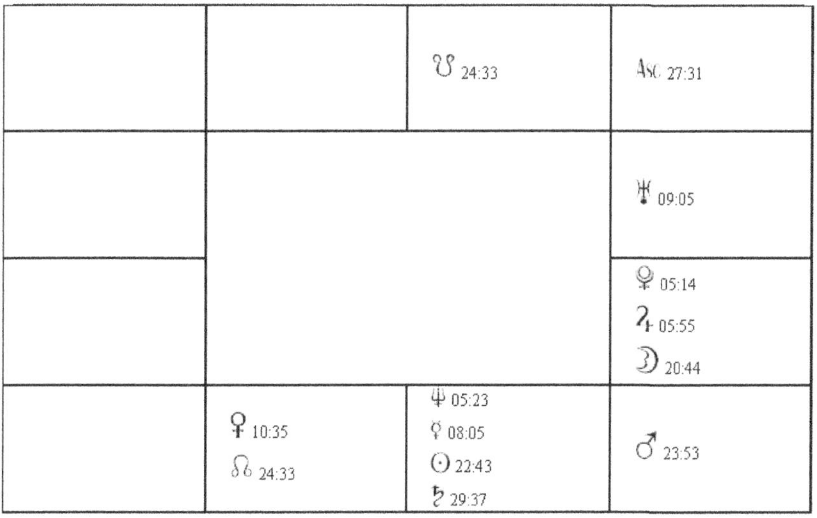

		☋ 24:33	Asc 27:31
			♅ 09:05
			♇ 05:14 ♃ 05:55 ☽ 20:44
	♀ 10:35 ☊ 24:33	♆ 05:23 ☿ 08:05 ☉ 22:43 ♄ 29:37	♂ 23:53

For major events to occur there are definite patterns of the planets to be recognized. A life-changing event occurs when there are many transits occurring simultaneously. The planets are the energy and indicators of certain specific things and people. Their aspects connect the planets in specific ways, but to truly understand what the event concerns takes a deep understanding of the houses. In world events we don't usually have a time of the event so we don't generally have access to the houses. But for prediction of an individual we have a time of birth therefore we can set up a chart with houses.

The birth chart is set up with the exact time of birth. This means the time and place of birth determines the houses. The beginning of a chart is based on the exact degree of the zodiac that is rising on the eastern horizon at the time and place of birth. As the earth turns on its axis each day all 12 signs of the zodiac cross the horizon. In terms of time each sign is on the horizon for two hours, therefore all 12 signs cross the horizon in a 24-hour day. The sign that is on the eastern horizon when the individual is born becomes the ascendant or rising sign. The exact time of birth will indicate the exact degree of the sign rising. In Vedic astrology the ascendant is called the lagna. The ascendant sign marks the 1st house. So if someone is born when the sign Cancer is on the eastern horizon then Cancer will be the sign of the ascendant, and is the sign on the 1st house. The chart is then set up with the following houses being ruled by the signs that follow in the natural order of the zodiac. This means the 2nd house is Leo, 3rd house Virgo, 4th house Libra, 5th house

Scorpio, 6th house Sagittarius, 7th house Capricorn, 8th house Aquarius, 9th house Pisces, 10th house Aries, 11th house Taurus and the 12th house Gemini. The degree of the ascendant is calculated by the exact time of birth. So the entire chart is calculated by the time, place, year and day of birth.

Once the ascendant and signs are set in the 12 houses, then the planets according to the signs they are in at this time are placed into the houses in the birth chart. For example, if Jupiter is in Taurus on the day of birth then with Cancer as the ascendant (1st house) it would be placed in the 11th house. The degrees of the planets at this time and place are included in the birth chart. This chart then becomes a map of ones life.

The houses in Vedic astrology and in this book are whole sign houses. This means the entire sign constitutes a house and the house cusps are contained within the house.

The planets at the time of birth are a part of this birth chart and the continual movement of the planets in relation to where they were at birth will be the key indicators with prediction. The continual movements of the planets are called the "Transits."

According to the signs on each of the house cusps the planet that rules the sign will rule that house. The moon rules Cancer therefore, if Cancer is the ascendant sign the moon rules the 1st house. So a planet according to the sign on each house rules that house. This is set up in each chart according to the ascendant sign. Each ascendant sign will have specific planets ruling each house. Based on the meanings of the houses, this will determine if a planet will give good or bad results.

Planetary Strength

Planets are stronger in their signs of rulership, and these must be noted.

Rulerships

Sun: Leo

Moon: Cancer

Mercury: Gemini/Virgo

Venus: Taurus/Libra

Mars: Aries/Scorpio

Jupiter: Sagittarius/Pisces

Saturn: Capricorn/Aquarius

Rahu/Ketu No rulerships

Outer planets no rulership

Planets are very strong to give their results in their signs of Exaltation and very weak in their signs of Debilitation. A planet in exaltation ruling difficult houses can sometimes magnify the difficulty for a house since it makes a house stronger, likewise it could weaken the effects of a difficult house when a planet is debilitated ruling a house. There are signs in which the planets are exalted and debilitated but there is also a particular degree that the planets are at their highest point of exaltation and debilitation. This point is the most powerful degree but the planets are still exalted and debilitated in these entire signs.

Exaltation and Debilitation

Sun - Aries/Libra 10 degrees

Moon - Taurus/Scorpio 3 degrees

Mercury - Virgo/Pisces 15 degrees

Venus - Pisces/Virgo 27 degrees

Mars - Capricorn/Cancer 28 degrees

Jupiter - Cancer/Capricorn 5 degrees

Saturn - Libra/Aries 20 degrees

Dispositors

Dispositors are extremely important when making predictions. The dispositor will give the heart and soul of the event. So when the dispositor of a planet is being set off by a transiting planet, it explains the reason why the event is occurring.

For example, transiting Jupiter is hitting Mars in the 4th house and Mars is in Capricorn. Saturn, as the ruler of Capricorn, is the dispositor of Mars and Saturn is in the 8th house. The event may be a move, but the underlying reason for the move is signified by Saturn being in the 8th house. Therefore the cause of the move (the reason why) is because of an inheritance (dispositor in the 8th) of the property.

Planets in their own sign become a focal point when looking at dispositors since many planets will be linked to this planet through dispositors. Therefore this becomes one of the most important planets in a chart. If it were the final dispositor of the chart, then this would be the most important planet of the chart indicating the focal point of a person's life. This means the house the final dispositor is in will prevail in importance and the focus of events in a life.

Chapter 2

The Houses (Bhavas)

An understanding of the meanings of the houses is the basis of astrology. Each house has specific meanings and these divisions will determine all areas of our lives. To look at these meanings and then relate them to each other is referred to as Bhavat Bhavam or the Derivative house system. When making specific predictions with transits the basic aspects should always be assessed, applying the transiting planets to the natal planets.

Additionally the transiting planets must be analyzed using the spatial relationships to the natal planets. The 6/8 relationship known as Shastastaka (unfortunate relationship) must not be over looked, for this aspect can indicate a serious event such as death or an accident. Major events concerning family members can be seen in our own chart using the principal of (bhavat/bhavam) from house to house with the transiting planets.

Bhavat/Bhavam (From House to House)

Bhavat bhavam is a Sanskrit phrase that means "from house to house." In Western astrology this is known as derivative houses. Here you will learn to utilize the basic meaning of the houses and apply them in relationship to each. For example, the basic meaning of the 2nd house is wealth and money. Therefore the 2nd house in numerical order to any of the houses will indicate the wealth or money acquired from that house. The 2nd house to the 7th house (which is the 8th house) will indicate the wealth and money of the spouse (7th house); the 2nd house to the 5th house (6th house) will indicate the financial prosperity of the children (5th house), and the 2nd house to the 10th house (11th house) will indicate financial gain through the career (10th house). And so on.

When counting from the house to house you must count the house you are beginning with as number one. So in counting the 2nd house from the 7th you must count the 7th house as one and the 8th house as two, and so the 8th house is the 2nd house from the 7th house.

The 12th house to any house indicates the end or final outcome to whatever the house in question represents. For example, the 6th house is the 12th house to the 7th house (marriage), so it represents the end of the marriage. The 3rd house is the end of the parents because it is the 12th house to the 4th house (parents).

The maraka houses derive their meaning from this exact principle. The maraka houses are the 2nd and 7th houses and are called the "killer houses." Since the 3rd house is our energy, will, and life force and the twelfth house is the house of loss, then the 2nd house is the loss of our life force. It is the twelfth from the 3rd. Similarly the 8th house is our length of life so the twelfth from the 8th (7th) would be the loss of life. Death of the mother is the 11th house because it is the 8th from the 4th (mother). Death of the father is the 4th house because it is the 8th from the 9th (father). The planets that rule the maraka houses are the maraka planets.

Grandchildren are the 9th house because they are our children's children, 5th from the 5th. Maternal aunts and uncles are the 6th house because they would be the 3rd house (siblings) from the 4th (mother). Paternal aunts and uncles are the 11th house because they are the 3rd (siblings) from the 9th (father). The maternal grandmother would be the 7th house, the mother's mother because this is the 4th from the 4th. The paternal grandmother would be the twelfth house because this is the 4th (mother) from the 9th (father).

In the case of twins that are born minutes apart with birth charts almost the same you would differentiate them by looking at the 3rd house as the younger sibling, and the 11th house as the elder sibling. In the elder twin's chart, the 3rd house would describe the younger twin and in the younger twin's chart the 11th house would describe the elder twin.

Let's say someone asks you about the health of their youngest brother's wife, because she is ill. You would look to the 3rd house (youngest brother) count seven houses (wife) from the 3rd house and arrive at the 9th house. You would then count six houses (health, illness) from the 9th house and arrive at the 2nd house. The planets in the 2nd house and the transits aspecting this house will reveal the answers.

Any family relatives and their situations can be assessed through rotating the chart to the appropriate house and taking that house as the ascendant. To read your spouse you would take the 7th house of your chart, rotate it so it becomes the ascendant and use the resulting chart as your spouse's chart. In other words the 7th house becomes your spouse's first house. You will be able to determine all the areas of life relating to your spouse in this way. The 9th house would be the ascendant to be read as your father's chart. The 4th house would become the ascendant for your mother's chart.

As another example, say you have three brothers and you are number two in the birth order of four boys. How do you assess which house is which brother?

The 3rd house is generally for the well-being of all siblings, but we know we have quite different relationships with each of them. There are also differences in their individual lives.

The 3rd house is the youngest sibling and the 11th house is the oldest sibling, but generally the 3rd house can be seen as all the siblings. To specify them look to the 3rd house for those that are younger and the 11th house for those that are older.

To read children in a chart, the first-born would be the 5th house, and the 2nd born would be the 3rd from the 5th (brother or sister to the first-born). Each child would be counted three houses from the previous one. So the third born would be the 3rd house from the 7th house, which is the 9th house. The house referring to each particular child can be seen as their ascendant. The entire chart (all twelve houses) becomes their chart using the ascendant arrived at for their first house. Thus, reading it as their individual chart. The transits and dashas will reveal more of their current situations.

In the case of first, second and third marriages or spouses, I have not found a particular system for this to work, maybe because divorce is not an option in India. Some say you look to the 3rd house from the 7th house (9th house) for the second marriage, and continue counting on three houses for each marriage. Personally I believe the 7th house will always reveal the current marriage. Even though the person we are married to may change, it is still our current marriage, and we only have one marriage partner at a time. Again the future dashas and transits will reveal the differences in the partners.

In the texts the principle of "Bhavat Bhavam" states that the number of the house from the lagna when counted again the same number of houses will give additional information pertaining to the original house. In other words, the 2nd house from the 2nd house is the 3rd house – the 3rd from the 3rd house is the 5th house and so on. For example, the 4th house from the ascendant rules the mother. Therefore, the 4th house from the 4th house (7th house) would be as relevant to the mother as the 4th house. The 9th house from the 9th house (5th house) will reveal more information about the father. Ironically, in both examples, the house arrived at (7th house- 4th house from the 4th house), (5th house 9th house from the 9th) are the mother's mother, and the father's father. The 8th house from the 8th house becomes the 3rd house, giving the 3rd house death inflicting qualities. What seems to happen is a perpetuation of each house by this sort of numerical duplication. The 6th house from the 6th house is the 11th house. The 11th house can reveal the result of illness and healing, or your enemy's enemy (your friend).

- The 2nd to any house represents gains acquired through that house that it is 2nd from.
- The 12th from any house represents losses through that house that it is 12th from.
- The 8th house from any house represents death through the house that it is 8th from.

Main Meaning of Houses and Important People in Applications

1. The 1st house is **the person** or the individual you are assessing
2. The 2nd house is **financial gains** or values
3. The 3rd house is **siblings, specifically the younger siblings**
4. The 4th house is the **mother**
5. The 5th house is **children, specifically the 1st born**
6. The 6th house is **health and accidents**
7. The 7th house is our **marriage partner** or business partner
8. The 8th house is major change or **death**
9. The 9th house is the **father** or grandchildren
10. The 10th house is **career** or notoriety, or in some cases the **father**

11. The 11th house is the **eldest sibling , friends or loss of the mother**

12. The 12th house is loss, **endings** or loss of children

Other People in a Chart for Major Events

1st House is the 3rd from the 11th house. This is the younger sibling to the eldest sibling. The **next eldest** in the birth order if one has siblings older. **It is the 6th from the 8th house and the 8th from the 6th**. The 1st house has always meant **injury to the physical body** when difficult planets are placed here. The 6th house is accidents and the 8th house can indicate death. It can also indicate the health of our physical body, and the condition of our constitution.

2nd House is the 8th from the 7th house. This house indicates the **death of the spouse** or the death of the marriage, **divorce**. Indications of this house are humiliation, disgrace or betrayal from the spouse.

3rd House is the 8th from the 8th house. This is another prominent house for death. **It is the 12th from the 4th house**. It is the endings or deaths of parents, of the past and of security. It is the house of the mother's death.

4th House is the 12th from the 5th house. This is endings for children, or the loss of children. It is the 8th from the 9th, the **death of the father**.

5th House is the 3rd from the 3rd house, indicating more about siblings. It is the sibling's sibling, the sibling **younger to you** but the next one older than the youngest, (2nd youngest to you).

It is the 9th from the 9th house. This is the father's father therefore, our **fraternal grandfather.**

6th House is the 12th from the 7th house. This house indicates the **end of the marriage** or possibly the death of the spouse. This house will indicate **divorce**.

7th House is the 3rd from the 4th house. This is your mother's siblings, so it represents your **maternal aunts and uncles**. **It is the 4th from the 4th house.** This is the house of our mother's mother or our maternal grandmother. **It is the 3rd from the 5th house.** This is the house that represents the **2nd born child** since it is the 3rd sibling from the 5th or the first-born. **It is the 3rd from the 5th** or the **3rd youngest sibling** from you.

<u>**8th House**</u> **is the 2nd from the 7th house**. This is the house of our **spouse's money** or wealth. It is the 8th from the 1st **our own death**.

<u>**9th House**</u> **is the 5th from the 5th house.** This is our children's children therefore; it is our **grandchildren. It is the 3rd from the 7th** or the 3rd born child.

<u>**10th House**</u> **is the 12th from the 11th house**. This is the house of endings for the eldest sibling. **It is the 7th from the 4th house**. It is our mother's spouse; therefore this house indicates how our **mother relates to our father**.

<u>**11th House**</u> **is the 8th from the 4th house**. This is a house of the **death or disgrace of the mother,** therefore it is the house to look for in adoption. **It is the 7th from the 5th house.** This house will indicate our **first-born child's spouse. It is the 5th from the 7th house** This can indicate your **spouse's children** from a previous marriage. **It is the 3rd from the 9th** or the **4th born child**.

<u>**12th House**</u> **is the 4th from the 9th house.** It is our father's mother; therefore our **paternal grandmother. It is the 8th from the 5th house**. This is the house of the **death or disgrace of children (particularly the first-born).** It could indicate the inability to have children. It is the 12th to the 1st therefore our **own endings**.

Chapter 3

Transits (Gochara)

Transits are one of the most important predictive tools used in astrology both East and West. The transit of a planet describes where that planet currently resides in the sky, and where it will continue to move in the future.

Transits can be referred to for past or future events. The sign (constellation) and degrees of a planet at a certain time are noted and compared to the birth chart. When the planets transit, or move, they aspect the planets in the birth chart. If there is an exact hit, an event occurs. Transits are the basis of most world predictions. It was by observing the configurations of the planets in the heavens that the ancients made their predictions for the future. We plan our future events according to the planetary movements from the time the Moon will be new or full to the retrograde cycles of Mercury, and many more.

Houses of Transits

A planet that enters different houses in the birth chart by transit will begin to activate that house and its meaning. When transiting Jupiter enters into the 4th house there may be an opportunity to move, or buy a new car, since the 4th house rules real estate, and cars. Jupiter is the great benefactor and seems to bring things into our lives.

Planetary Aspects/Drishti of Transits

If a transiting planet forms an aspect to a natal planet then the house the natal planet is in will be activated as well as the houses that the natal planet rules. The aspects the transiting planets give follow the same rules as in the natal chart.

Full aspects are considered 100 percent effects in influence. There are weaker aspects that have effects of 75-50 percent.

Aspects are connectors of planetary and house energies.

Aspects are always counted in a forward direction.

Planets aspect houses even though no planets reside there.

Planets in the same sign/house are in aspect (conjunction).

Planets in opposite signs/houses are in aspect.

Mars' special aspects are 4, (7), and 8 signs/houses from its position.

Jupiter's special aspects are 5, (7), and 9 signs/houses from its position.

Saturn's special aspects are 3, (7), and 10 signs/houses from its position.

1. Rahu's and Ketu's special aspects are 5 and 9 signs/houses from their positions.
2. Planets are either natural benefics or natural malefics. The natural benefics are Jupiter, Venus, Mercury, and Moon. The natural malefics are Mars, Saturn, Rahu, Ketu, and Sun.
3. Planets carry the meanings of the houses they rule. Natural malefics become functional benefics if they rule trikonal houses (1, 5, 9). Natural benefics become functional malefics when they rule the dusthana houses (3, 6, 8, 12), and not a trikonal. When a planet rules both a dusthana and a trikonal, the planet is still considered benefic. The trikonal house outweighs the dusthana house.
4. A planet that aspects a house it rules empowers that house, and the matters ruled by that house. It operates like a planet in its own sign in the house it aspects.

Planets can mutually aspect each other. This gives them a two-way connection, each reinforcing the other.

5. Sambandha is when planets are mutually aspected and in mutual reception. This means a complete connection.

Planets that are out of sign but very close in degrees still influence each other. Example: Jupiter 29 degrees of Scorpio, and Mars at 0 degrees of Sagittarius.

The aspects from the Moon give further clarification to the chart. This means making the Moon as the ascendant. This is called Chandra Lagna. All the planets placed from the Moon using the moon's sign as the 1st

house is to be used for prediction. In India the transiting planets from the Moon are revered even more important than from the ascendant. I use both ascendants in prediction.

6. The transiting planets, aspecting the natal planets, trigger life events. The transiting planet will carry the nature of its placement in the natal chart. This involves its rulership of houses as well as the natal house it resides in and aspects it receives.

Personal Planets

The Sun and Moon are the most personal in the individual's chart; they are called the lights in a chart. Next are the personal effects of personality: Mercury, Venus, and Mars affect our thinking process and our relationships. Jupiter and Saturn are called the social planets; they affect our lives on a social level with society.

The Sun and the Moon represent the duality of our nature on earth, for the Sun and Moon reflect the male/female sides of us. They represent the father and mother, day and night, giving and receiving energy, so they represent the true essence of our lives.

Mercury, Venus, and Mars pertain to our relationships, as in love and the communication of ideas. Venus and Mars deal with the power of attraction as sexual energy, and Mercury shows how we communicate. These are an essential part of our connections to others. Both Mercury and Mars pertain to siblings, which are our first relations in childhood.

Jupiter and Saturn pertain to the social aspect of our lives as in community and opportunities for growth. Jupiter gives opportunities but Saturn gives the disciple to achieve our goals, so both are essential to our growth in this reality. We need both Jupiter and Saturn to balance our world. They work together to get any work accomplished.

The outer planets Uranus, Neptune and Pluto are not personal planets; they relate to events on a mass level. They move so slowly that they shape trends and generations in certain signs and aspects. They are essential in predicting world events since they rule the collective unconscious. Their placements in a natal chart shape generations of people as they reflect certain times and eras. The generations born with their signs and configurations have these qualities innate in their nature.

In an individual's chart these planets most definitely affect any personal planets when they are in aspect. Such as Uranus conjunct the Sun will make someone rebel against authority figures or their father.

Jupiter/Saturn Year's Focus by Transit

The most important annual transits to focus on are those of Jupiter and Saturn. These two planets will give the overall status of the year. Look to the house in which Jupiter resides for the year, and next look to the house that Saturn is influencing; the area of life these houses rule will predominate. The houses they aspect will also be activated. The slower the planet moves, the more lasting the imprint or experience it produces.

The houses and planets that Jupiter aspects by its placement will expand and grow. Saturn has the opposite effect by way of causing restriction and limitation. The houses where these planets are placed will be the most effected, but the houses they aspect are also influenced.

They both form conjunctions and oppositions and both have their own special aspects. The houses that both Jupiter and Saturn aspect will bring the fruits of those houses. Saturn gives discipline and Jupiter brings opportunities, therefore this is a powerful combination for manifestation. Jupiter's special aspect is the trine (5, 9) and Saturn's special aspect is the forward sextile and backwards square or (3, 10). For example, if Jupiter is transiting in Gemini and Saturn is transiting in Libra. The ascendant is Gemini so Jupiter is in the 1st house and Saturn is in the 5th house. Jupiter in Gemini is in the 1st, and aspects the 5th, 9th and 7th houses. Saturn in Libra is in the 5th house and aspects the 11th, 7th and 2nd house. So in this case the 5th and 7th houses are aspected by both Jupiter and Saturn. These are the houses that will produce the most powerful and good results from the year. But the houses that Saturn aspects alone will bring endings, constriction, losses and setbacks, while the houses that Jupiter aspects alone will bring expansion, opportunities and gains.

Jupiter's aspect to Planets

Jupiter conjunct, opposite, or trine (5, 9) the Sun: expansion, feelings of greatness and importance, promotions, opportunities, optimism, over-estimation, exaggeration, and expanding too quickly.

Jupiter conjunct, opposite, or trine (5, 9) the Moon: Expanded feelings for good or bad, deep feelings, and opportunities for love.

Jupiter conjunct, opposite, or trine (5, 9) Mercury: opportunity for travel, going on new journeys, learning new information, time to make plans, and seeing the future clearly.

Jupiter conjunct, opposite, or trine (5, 9) Venus: Opportunity for new love and romance, creativity, buying new luxury items like a car.

Jupiter conjunct, opposite, or trine (5, 9) Mars: New ideas, expansion in career, surges of energy, and competitive drive.

Jupiter conjunct, opposite, or trine (5, 9) Jupiter: Travel plans, expanding ideas and new perceptions of the future.

Jupiter conjunct, opposite, or trine (5, 9) Saturn: opportunities for work, sense of discipline, and manifestation of new projects.

Jupiter conjunct, opposite, or trine (5, 9) Rahu: Expanded ideas and opportunities, windfalls, luck, overextending oneself, attraction of a marriage partner, and problems with children.

Jupiter conjunct, opposite, or trine (5, 9) Ketu: Inner search, internalizing feelings, spiritual partner, and sense of deep loss.

Saturn

Saturn conjunct, opposite, and (3, 10) the Sun: Loss of energy and vitality, low self-esteem, focus and discipline, health issues or setbacks, and issues with father.

Saturn conjunct, opposite and (3, 10) the Moon: depression, pessimistic outlook, victim, and issues with mother, sadness, and seriousness.

Saturn conjunct, opposite and (3, 10) Mercury: postpone or delays in travel, focus and concentration for writing, serious minded and good sense of reality, and misunderstandings in communications.

Saturn conjunct, opposite and (3, 10) Venus: loneness, alienation from partners, break ups, and problems relating to others.

Saturn conjunct, opposite and (3, 10) Mars: set backs and delays, obstacles, frustration, slow progress, death and violent endings, persistence and patience for success.

Saturn conjunct, opposite and (3, 10) Jupiter: Loss and setbacks in work, feeling beat down, no opportunities, loss of hope, and overcoming great odds or obstacles.

Saturn conjunct, opposite and (3, 10) Saturn: Sense of maturity and growth, making serious plans, endings, and feeling old.

Saturn conjunct, opposite and (3, 10) Rahu: Growth and expansion from hard work, gains, opportunities, and disruptions to career.

Saturn conjunct, opposite and (3, 10) Ketu: Loss and frustration, sadness and despair, sickness, disease, and death.

Stations of Faster Transiting Planets

The faster-moving planets will produce more fleeting everyday experiences, but it is when these faster-moving planets slow down and turn retrograde or direct that their impact is felt.

Watch for the degree that planets become stationary, as this marks a sensitive, potent point that stays active till the next retrograde.

The house in which Mercury stations will be a major focus for over 2 months; because in it's back and forth movement of retrogression Mercury will stay in the same sign/house throughout the entire time.

When Venus goes retrograde it remains in the same sign for 4 months, and Mars for 7 months, so these sign/houses in that year must be analyzed.

Remember that when a planet slows down and stations it is drawing attention to itself. It has something important to reveal. Notice the houses these planets remain in for these longer durations of time in the retrograde process because these are areas of life that that are the most eventful during this time.

Moon as the Second Hand of the clock in Prediction

When there is an event that is climatic and fundamental as in a death, there will always be a number of transiting aspects transpiring, but the trigger that times the exact day is usually the Moon.

It has been said that the outer planets are like the hour hand on a clock, the inner planets are like the minute hand, but the fast hand for the seconds is the Moon.

The planets in transit are the timing devices in a chart. The Moon should always be observed each month in terms of its new Moon and full Moon phases.

The house that is activated during the new Moon will give an idea of what new projects will be initiated during that month. The houses activated during the full Moon will reveal the outcome of the new Moon's development.

Remember the new Moon is when the Sun and Moon are conjunct, so only one sign/house is activated. A full Moon occurs when the Sun and Moon are in opposition, two weeks following a new Moon, and therefore two opposing houses will be activated.

Planets that are in close aspect by conjunction or opposition to the lunation also become activated, and tip off events relative to the meanings of those planets and their positions in the natal chart.

Eclipses are especially potent new and full Moons and will have a powerful effect if they fall close to natal planets in the chart.

Rahu and Ketu in Prediction

Aside from all else, the nodal axis of the Moon will reveal the most pungent events of the year. Always note in what sign/houses the eclipses fall for the year, for it is here that most changes will take place. Transiting Rahu and Ketu will fall in opposing signs activating two opposing houses. There will be gains (Rahu) with losses (Ketu) associated with these signs/houses. As mentioned before, transiting Rahu and Ketu will activate the houses in the same way as they do in the natal chart. They always bring a quality of fate and destiny.

Here is what to look for:

The houses that Rahu and Ketu occupy

The houses of their dispositors

The houses ruled by the planet(s) that conjoins Rahu or Ketu.

One or more of these houses will be connected to the destiny and fate of the events and karma.

Rahu and Ketu aspect to Personal Planets

Rahu

Rahu conjunct the Sun: addictive personality, excessive, powerful, connections with affluent people, alcoholic father, life of extremes, and father may be from a foreign country.

Rahu conjunct the Moon: obsessive and compulsive mind, mother with emotional problems or addictions, and emotionally disturbed.

Rahu conjunct Mercury: Technically advanced mind, active mind, opportunities to travel, and connections with foreign lands.

Rahu conjunct Venus: sudden love attractions and obsessions, marriage to a foreigner, problems in relationships, and strong interest in beauty products and art.

Rahu conjunct Mars: Aggression, athletic skills, excessive sexual appetite, problems with brothers and sisters, war and fighting, attacks with weapons, and terrorists.

Rahu conjunct Jupiter: Expanded ideas and opportunities, windfalls, luck, overextending oneself, attraction of a marriage partner, and problems with children.

Rahu conjunct Saturn: Growth and expansion from hard work, gains, opportunities, and disruptions to career.

Ketu

Ketu conjunct the Sun: humble and meek, loss around the father, no self-esteem, introvert, and disease producing.

Ketu conjunct the Moon: Complicated personality, intuitive, psychic, unusual mother, introverted, and loss around women.

Ketu conjunct Mercury: Intuitive, lack of communication, and problems around travel.

Ketu conjunct Venus: loss around love and relationships, ascetic, spiritual or unusual partner, eye for art, and problems with vehicles or travel.

Ketu conjunct Mars: Inner torment, burning desire, deep-seated anger, paranoid, terrorists, accidents, endings and death.

Ketu conjunct Jupiter: Inner search, internalizing feelings, spiritual partner, and sense of deep loss.

Ketu conjunct Saturn: Loss and frustration, sadness and despair, sickness, disease, and death.

Outer Planets Transits

The outer planets Uranus, Neptune, and Pluto will have a powerful affect on planets they conjunct, oppose or square. The more personal the planet being hit the more it affects the individual personally. The most personal planets are Moon, Sun, Mercury, and Venus, while the personal points to be watched are the ascendant degree (for self) in the first house, and the midheaven degree (for career) in the 10th house. All these will involve long-term, life-changing events. The houses they tenant, as well as the houses the natal planets rule, come into play involving the event that transpires.

There are three transit crossings if a natal planet is hit within the year. Jupiter and Saturn may make three crossings to a natal planet because of the retrograde process, but not always. The first hit is the initial incident, the second hit usually intensifies the event and the third hit finishes off and finalizes the experience. Outer planets hitting outer planets will not be such a personal experience; they will be generational, affecting a whole group of individuals, and may be spread out over a period longer than a year.

The transiting outer planets aspecting the natal outer planets will not generally cause any real effect, mainly because it would be generational. They move too slowly to be personal. This means a person's natal Pluto will be in the same sign for about 12 years; so when transiting Pluto makes a square to natal Pluto it will indicate a change in life that everyone goes through at the same time and will have an effect on the generation of people that it is influencing.

So that means we all experience the transiting planets aspect to the natal positions in life at the same crossroads of life, Uranus squares Uranus at age 21, Neptune squares Neptune at the late 30s to 45, and Pluto squares Pluto at 39-46. These are all times when we have life changes and crises. And there are longer transits such as Uranus aspect to Neptune or Pluto, and Neptune to Uranus and Pluto or Pluto to Uranus and Neptune. These transits influence world events and of course the world events have an effect on us personally. The transiting aspect of the outer planets to personal planets will have a huge effect in triggering events. Again, the personal planets are Sun, Moon, Mercury, Venus, Mars, Jupiter, Saturn, Rahu and Ketu.

Secondary Transiting Influences

There is a secondary influence that can be applied. The transiting planets can be used in relation to the signs they rule in a chart. When the transits form aspects to each other in the heavens these aspects will relate personally to an individual according to the houses that the transiting planets rule in a chart.

For example, if Saturn and Mars are in opposition in the sky, then the houses ruled by both Saturn and Mars in a person's chart will become activated by this transit. A Gemini ascendant has Mars as ruler of the 6th and 11th houses. When Saturn aspects Mars there could be setbacks and disappointments in the area of friends (11th house), and work (6th house). Likewise Mars aspecting Saturn will cause problems to the houses Saturn rules. With Gemini ascendants Saturn rules the 8th and 9th houses so problems with the father (9th house) or inheritances (8th house) are the likely possibilities. When there are difficult transits in the sky everyone will be affected in personal ways. The macrocosm always relates down to the microcosm.

Transiting Planets Relate to Natal Meanings

A transiting planet will carry the effects of its natal placements and rulership. As to the quality of the transiting planets, some look to the natal placements as to the kind of effect they will produce. This can give a clearer idea to specific predictions.

For example, if transiting Saturn is in the 11th house and the ascendant is Taurus, then it will activate the meanings of the 9th and 10th houses as well as its own nature in the natal chart, (the house it is placed in natally, and the aspects it receives). If natal Saturn is in the 3rd aspected by Jupiter, transiting Saturn will bring to the 11th house its rulership of the 9th and 10th houses, as well as the 3rd house placement, the influence of Jupiter's aspect. Therefore, Saturn's transit can bring travel and learning (3rd, 9th house and Jupiter) to the 11th house of friends or great gains. Or Saturn could bring about travel and learning (3rd, 9th) with friends (11th) for the pursuit of career goals (10th).

Outer Planets' Transits to Natal Planets

The slower a planet moves the more powerful the effects. This means the outer planets have great intensity and long-range effects and the stationing degree of all the planets must be noted in terms of making precise predictions for the year in question.

In the order of Importance the outer planets aspecting a personal planet will have the greatest impact on life for that year. But they last for long periods of time, so the timing of exact events on a certain day takes into account faster moving planets to trigger the slower moving transits.

The next and most important variables are the transits of Jupiter and Saturn, and of equal importance are the effects of Rahu and Ketu as they aspect the natal planets.

For the outer planets the conjunction, opposition and square must be taken into account. The conjunction is the most intense but the opposition is the most difficult and the squares are very stressful.

Outer planets' aspects to natal outer planets are not as important. The aspects that form between the outer transiting planets show the trends of the masses and turning points in life that everyone experiences at the same time. They are imperative to understanding global currents. As they form conjunctions, oppositions and squares to each other the world is in crises. They are the key features for making world predictions. The outer planets do not rule signs. The old rulerships are used: Mars rules Scorpio, Saturn rules Aquarius, and Jupiter rules Pisces. Their slow movement represents entire generations of people. This means that an aspect would be affecting an entire generation. Pluto opposing natal Uranus would be in effect for those born within a 12-year span. This is not a personal effect; it is more a generational effect!

Here are some of the effects that can be produced for the transits of the outer planets to personal planets. The transits are temporary and the natal positions are permanent parts of the character.

Uranus

Uranus conjunct, opposite, or square the Sun: extreme nervousness, accidents, huge lifestyle or residential changes, and problems with authority.

Uranus conjunct, opposite, or square the Moon: emotional conflicts and problems with women, unsettling emotional disturbances, changing the mind and opinions, and an unpredictable mother.

Uranus conjunct, opposite or square Mercury: Brilliant ideas, flashes of insight, unstable thoughts, inability to concentrate, and unexpected travel plans.

Uranus conjunct, opposite or square Venus: Change of heart in relationships, breakups, divorce, and new love affairs.

Uranus conjunct, opposite or square Mars: accidents, unexpected sudden danger concerning weapons or fire, and breakdowns in machinery.

Uranus conjunct, opposite or square Jupiter: Sudden windfalls, new freedom and opportunities, and explosive events.

Uranus conjunct, opposite or square Saturn: Sudden catastrophes, breakdown of the status quo, and the end of old patterns that occur suddenly.

Neptune

Neptune conjunct, opposite or square the Sun: Delusions of grandeur, interest in mysticism, spiritual or delusional, dishonesty, and cheating.

Neptune conjunct, opposite or square the Moon: delusional mother, deception from females, deep imagination or deep delusions, untruthful, artistic, careful of scams and scam artists.

Neptune conjunct, opposite or square Mercury: Be careful signing contracts, con artists, travel to foreign lands, inability to find your way, and getting lost.

Neptune conjunct, opposite or square Venus: delusions regarding relationships, feels like a spell is cast but wears off when the transit is over, inability to see reality, and becoming artistic.

Neptune conjunct, opposite or square Mars: deception from powerful enemies, unknown diseases and hard to diagnose illnesses.

Neptune conjunct, opposite or square Jupiter: Imaginations of grandeur, big visions and travel to mystical places.

Neptune conjunct, opposite or square Saturn: awakening to reality, rude awakenings, change in the personal environment and habits.

Pluto

Pluto conjunct, square or opposite the Sun: powerful sense of ego, huge changes that transform the life forever, humbling and humiliation, and having to surrender a need to control.

Pluto conjunct, square or opposite the Moon: sense of being controlled, controlling women, dark night and emotional transcendence.

Pluto conjunct, square or opposite Mercury: obsessive or controlling thoughts, discipline, focus and self-destructive thoughts.

Pluto conjunct, square or opposite Venus: controlling partners, betrayal, dark sexuality and cheating partners.

Pluto conjunct, square or opposite Mars: anger, violence, dangerous events, accidents, impulsive, obsessions and murder.

Pluto conjunct, square or opposite Jupiter: massive or extreme power, feelings of greatness, over-exaggeration and big money.

Pluto conjunct, square or opposite Saturn: destruction, dissolution, death, endings and breakdown of old patterns.

Review

The transiting planets according to their house placements and the houses they aspect affect the area of life these houses rule over. The natal planets that they are aspecting are affected as well in terms of the houses they are in as well as the houses the planets rule, and the core meanings may involve the dispositors of the planets being aspected.

Many times more than one planet is affecting a certain house, indicating many events concerning this house.

Mars as a faster moving planet sets things off. It is a trigger just like a gun, and is particularly important in accident and violent death charts. You will see many dangerous events that fall under the exact aspects of Mars. It indicates aggression, high energy, impatience, impulsiveness, fights, anger and war, and also rules all weapons, fire and explosions. So it is no surprise that Mars is involved in violent attacks. Ketu is said to be like Mars while Rahu is like Saturn, so Ketu conjunct Mars can also be involved in terrorist attacks.

The degrees where Mars stations are very powerful, and they always predict an event. The nature of the event will depend on the house Mars is transiting, the planets it is aspecting and the houses that these planets rule.

As the faster moving planets Venus and Mercury transit over the natal planets in a birth chart they will indicate daily events. As Venus and Mars have contact with one another they can bring out love and attraction. But it is not until they slow down in motion in preparation to go retrograde or direct that they have a more enduring, lasting effect. If they conjoin a personal planet while stationing then a powerful event will occur.

The moon is the final denominator in making a prediction. It is actually the relationship between the Sun and Moon that determine many of the world events that occur over time. The phases of the Moon can dictate the feelings and senses of people around the world. The new Moon represents new beginnings and the full Moon signifies projects that initiated during a new Moon come into fruition. The onset of a new Moon brings in a new beginning, and the planets in relationship to the new Moon can determine the developments for that particular month. A new Moon conjunct Uranus will bring on change and sudden upsets for the on-going month. A new Moon conjunct Jupiter can bring optimism and opportunities. But a new Moon conjunct Mars can bring anger, discord and aggression. The Full Moon will shed light on the beginnings that were initiated 2 weeks before during the New Moon.

Transits can give us pertinent information in prediction. From the grand cycles of precession, to the cycles of the outer planets Uranus, Neptune and Pluto, to the cycles of Saturn and Jupiter combined with the fated events of Rahu and Ketu. Next proceed to the cycles of Mars, then Venus and Mercury, and lastly to the Sun and Moon cycles. We have all these cycles performing their dance of give and take, and here we have the very complicated results of the effects that play out on mankind and on our individual lives. This is astrology!

Chapter 4

Planetary Dashas

The predictive tool used in Vedic astrology to time the events and cycles in a lifetime is the Dasha system. The main dasha system used by most astrologers is the Vimshottari Dasha system.

How the Dasha System Works

The dasha system is based on the nakshatras, which are the true essence of Vedic astrology. There are 27 nakshatras in the zodiac. They are smaller divisions than the signs. They divide up the entire 12 sign zodiac of 360 degrees into portions of 13 degrees and 20 minutes, whereas each of the 12 zodiacal signs is 30 degrees. Each of these nakshatras has a specific meaning and is ruled by a planet. Then the planet that rules the nakshatra has a designated number of years. Adding up all the allotments of years of each nakshatra's ruling planet the grand total of 120 years is the final duration of a lifetime. There is a specific order that the planets always follow. The initial starting cycle begins according to the nakshatra where your natal moon is placed. This is the reason why Vedic astrology is called a Lunar based system. The Nakshatras are often referred to as the Lunar Mansions because the Moon's rate of speed is related to the nakshatras. The Moon moves 13 degrees 20 minutes per day, therefore residing one day in each nakshatra, even though the Moon stays in one sign for 2 ½ days.

There are 9 cycles based on the 9 planets that rule the nakshatras. These are what equate to 120 years. These 9 cycles repeat 3 times through the 27 nakshatras.

The first nakshatra (Ashwini) is ruled by Ketu, followed by Venus, Sun, Moon, Mars, Rahu, Jupiter, Saturn, and Mercury. The same sequential order is then twice repeated to complete all 27 nakshatras. Each dasha or planetary cycle has a different length of years: Ketu is 7 years, Venus 20 years, Sun 6 years, Moon 10 years, Mars 7 years, Rahu 18 years, Jupiter 16 years, Saturn 19 years, Mercury 17 years.

Once the order is established, there are sub cycles that come into play that follow the same sequential order as the grand cycles. These cycles are called the maha dashas and the bhukti. These cycles can be divided down into many smaller cycles but they become more and more vague. Many use the grand cycle with the Bhukti and sometimes the Antara Dasha -- the 3rd level down -- is used, but lower than that it gets too obscure. The bhukti cycle is the best indicator of the events relevant in the life.

The Nakshatras

	Nakshatra		**Degrees**		
1	Ashwini	"the horse woman"	00:00 ♈ to 13:20 ♈	Ketu	7
2	Bharani	"the bearer - of new life"	13:20 ♈ to 26:40 ♈	Venus	20
3	Krittika	"the one who cuts"	26:40 ♈ to 10:00 ♉	Sun	6
4	Rohini	"the red one"	10:00 ♉ to 23:20 ♉	Moon	10
5	Mrigashira	"head of a deer"	23:20 ♉ to 06:40 ♊	Mars	7
6	Ardra	"the moist one"	06:40 ♊ to 20:00 ♊	Rahu	18
7	Purnavasu	"return of the light"	20:00 ♊ to 03:20 ♋	Jupiter	16
8	Pushya	"to nourish"	03:20 ♋ to 16:40 ♋	Saturn	19
9	Ashlesha	"the embracer"	16:40 ♋ to 30:00 ♋	Mercury	17
10	Magha	"the great one"	00:00 ♌ to 13:20 ♌	Ketu	7
11	Purva Phalguni	"the former reddish one"	13:20 ♌ to 26:40 ♌	Venus	20
12	Uttara Phalguni	"the later reddish one"	26:40 ♌ to 10:00 ♍	Sun	6
13	Hasta	"the hand"	10:00 ♍ to 23:20 ♍	Moon	10
14	Chitra	"the bright one"	23:20 ♍ to 06:40 ♎	Mars	7
15	Swati	"the sword or independence"	06:40 ♎ to 20:00 ♎	Rahu	18
16	Vishakha	"the forked shaped"	20:00 ♎ to 03:20 ♏	Jupiter	16
17	Anuradha	"the discipline of the divine spark"	03:20 ♏ to 16:40 ♏	Saturn	19
18	Jyeshta	"the eldest"	16:40 ♏ to 00:00 ♐	Mercury	17
19	Mula	"the root"	00:00 ♐ to 13:20 ♐	Ketu	7
20	Purva Ashadha	"early victory"	13:20 ♐ to 26:40 ♐	Venus	20
21	Uttara Ashadha	"latter victory"	26:40 ♐ to 10:00 ♑	Sun	6
22	Shravana	"the ear"	10:00 ♑ to 23:20 ♑	Moon	10
23	Dhanishta	"the richest one"	23:20 ♑ to 06:40 ♒	Mars	7
24	Shatabishak	"the hundred healers"	06:40 ♒ to 20:00 ♒	Rahu	18
25	P: Bhadrapada	"the former happy feet"	20:00 ♒ to 03:20 ♓	Jupiter	16
26	U: Bhadrapada	"the latter happy feet"	03:20 ♓ to 16:40 ♓	Saturn	19
27	Revati	"the wealthiest one"	16:40 ♓ to 30:00 ♓	Mercury	17

Vimshottari Dasha and Bhuktis Sequence									
Planet	**Ketu**	Planet	**Venus**	Planet	**Sun**	Planet	**Moon**	Planet	**Mars**
Y/M/D	Bhuktis	Y/M/D	Bhuktis	Y/M/D	Bhuktis	Y/M/D	Bhuktis	Y/M/D	Bhuktis
0/4/27	☋ ☋	3/4/0	♀ ♀	0/3/18	☉ ☉	0/10/0	☽ ☽	0/4/27	♂ ♂
1/2/0	☋ ♀	1/0/0	♀ ☉	0/6/0	☉ ☽	0/7/0	☽ ♂	1/0/18	♂ ☊
0/4/6	☋ ☉	1/8/0	♀ ☽	0/4/6	☉ ♂	1/6/0	☽ ☊	0/11/6	♂ ☊
0/7/0	☋ ☽	1/2/0	♀ ♂	0/10/24	☉ ☊	1/4/0	☽ ♃	1/1/0	♂ ♃
0/4/27	☋ ♂	3/0/0	♀ ☊	0/9/18	☉ ♃	1/7/0	☽ ♄	0/11/27	♂ ♄
1/0/18	☋ ☊	2/8/0	♀ ♃	0/11/12	☉ ♄	1/5/0	☽ ☿	0/4/27	♂ ☿
0/11/6	☋ ♃	3/2/0	♀ ♄	0/10/16	☉ ☿	0/7/0	☽ ☋	1/2/0	♂ ☋
1/1/0	☋ ♄	2/10/0	♀ ☿	0/4/6	☉ ☋	1/8/0	☽ ♀	0/4/6	♂ ♀
0/11/27	☋ ☿	1/2/0	♀ ☋	1/0/6	☉ ♀	0/6/0	☽ ☉	0/7/0	♂ ☉
7	Yr Total	20	Yr Total	6	Yr Total	10	Yr Total	7	Yr Total

Planet	**Rahu**	Planet	**Jupiter**	Planet	**Saturn**	Planet	**Mercury**		
Y/M/D	Bhuktis	Y/M/D	Bhuktis	Y/M/D	Bhuktis	Y/M/D	Bhuktis	Y/M/D = Time in	
2/8/12	☊ ☊	2/1/18	♃ ♃	3/0/3	♄ ♄	2/4/27	☿ ☿	Years/Months/Days	
2/4/24	☊ ♃	2/6/12	♃ ♄	2/8/9	♄ ☿	0/11/27	☿ ☋		
2/10/6	☊ ♄	2/3/6	♃ ☿	1/1/9	♄ ☋	2/10/0	☿ ♀		
2/6/18	☊ ☿	0/11/6	♃ ☋	3/2/0	♄ ♀	0/10/6	☿ ☉		
1/0/18	☊ ☋	2/8/0	♃ ♀	0/11/12	♄ ☉	1/5/0	☿ ☽		
3/0/0	☊ ♀	0/9/18	♃ ☉	1/7/0	♄ ☽	0/11/27	☿ ♂		
0/10/24	☊ ☉	1/4/0	♃ ☽	1/1/9	♄ ♂	2/6/18	☿ ☊		
1/6/0	☊ ☽	0/11/6	♃ ♂	2/10/6	♄ ☊	2/3/6	☿ ♃		
1/0/18	☊ ♂	2/4/24	♃ ☊	2/6/12	♄ ♃	2/8/9	☿ ♄		
18	Yr Total	16	Yr Total	19	Yr Total	17	Yr Total		

Steps to Interpret the Dashas

The big picture and overall general trends are seen through the Dashas.

The grand cycle is the Maha dasha

The sub cycle is the Bhukti

There are actually many smaller sub-cycles. You can reduce it down to 7 sub-cycles but they are too insignificant. You only need 2 levels, and the way that they relate to each other.

Most Important Points

7. The house the dasha ruling planet is in (Both grand (maha dasha) and sub cycle (Bhukti) ruling planets).
8. The houses the dasha ruling planets Rule.
9. The aspect between the 2 planets ruling the cycles (Dashas). This means counting degrees from the maha dasha ruling planet to the bhukti ruling planet. An easy way to count degrees is to simply count the number of signs from planet to planet.

Using Transits with the Dashas

The most important planets to observe in the chart are initially the maha dasha ruling planet and the bhukti planet in terms of the transits. This means you will give more importance to the 2 transiting planets of the maha dasha planet and the bhukti planet. So if you are in the Jupiter maha dasha, Rahu bhukti then transiting Jupiter and Rahu are the most important transiting planets. Next the most important natal planets to be assessed in terms of being aspected by the transits are these planets' positions in the natal chart. So natal Jupiter and natal Rahu when aspected by the transiting planets are more important than other natal planets, but the other transits do matter. Only these are of more importance during the dasha/bhuktis. This is the way to understand what takes priority in predicting events.

The planets take on the energy of the houses that they rule. For example, Jupiter is malefic for a Taurus Ascendant because it rules the 8th house and the 11th house. When it rules the 8th house and not (1, 5 or

9) it is a malefic planet for that chart. But Saturn is a benefic for a Taurus Ascendant because it rules the 9th and 10th houses.

The houses that are always good are 1, 5, and 9.

The difficult houses are 6, 8 and 12

If a planet rules both a difficult and good house, the good house always over-rides the bad house. Gemini ascendant Saturn rules both the 8th and 9th houses, but Saturn is good because it rules the 9th, which over-rides the 8th house.

Counting from planet to planet:

1/1 Conjunction = very intense, if in a benefic house it can be great, but in a bad house malefic.

2/12 = gains and losses.

3/11 = Positive gains and improvement.

4/10 = action and advancement, big changes.

5/9 = Easy movement forward.

6/8 = very difficult, injuries.

7/7 = Opposition, controversy, (depends on the planets as to good or bad).

Review

Look to the maha dasha ruling planet. This indicates the focal point for the duration of this cycle. The house the maha dasha ruler is in will be a major focus. Additionally the houses this planet rules will be a major focus.

Since these cycles are so long, the way to look at the pivotal points and events occurring in a life is to focus on the Bhukti ruler. Since the maha dasha is the reference point, then the bhukti ruling planet in relationship to the dasha ruler is the determining point of prediction. So the maha dasha ruling planet and its house/sign becomes the starting point in a chart. It is the new starting point or the new ascendant. So as the Bhukti changes so does the focus, but through the eyes of the starting point of the maha dasha ruler.

The general rule is that you can view the entire maha dasha period by viewing the other planets placements from the maha dasha ruler to understand the effects of this entire cycle. For example, if there are planets 7th from the maha dasha ruler then relationship issues for good or bad will come up.

The next step is to focus on the maha dasha ruling planet in transit to the birth chart. This will be the most important transiting planet to focus on. So if you are in Jupiter maha dasha and Venus bhukti then the transits of these 2 planets have a stronger impact on the natal planets.

Next pay specific attention to the dasha ruling planets (Maha Dasha and Bhukti) in the birth chart and the contacts that a transit may make to these 2 specific planets. So if you are in Saturn maha dasha and mercury Bhukti then these 2 planets are ultra sensitive to the aspects of a transiting planet.

Chapter 5

Using Divisional Charts

The predictive value of the dashas' rulers in the divisional charts can make a specific prediction brilliant. The problem is that many people do not have an accurate birth time. But it can be a means to find the proper birth time by analyzing past events in relation to the dasha rulers in these charts. If there is a proper birth time these charts can be used in accordance to the dasha ruling planets. The divisional charts are used in the same way the birth chart is used in terms of the dashas.

The transiting planets are not used and not necessary in this case. All that needs to be accessed is the maha dasha ruler and the bhukti: the houses they occupy, the houses they rulé and the relationship these planets have to each other. So this entails making the maha dasha the ascendant and counting how many houses/signs the bhukti ruling planet goes from the maha dasha ruler. While dissecting these divisional charts the aspects and yogas of the planets must be noted as well. But for quick reference note the house placement, the house ruler and their relationship to each other. For example if you are in the maha dasha/Bhukti of Mars and Jupiter and those two planets are conjunct in the 10th house of the Dashamsha chart then you know this predicts a rise in opportunities in the career. The Dashamsha chart is the divisional chart for career.

Below is a list of the divisional charts to be assessed for prediction. All other divisional charts are too obscure and not generally used in prediction. The other charts are important but not for our purposes here.

The Divisional charts (also called Vargas) are divisions of the birth chart used to peer deeper into specific issues of a life. This is what makes Vedic astrology such a powerful predictive tool.

Divisional Charts, also known as the Vargas

Vargas are the various divisions of the 30-degree segments of a sign. Each varga or divisional chart gives a more detailed look, magnifying specific areas, and is used to view just one aspect of a person's life at a time. Vargas are very sensitive to time, and if the birth time is incorrect by minutes they can result in an inaccurate chart. I am leery to use them unless I know the birth time is correct, although of course some astrologers use them to rectify a birth time.

Most astrologers use only some of the main 16 divisional charts. These can certainly fine-tune your analysis. If you want more specific information about your career you would use the career chart (Dashamsha chart), but you must not read any issue other than career from it. By far the most important divisional chart is the navamsha chart, which reveals the spiritual essence and the deeper truth of an individual. The real clues to the outcome of a person's life are in the navamsha. The maha dasha ruler and bhukti ruler must always be reviewed in the navamsha, for it will reveal information as to the outcome of the life, and indicate the inner quality of the cycles. The houses these rulers tenant will reveal which areas of life will be the driving inner force of that period. Transits are not applicable to the divisional charts because they must be converted to their divisions before they can be referred to, and so generally they are not used in this way.

Rashi Chart

The Rashi chart (D-1) is the original birth chart, 30 degrees of a sign divided by one. This represents the whole person and contains within it everything of their past, present and future. The divisional charts are all derived from this one chart. The strength of the Rashi planets can be analyzed by the signs they occupy in the divisional charts, and usually there will be one planet that consistently goes to strong placements in the majority of the Vargas. This indicates that the planet gives good results. The Vargas must always be used in relationship to the Rashi, the chart from which they are all derived.

Dreshkana Chart

The Dreshkana chart (D-3) divides the 30-degree sign into three parts of ten degrees each. It is used to fine-tune issues of the 3rd house, taking a closer look at siblings, courage, energy and life force. Mars is the most important planet in this chart.

The signs in the Dreshkana chart remain in the same element. The first ten degrees will be in the sign ruled by the planet, the second ten degrees will be in the next sign of the same element (or five signs away), and the last ten degrees will be in the last sign of the same element (or nine signs away). For example, if Venus is 11 degrees of Scorpio in the Rashi, the first ten degrees in the Dreshkana will be Scorpio (water), the second ten degrees will be Pisces (water), and the last ten degrees will be Cancer (water). Venus is in Pisces in this Dreshkana chart.

Charturtamsha Chart

The Charturtamsha chart (D-4) divides the 30-degree sign into four parts of 7.30 degrees each, and is used to fine-tune issues of the 4th house. It reveals further information on happiness, home, mother, real estate and any fixed assets.

The four divisions are all in the same quality (cardinal, fixed or mutable) starting with the first 7.30 degrees in the sign the natal planet occupies. A planet in Cancer in the Rashi requires that the first 7.30-degree division will be Cancer, the second 7.30-degree division will be Libra, the third 7.30-degree division, Capricorn, and the last 7.30-degree division, Aries. For example, if Mars is 12 degrees of Cancer in the Rashi it will be in Libra in the Charturtamsha chart.

Trimshamsha Chart

The Trimshamsha chart (D-30) divides the 30-degree sign through a unique calculation into five parts of approximately six degrees each and is used to fine-tune the 6th house. It indicates accidents, health, obstacles and enemies.

The planets are calculated differently according to whether they occupy odd-numbered signs or even-numbered signs in the Rashi. For an odd-numbered sign the first five degrees are ruled by Mars (Aries), the next five by Saturn (Aquarius), the next eight degrees by Jupiter (Sagittarius), the next seven degrees by Mercury (Virgo), and the last five degrees are ruled by Venus (Taurus). In even-numbered signs the above order is reversed, starting with Venus as the first five degrees. The Sun, Moon, Rahu and Ketu are not taken into account when interpreting the Trimshamsha chart. It is Saturn that will indicate the biggest challenges.

Saptamsha Chart

The Saptamsha chart (D-7) divides the 30-degree sign into seven parts of 4.17 degrees each. It pinpoints issues with children, creativity and intelligence.

If the natal planet is in an odd-numbered sign, the Saptamsha divisions start with that sign and continue in zodiac order. If the planet is in an even-numbered sign the Saptamsha starts with the opposite sign. Jupiter is the planet to note in this chart.

Navamsha Chart

The navamsha chart (D-9) divides the 30-degree sign into nine parts of 3:20 degrees each. This is the most important divisional chart of all, and Vedic astrologers automatically compare this chart to the Rashi chart to determine the results of a person's life.

The Navamsha chart is called the fruit of the tree. It reveals the future outcome of a person's life, promising to manifest the potential in the Rashi chart. We seem to become the navamsha chart as we grow older. These are the issues of the 9th house, the house of luck, fortune and spiritual pursuits. If a planet is in the same sign in both the birth chart (rashi) and the navamsha it is vargottama, meaning it gains strength and is a more powerful planet in the Rashi. Some also refer to the navamsha as the spouse who is the mirror of yourself.

To calculate the navamsha of a planet, the first 3:20 degrees begin with the first quality (cardinal, fixed, mutable) of the element the planet is in, and then the following divisions continue with the zodiacal signs in order regardless of quality or element. For example, if Venus is 10 degrees of Scorpio in the Rashi, the first navamsha will be Cancer (the cardinal sign of the same element), the second navamsha will be Leo, the third Virgo, the fourth Libra, the fifth Scorpio, the sixth Sagittarius, the seventh Capricorn, the eighth Aquarius, and the ninth navamsha is Pisces. Because Venus was in the fourth division (by nine) of its Rashi sign, Venus falls in the fourth navamsha of Libra here.

Dashamsha Chart

The Dashamsha chart (D-10) divides the 30-degree sign into ten divisions of three degrees each. It is referred to as the career chart, as it focuses on the 10th house and can indicate social standing, status and ambition as well as revealing the type of career best aspired to. It can also indicate fame in this area.

With odd-numbered signs the Dashamsha divisions begin with the sign being divided, then the other signs follow in their natural order. From an even-numbered sign the Dashamsha divisions begin with the sign located nine signs further around the zodiac, then follow in natural order.

The planet that rules the 10th house in the Rashi chart will be the most important planet to be analyzed in the Dashamsha chart, giving important clues as to what career an individual should pursue. The Sun is also an important consideration, as is the planet that rules the Rashi ascendant.

Dwadashamsha Chart

The Dwadashamsha chart (D-12) divides the 30-degree sign into twelve parts of 2:30 degrees each. It starts with the ruling sign, and continues through the 12 signs of the zodiac in their natural order.

This chart gives the deeper essence of the twelfth house, including details of the past incarnation and what karmas are to be worked on in this lifetime. It can reveal talents or gifts brought from past lives, as well as fears or difficulties. The most important planet to be assessed here is the Sun, because the Sun is our soul essence, spirit, and the ego, which must be overcome.

This is also the chart to use to find information on the parents, for we never escape their imprint on our early conditioning, and before this incarnation we choose them so we can experience certain karmas. All this develops coping and learning skills for our future.

Shodhashamsha Chart

The Shodhashamsha chart (D-16) divides the 30-degree sign into 16 parts of 1:52'30" each. It focuses on 4th house matters especially the means of transport. I use this chart to determine when someone will buy a car. It can be used to assess any fixed assets.

Sadhe Sati

Sadhe Sati is the seven and a half year period of the transit of Saturn in the sign before, sign of, and sign after the natal Moon. This is considered a difficult time in life, especially the 2½-year period when Saturn is in the sign of the natal Moon.

Transits from the Moon (Chandra Lagna)

In India the transits are always assessed from where the natal Moon is in a birth chart. In actuality each planet could be isolated and deemed as the new ascendant, but essentially what is happening in this event is that each planet is made the subject of attention, and the other planets in the birth chart (as well as the transiting planets) are seen in relation to that planet. Therefore as each planet is the focal point, this reveals how it prospers in the life of an individual. This will reveal the aspects of that planet as the stirra karaka. Stirra karaka means the fixed properties that the planet represents, and especially the people that they represent in our lives.

Stirra Karakas

Moon: mother, emotions.

Sun: father, physical constitution and work.

Mercury: aunts and uncles, communications.

Venus: marriage partner for a man, relations.

Mars: Siblings, real estate.

Jupiter: children, expansion.

Saturn: elderly people, restrictions.

To refine the predictions in a chart looking at the transiting planets both from the Moon and the natal ascendant really fine-tunes a prediction because if a prediction can be made using both the ascendant and the Moon as the ascendant you can make a solid prediction. This is because what you are able to assess are the emotions and the mind of an individual. This reveals their inner world in terms of happiness, and will reflect the events in their life.

Then there are many who use the Sun as the ascendant for the Sun is the ego and sense of your spirit, and so is a sense of who you are. Actually there is a system in Vedic astrology called the Sudarshan chart that looks at all 3 ascendants before making a prediction, the ascendant, Moon and Sun.

Pattern step by step in each chart:

Maha dasha ruler and Bhukti:

1. Houses they occupy
2. Houses they rule
3. Their special relationship to each other
4. Transits of these planets
5. Natal placements and the aspects they receive from the transiting planets.
6. Houses they occupy in the Divisional Charts and in relationship to each other
7. Transits are not used in the Divisional charts - only dasha rulers - focus on the maha dasha ruler and bhukti

Putting it all together the lives of the Kennedy Family will prove this power of Prediction

Part V

The Kennedy Family
The Power of Prediction

Chapter 1

Joseph Kennedy Sr.

The Kennedy Family

The Kennedy families have the most dramatic extremes of life's experiences with well-documented events. Therefore their lives will demonstrate the techniques outlined in the previous chapters on prediction.

Joseph Kennedy the father of the Kennedy clan must have a powerful chart indicating a rise and fall throughout life. There were many successes along with many tragedies.

He was an American entrepreneur and financier, the founder of a dynasty of Kennedys. He was the U.S. Ambassador to the Court of St. James 1937-1940. He included early film making in his ventures.

He married Rose Fitzgerald on 10/07/1914; his children included President John F. Kennedy, Senators Edward (Ted) Kennedy, and Robert Kennedy, who was Attorney General under John F. Kennedy, and a U.S. Senator. Joseph Kennedy died on 11/18/1969, Hyannis Port, MA.

7th h. 21	8th h. 23	9th h. 31	10th h. 37
♓	♈	♆R 10:01 Roh ♇R 13:40 Roh ♉	♊
6th h. 32 ♒	Joseph P. Kennedy Sr. Thu 09-06-1888 07:06:00 Boston, Massachusetts USA Timezone: 5 DST: 0 Latitude: 42N21'30 Longitude: 71W03'35 Ayanamsha : -22:17:54 Lahiri		11th h. 32 ☊ 07:25 Pus ♄ 22:13 Asl ♋
5th h. 27 ☋ 07:25 USh ♑			12th h. 24 ☉ 21:58 PPh ☽ 25:54 PPh ♌
♐ 4th h. 23	♂ 04:51 Anu ♃ 07:06 Anu ♏ 3rd h. 28	♎ 2nd h. 25	☿ 03:41 UPh ♀ 07:30 UPh Asc 12:44 Has ♅ 23:16 Has ♍ 1st h. 34

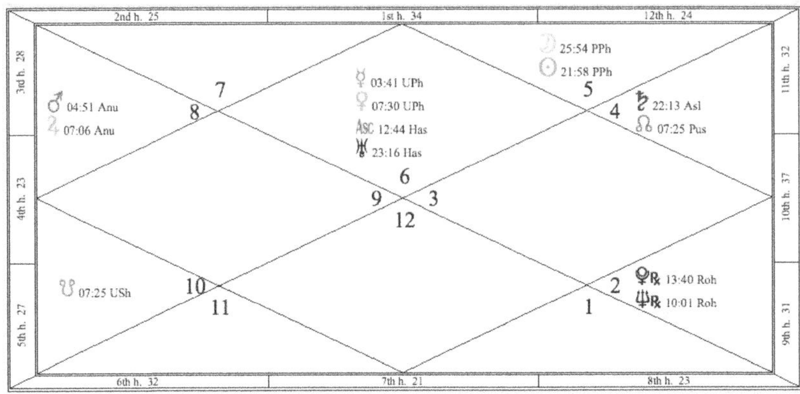

Born on September 6, 1888, in Boston, Massachusetts, Joseph P. Kennedy is best known for being the father of three political leaders: President John F. Kennedy, U.S. Senator Ted Kennedy, and Robert Kennedy, U.S. Senator and Attorney General. He died in his home state on November 18, 1969.

In 1914, Joseph P. Kennedy married Rose Fitzgerald; the couple would eventually raise four sons, Joseph Patrick "Joe" Jr. (born in 1915), John Fitzgerald (born in 1917), Robert Francis (born in 1925) and Edward "Ted" Moore (born in 1932), and five daughters: Rose Marie "Rosemary" (born in 1918), Kathleen Agnes "Kick" (born in 1920), Eunice Mary (born in 1921), Patricia (born in 1924) and Jean Ann (born in 1928). The Kennedy children were encouraged to read The New York Times at an early age, and only national issues were discussed during dinner.

Birth Chart Analysis of Joseph P Kennedy Sr.

With Virgo as the ascendant, Mercury is the ascendant ruler and is in the 1st house, exalted. This denotes a strong and vital character with a keen intelligence. The debilitation of Venus is uplifted due to its conjunction with exalted Mercury in the 1st house. Venus conjunct Mercury gives him the Midas touch in terms of making money, for Venus rules the 9th house of luck and fortune. As Venus is conjunct exalted Mercury, ruler of the 1st house this is a powerful Dhana yoga bringing him wealth and fortune. Dhana yogas represent money and wealth in a chart. They consist of the rulers of the money houses coming together 1,2 11, 5 and 9.

Mars and Jupiter in conjunction in the 3rd house empower his courage to overcome all obstacles. This gives a competitive drive and ambition but is not good for relations with other siblings. Mars in the 3rd house causes contention and problems with other brothers or sisters.

Joseph Kennedy was driven to succeed as a businessman, leader and politician. He became a bank president by age 25, also holding positions as a shipyard manager and movie studio owner. By age 30, he was a millionaire. This is due to the powerful Saturn and Rahu conjunction in the 11th house of gains and politics. And he had many associations with foreign countries, as he was the first Irish-American ambassador to Britain 1938 - 1940, with the powerful Sun and Moon conjunction in the 12th house of foreign affairs.

But the most notable accomplishments of success came from his children. His destiny of greatness and loss can be seen through the triumph and defeat of his children. The 5th house is the house of children and Ketu in the 5th house indicates loss through his children. Wherever Ketu is in a chart indicates the place where we feel something is always missing, constantly trying to fill this emptiness or void. So this is a house that has intense activity. There certainly was a great loss in the area of children with Ketu here for 4 of his children died violently while he was still alive. His oldest son Joseph and second daughter Kathleen died in a plane crash, and sons John Fitzgerald and Robert were assassinated. Also his mildly mentally retarded daughter who had a lobotomy became severely retarded. The success and power gained by his children is seen from Saturn ruler of the 5th house conjunct Rahu in the 11th house of gains and politics. Rahu gives material power but with a price to pay. The dispositor of both Saturn and Rahu in Cancer is the Moon. The Moon is in the 12th house of loss with the Sun in Leo. So both the Sun and Moon as the lights in the chart are both in the house of loss. The Sun in its own sign Leo indicates great loss for it is the ruler of this house.

Another serious indication of his fate and destiny with his children involves the Kala Sarpa yoga. This means all the planets are on one side of Rahu and Ketu. Kala Sarpa gives life a certain destiny, intensifying all the yogas and power of a chart for good or bad. Interestingly, Rahu is conjunct Saturn the ruler of the 5th house (children) and in the 11th house, the house of power and gains. But the most significant notation here is that Rahu is moving away from Saturn meaning it has burned or crossed over Saturn meaning that the indications of Saturn are destroyed

Another indication in his chart concerning the death of children can be seen as Jupiter the karaka of children is in the 3rd house with Mars. Jupiter is exactly aspected by Rahu as well. Rahu is an affliction when it aspects planets. Mars rules the 8th house of death, and both situated in the 3rd house indicates death, for the 3rd house is also a house of death because it is the 8th from the 8th house. This is a double emphasis around the death of children.

Additionally another clue around the death of his children can be seen from the 5th house by viewing the 5th as the 1st house. To focalize any house and the outcome concerning the effects of a house look at that house as the 1st house. Therefore, viewing the 5th house as the 1st house posits the Sun and Moon in the 8th house. Remember that the 12th house in any chart is the 8th house from the 5th house and will bring issues of loss for children depending on the planets in this house. It is noteworthy that the Sun in Leo puts the ruler of the 8th in the 8th with the Moon. This is very telling of great loss through children.

There is hardly the need to analyze the divisional charts to understand his karmas with his children, but to confirm this finding in the navamsha chart, Mars is in Leo in the 5th house of children indicating strong powerful children. But the ruling planet of the 5th house is the Sun, which is debilitated in Libra and is aspected by Saturn. Also, Jupiter the karaka of children is conjunct Rahu. If the planets from the navamshas chart are reinserted into the birth chart, Mars a violent planet in Leo in the navamsha goes into the 12th house with the Sun and Moon.

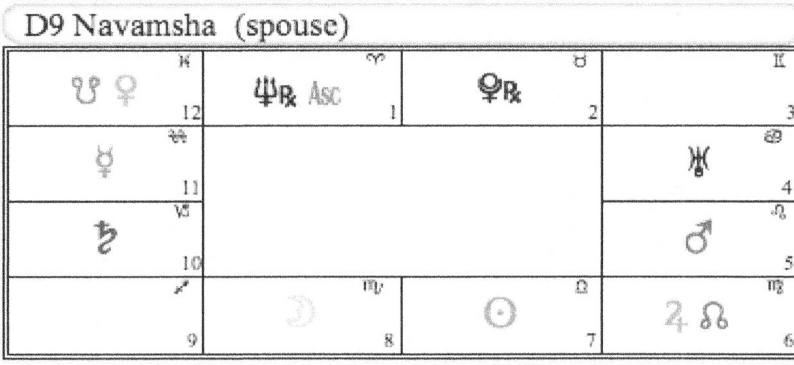

D9 Navamsha (spouse)

♓ ☋ ♀ 12	♈ ♆℞ Asc 1	♉ ♇℞ 2	♊ 3
♒ ☿ 11			♋ ♅ 4
♑ ♄ 10			♌ ♂ 5
♐ 9	♏ ☽ 8	♎ ☉ 7	♍ ♃ ☊ 6

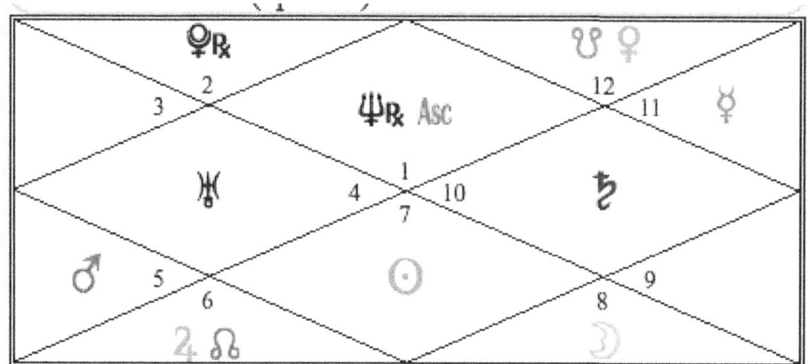

In the Saptamsha chart for children the karaka for children, Jupiter rules the 8th house and is conjunct Mars and Saturn, plus Rahu aspects them. Jupiter is aspected by 3 first-rate malefics causing great destruction to the area that this planet rules, which is children.

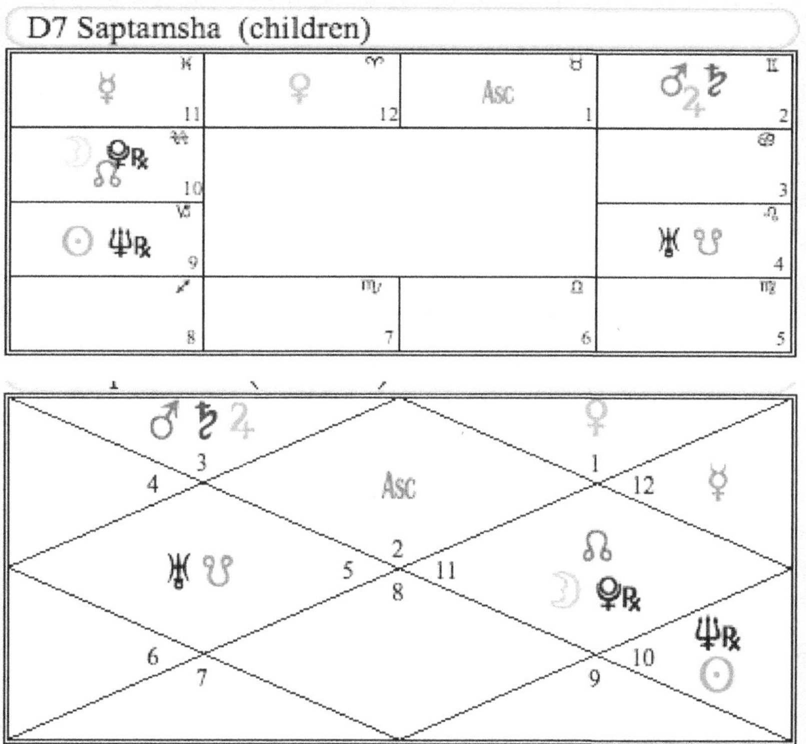

In reviewing this analysis looking particularly at the destiny of his children, the analysis of his birth chart clearly points to tragedy. This is revealed step by step by assessing:

planets placed in the 5th house

planets ruling the 5th house

planets aspecting the 5th house

dispositors of the planets ruling the 5th house

karakas for the item in question (children/Jupiter)

Looking from house to house, from the 5th house (looking at the 5th house as the 1st house), the 12th house is the 8th from the 5th house. Next, if we analyze the navamshas chart and the divisional chart that represents the area of life in question, which is the Saptamsha chart for children the result is clear.

Now with this analysis let's see how to time these events in the chart. How could we predict these events?

Joseph Kennedy lost 4 of his children violently while he was still living. The oldest, Joseph died in a plane crash August 12th 1944, daughter Kathleen, his 4th child (2nd daughter) died in a plane crash May 13, 1948, John F. Kennedy was assassinated November 22, 1963, and Robert (Bobby) was assassinated June 5, 1968.

Joseph Patrick Kennedy Junior dies in a post-World War II airplane crash on August 12th 1944. He was the oldest and Joseph's hopeful for President of the United States. This had to be a horrific day for Joseph P. Kennedy senior.

Joseph Senior's maha dasha was Jupiter and bhukti was Rahu. Notice Rahu exactly aspects Jupiter indicating a karmic event. What comes into play with these dasha rulers are the planets that are involved by aspect. Jupiter conjoins Mars, ruler of the 8th house, and Rahu is with Saturn ruler of the 5th house. Don't forget Jupiter is the karaka for children all by itself. Since Rahu and Ketu do not rule houses, their dispositors and the planets they conjunct come into play during the activation of their dashas. Therefore, Saturn is activated by its conjunction to Rahu and the aspect to Jupiter. The dispositor of Rahu is activated and Rahu in Cancer activates the Moon. His Moon is in the 12th house of loss and it is the 8th house from the 5th house indicating the possible death of a child.

♃ - ☊	Fri	06-02-1944
♄ - ♄	Sun	10-27-1946
♄ - ☿	Sat	10-29-1949
♄ - ☋	Wed	07-09-1952
♄ - ♀	Mon	08-17-1953
♄ - ☉	Wed	10-17-1956
♄ - ☽	Sun	09-29-1957
♄ - ♂	Thu	04-30-1959
♄ - ☊	Wed	06-08-1960
♄ - ♃	Mon	04-15-1963

The dasha rulers should always be observed in the divisional charts concerning the matters of interest. Looking at the navamsha chart Jupiter and Rahu are conjunct in the 6th house of struggles and accidents. In the Saptamsha chart (children) Jupiter as the karaka for children is afflicted by 3 malefics. It is conjunct both Mars and Saturn and aspected by Rahu the bhukti ruler. Also Jupiter does rule the 8th house in the Saptamsha chart. The aspect of Rahu and Jupiter seem to remain in aspect throughout most of the divisional charts. Look at the Trimshamsha (D30) chart for misfortunes: Jupiter is again with Rahu in the 6th house.

The transits are the denominator for the timing of events in a life. This is so clear on this day of his oldest son's death. August 12, 1944 transiting Jupiter (maha dasha ruler) was 10 degrees of Leo in the 12th house of loss (8th house from the 5th). Rahu the Bhukti ruler was 4 degrees of Cancer, which just crossed over natal Saturn and Rahu. This means transiting Ketu the indicator of loss was in the 5th house of children. This is a nodal return.

Remember, Rahu and Ketu give the results of the planets they are conjunct and their dispositors since they do not rule houses. In this case the Moon is the dispositor of Rahu. On this fateful day transiting Mars was exactly on his natal Moon in the 12th house (8th from the 5th). Transiting Mars conjunct natal Moon is also aspecting his natal Jupiter (karaka of children and the maha dasha ruler) and natal Mars, ruler of the 8th house. Transiting Saturn was aspecting the Sun and Moon by its 3rd aspect. So both Mars and Saturn were aspecting both his natal Sun and Moon. In his natal chart Mars is the indicator for death, as Mars rules the 3rd house (8th from the 8th) and the 8th house.

Transiting Ketu in the 5th house is exactly aspecting his natal Mercury ruler of his chart, indicating the great lost he felt from this horrible event. Plus, Ketu is aspecting his ascendant and Venus.

Last but not least, always analyze the birth chart from the Moon when looking at the transiting planets. With his natal Moon in Leo transiting Rahu and Sun were in the 12th house from the Moon. Mars was conjunct the Moon, ruler of the 12th house from the Moon. Rahu is aspecting the 8th house while in the 12th house.

Transits: Death of Joseph Kennedy Jr.

7th h. 28	8th h. 29	9th h. 30	10th h. 41
♓	♈	☽ 12:39 Roh ♅ 19:28 Roh ♉	♄ 13:25 Ard ♊
6th h. 27 ♒	Death of Joseph Kennedy Jr. Sat 08-12-1944 12:00:00 London England Timezone: 0 DST: 2 Latitude: 51N30'00 Longitude: 00W07'00 Ayanamsha : -23:04:46 Lahiri		☊ 04:27 Pus ♇ 15:36 Pus ☉ 26:27 Asl ♋ 11th h. 29
5th h. 29 ☋ 04:27 USh ♑			♀ 09:13 Mag ♃ 10:33 Mag ☿ 23:43 PPh ♂ 26:20 PPh ♌ 12th h. 21
♐	♏	♎	♆ 09:19 UPh ASC 21:26 Has ♍
4th h. 29	3rd h. 23	2nd h. 27	1st h. 24

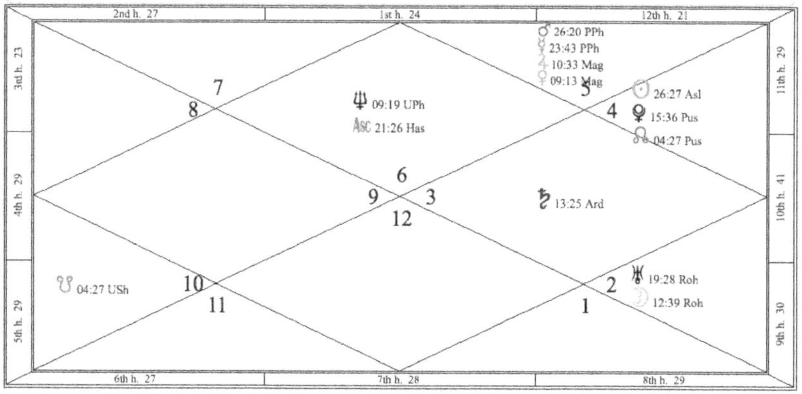

Next he lost his daughter Kathleen Kennedy in another plane crash May 13, 1948.

He had just entered his Saturn maha dasha In October 1946, so he was in a Saturn maha dasha and a Saturn Bhukti.

Look at Saturn exclusively in this case and you will see the reason why he lost two children tragically in this maha dasha (Kathleen and John F. Kennedy). His Saturn is the ruler of the 5th house and is conjunct Rahu, and aspects the Ascendant, Mercury and Venus. Saturn's dispositor is the Moon located in the 12th house.

In the navamsha, Saturn is in the 10th house in Capricorn, indicating the great rise of his son John F. Kennedy as President of the United States during this dasha. But Saturn does aspect the Sun ruler of the 5th house. This is not sufficient to call the death of a child but looking at the Saptamsha chart, Saturn is in the 2nd house with Mars and Jupiter. Jupiter is the karaka for children and ruler of the 8th house of death. Mars rules the 12th house of loss. So the rulers of the 8th and 12th house surround Saturn in the Saptamsha.

The transit of Saturn must be the focal point while he was in the Saturn maha dasha and the Saturn bhukti. Transiting Saturn was at 23 degrees on the day of her death. Here transiting Saturn was conjunct his natal Saturn and Rahu. Saturn is the ruler of his 5th house conjunct Rahu. His natal Saturn brings the karma of the death of children with Rahu, and the fact that it is the key factor of his destiny being conjunct Rahu with the Kala Sarpa Yoga.

Transiting Mars and Jupiter play a huge part in the devastation, as they were in exact aspect. Transiting Jupiter was 4 degrees Sagittarius and Mars was 4 degrees Leo. Transiting Mars was exactly aspecting natal Mars ruler of the 8th house, and natal Jupiter, the karaka of children. Rahu and the Sun were transiting the 8th house.

The culprit of suffering comes through his Saturn conjunct Rahu involved in the Kala Sarpa yoga.

Transits: Death of Kathleen Kennedy

9th h. 27	10th h. 36	11th h. 33	12th h. 19
♓	☊ 20:54 Bha ☉ 29:26 Kri ♈	☿ 15:10 Roh ♉	♅ 01:09 Mrg ♀ 10:59 Ard ☽ 25:15 Pun ♊
8th h. 29 ♒	Death of Kathleen Kennedy Thu 05-13-1948 12:00:00 Paris France Timezone: -1 DST: 0 Latitude: 48N52'00 Longitude: 02E20'00 Ayanamsha : -23:07:56 Lahiri		1st h. 28 ♇ 19:30 Asl ♄ 23:14 Asl ASC 29:30 Asl ♋
7th h. 23 ♑			2nd h. 23 ♂ 04:44 Mag ♌
♃℞ 04:36 Mul ♐	♏	☋ 20:54 Vis ♎	♆℞ 17:27 Has ♍
6th h. 23	5th h. 29	4th h. 35	3rd h. 32

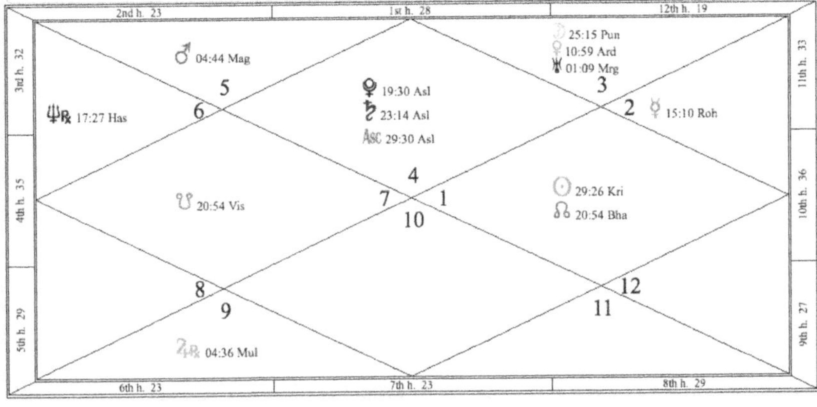

In November of 1963, one of the worse tragedies occurred for the United States of America. I witnessed the world in deep sorrow as I was in the exact place President Kennedy was killed in Dallas Texas. My mother and sisters were there in downtown Dallas during this horrific and tragic event, so this hits home for me. I Remember my neighbor across the street, whom I knew so well, Doctor Malcolm Perry was the President's doctor at the time of this shooting. I will never forget the sadness and tears everyone felt here in Dallas.

As for John Fitzgerald Kennedy his father lost his heir to the Presidency and the sadness he endured was devastating. He was in a Saturn maha dasha and a Jupiter bhukti. Knowing his birth chart we know that his Jupiter is with Mars, ruler of the 8th house in the 3rd house (8th from the 8th). Both Jupiter and Mars are in Scorpio, so Mars is the dispositor of Jupiter and of course is the ruler of the 8th house. From the Moon, Jupiter rules the 8th house counted from the natal Moon.

In his navamsha and trimshamsha (misfortune) Jupiter is with Rahu, and in his Saptamsha (children) Jupiter is with Mars and Saturn.

The transits will clinch the timing of this event during this time. Interestingly enough transiting Saturn was exactly opposite the same degree from the time Kathleen was killed. At the time of her death Saturn was 23 degrees Cancer and at the time of President Kennedy's death Saturn was 23 degree Capricorn. This is within 1 degree of Joseph Kennedy's natal Saturn at 22 degrees Cancer. But here we have transiting Saturn in the 5th house of children opposing natal Saturn in the 11th house ruling the 5th house. Also, it is aspecting Ketu in the 5th house.

The transiting Moon was in Capricorn in the 5th house triggering the effects of this event on this day.

Transiting Jupiter was in Pisces 16 degrees aspecting natal Saturn (dasha ruler), Rahu, and natal Mars and Jupiter. It is transiting the 8th house from the Moon.

Transiting Mars and Sun are in Scorpio aspecting natal Jupiter and Mars. Transiting Mars is activating natal Mars as the 8th house ruler and Jupiter karaka for children.

The outer planets are to be considered when there is an exact aspect, and in this case Neptune was involved in an exact square to natal Saturn. Remember Saturn is crucial in this event since it is the maha dasha ruler, and ruler of the 5th house, and conjunct Rahu in the Kala Sarpa Yoga. I use the conjunctions, oppositions and squares of the outer planets. On this day Neptune was 22 degrees Libra, exactly square natal Saturn at 22 degrees Cancer. Neptune is always involved in hidden secrets and will remain an unsolved mystery. Neptune pertains to deception, deceit, denial and illusions. And to this day this mystery is still unresolved, and the truth will never be uncovered because the people who are involved cannot be accused. Being from Dallas I have some very real suspicions. Just remember that if it were the mafia or the communists there would be no problem revealing this truth, but the truth is so involved with the inside that it must never be revealed. That is all I will say for now.

Transits John F. Kennedy Assassination

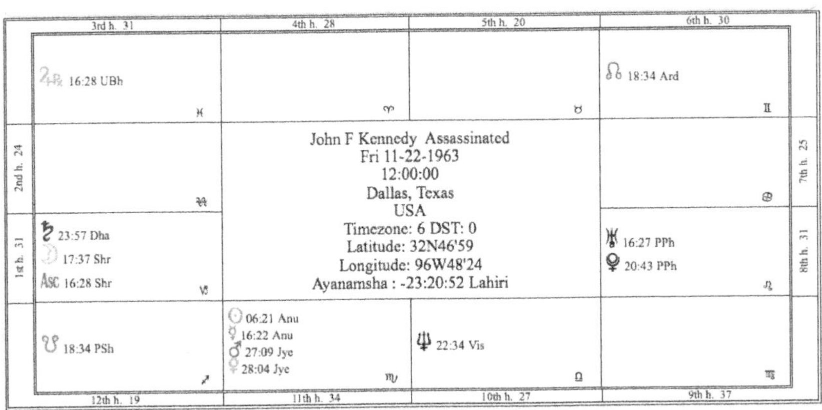

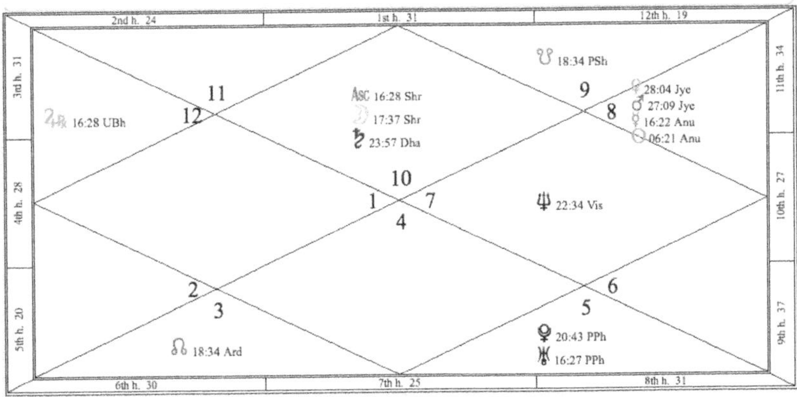

Robert Kennedy was assassinated June 5, 1968 as he was running for President. His father Joseph Kennedy was in a Mercury Maha dasha and a Ketu Bhukti. His Mercury is strong in Virgo in the 1st house so he was probably proud of Bobby's run for President, but as he went into the Ketu bhukti this activated the cycle of loss with children, noting that his Ketu is in the 5th house (children). Ketu is in Capricorn, and so the dispositor is Saturn; and this ignites the karmic destiny of this ill-fated Saturn. In processing the transits, it is no surprise that transiting Rahu was aspecting Saturn. He was in a nodal return again.

☿ - ☋	Sun	03-24-1968
☿ - ♀	Fri	03-21-1969
☿ - ☉	Thu	01-20-1972
☿ - ☽	Sat	11-25-1972
☿ - ♂	Sat	04-27-1974
☿ - ☊	Thu	04-24-1975
☿ - ♃	Thu	11-10-1977
☿ - ♄	Sat	02-16-1980
☋ - ☋	Tue	10-26-1982
☋ - ♀	Fri	03-25-1983

In his navamsha, Mercury is placed nicely in the 11th house, but rules the 6th house of struggles, and Ketu is in the 12th house of loss. Mercury is debilitated in the Saptamsha chart and Ketu is in Leo. A revealing trick to further see how the divisional charts affect the natal birth chart is to take the placements of the planets in the divisional charts and place them back into the birth chart. Ketu in Leo in the Saptamsha chart is placed back into the 12th house (birth chart) of loss where it conjoins the Sun and Moon. This is a very sad and powerful predictor of great losses around children.

The transiting planets once again line up to reveal this fateful day in the life of Joseph Kennedy. Transiting Saturn was 28 degrees Pisces in the 8th house from the Moon as it was aspecting his ascendant, natal Mercury and Venus. Also transiting Rahu is with transiting Saturn in Pisces at 23 degrees, exactly aspecting natal Saturn (dasha ruler, ruler of the 5th house, conjunct Rahu involved in the Kala Sarpa yoga).

Transiting Jupiter was 5 degrees Leo approaching his Sun and Moon in the 12th house aspecting the 8th house. But the most significant triggering aspect on that day was transiting Mars at 25 degrees of Taurus where it exactly aspected his natal Moon at 25 degrees Leo. It was also aspecting the natal Sun, Mars and Jupiter. Every time a child died he had the transiting planets aspecting critical natal points Moon, Sun, Mars, Jupiter, Saturn and Rahu and Ketu! Each time there was an exact hit of a major natal planet!

As for the outer transiting planets on this day, Pluto was exactly conjunct his natal Moon at 25-26 degrees Leo. Pluto concerns death and conspiracy. It is involved with issues of power and money.

Transits: Robert (Bobby) Kennedy Assassinated

3rd h. 39	4th h. 25	5th h. 24	6th h. 34
♄ 28:59 Rev ☊ 23:32 Rev ♓	♈	♀ 17:08 Roh ☉ 21:15 Roh ♂ 25:48 Mrg ♉	☿ 08:34 Ard ♊
2nd h. 30 ♒	Robert Kennedy Assassinated Wed 06-05-1968 00:16:00 Los Angeles, California USA		7th h. 26 ♋
1st h. 30 Asc 29:02 Dha ♑	Timezone: 8 DST: 1 Latitude: 34N03'08 Longitude: 118W14'37 Ayanamsha : -23:24:53 Lahiri		8th h. 23 ♃ 05:14 Mag ♇ 26:45 UPh ♌
♐ 12th h. 23	♆℞ 01:12 Vis ♍ 11th h. 34	♎ 10th h. 30	♅ 01:39 UPh ☽ 05:07 UPh ☋ 23:32 Cht ♍ 9th h. 19

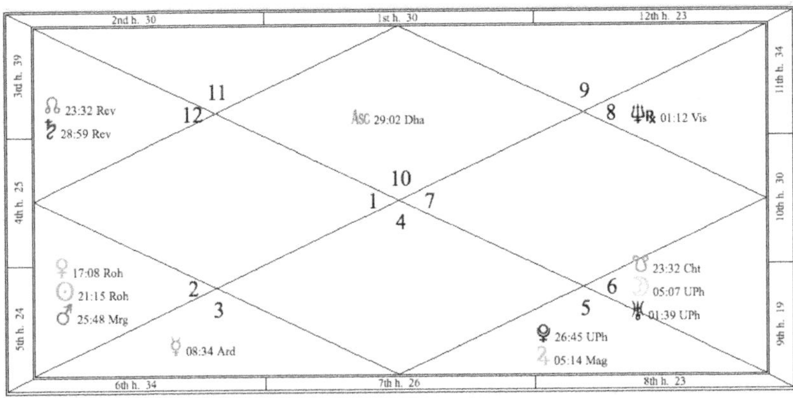

It was on November 18th of 1969 that Joseph Kennedy died. He was in Mercury maha dasha and Venus Bhukti. In terms of the dashas involved in death there are always maraka planets involved as a dasha ruler. As he was in Mercury maha dasha Mercury is strong, but it is conjunct Venus - the ruler of the 2nd house. The maraka houses are the 2nd and 7th houses. Planets that are in or rule the 2nd or 7th houses are maraka planets (maraka means "killer") So, Venus rules the 7th house making it a maraka planet, and it is conjunct the maha dasha ruler Mercury. Also, in the divisional chart of misfortunes, Trimshamsha D-30 both Venus and Ketu are in the 7th house (maraka).

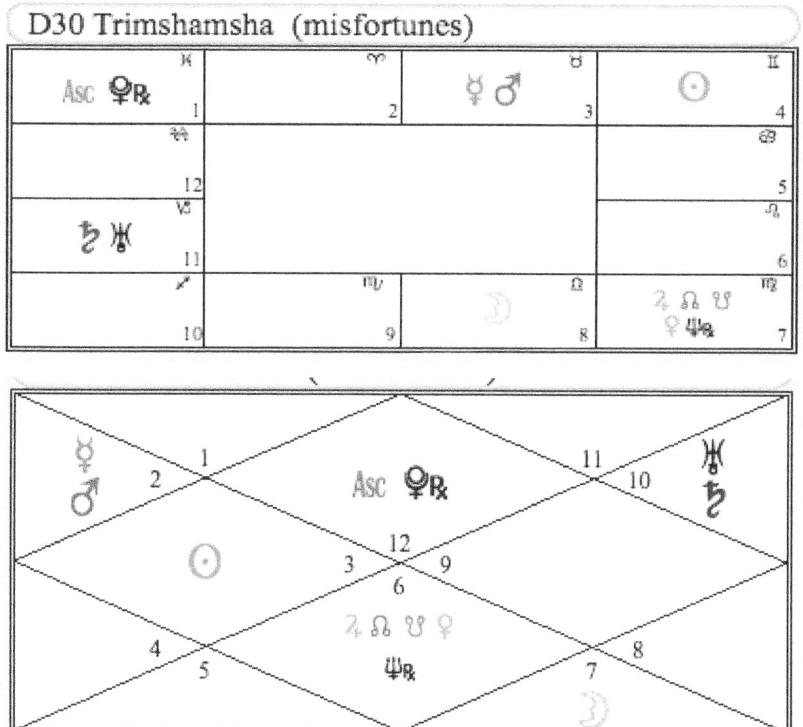

It is the transits that always reveal the fate. On this day that he left the world transiting Sun, Moon, Mercury and Venus were in the 2nd house (maraka). Transiting Saturn was at 11 degrees Aries in the 8th house of death, aspecting natal Ketu. Natal Ketu activates natal Saturn as Ketu's dispositor. Transiting Mars was 9 degrees Capricorn, 2 degrees from natal Ketu. Transiting Jupiter was in the 1st house at 29 degrees representing his freedom from this world. But most interestingly, transiting Ketu was exactly on his natal Moon at 25-26 degrees Leo. Ketu represents the liberation of the soul from this world, especially in the 12th house of endings.

Looking at the exact hits of the transiting outer planets, this was truly a predictable death, for transiting Uranus was on the ascendant representing a sudden shift from this world. Interestingly, I have found Neptune to be specifically involved with death. Transiting Neptune was 4 degrees of Scorpio exactly conjunct natal Mars in the 3rd house (8th from the 8th) ruler of the 8th house. There may have been a mystery surrounding his death or life but one thing for sure - he finally found peace from the torments of this world.

Transits: Death of Joseph Kennedy Sr.

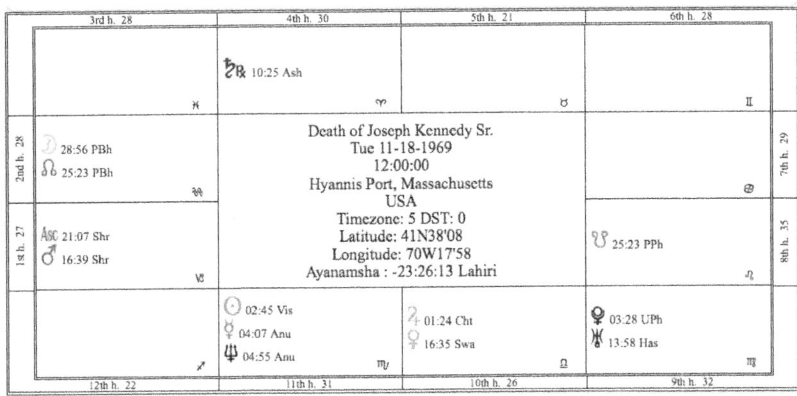

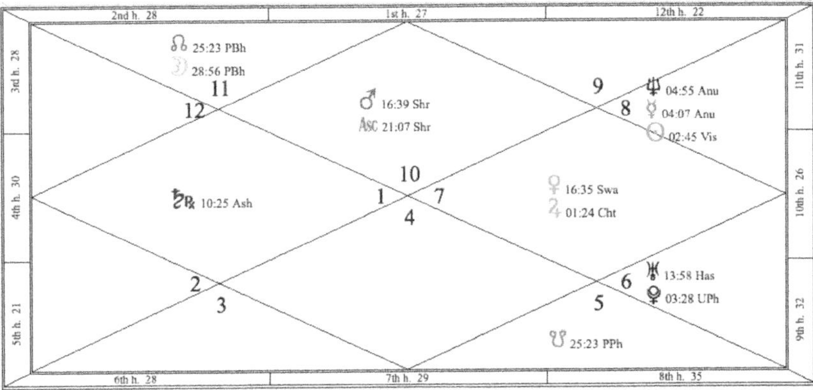

Chapter 2

John Fitzgerald Kennedy

John F. Kennedy was the 35th President of the United States of America, inaugurated as President on January 20th, 1961 and assassinated on November 22nd, 1963. As one of our most charismatic Presidents, he had affairs with Hollywood movie stars. He is known for his great achievements and accomplishments with civil rights in America, and is historically known for creating monumental changes in transformational times.

His family seemed to be under a curse with tragedy after tragedy. His older brother Joseph was killed in WWII in 1944, his older sister Kathleen died later in a plane crash in France in 1948, his mentally retarded sister had a botched operation leaving her brain dead, and his wife Jacqueline had two still born babies, one in 1956, and another in 1963 while in the White House. John F Kennedy was assassinated in 1963 and his brother Robert Kennedy was assassinated 1968, his youngest brother Ted survived a plane crash where the pilot and his aides died in 1964, and a car crash and a scandal in1969 that Ted never overcame. In 1999, his son John Kennedy JR was killed in a plane crash.

Aside from such great loss the place of his greatest achievement was the Presidency of the United States where he will go down in history forever. The 10th house is the house of Presidents, kings and rulers. President Kennedy has Ketu in his 10th house indicating transformational change. He did great things to change the world but the career he chose brought him great loss. For this is an indication of his assassination. As Ketu (the indicator of loss) is in Gemini, Mercury, ruler of Gemini is in the 8th house of death. Mercury and Mars both in Aries are in the 8th house, and Mars rules the 8th house of death.

This is a very ominous chart for life and death but does indicate a life of surrender and empowerment for the world. He sacrificed his life for the betterment of humanity. Powerful planets in the 8th house indicate strong charisma and magnetism. Hollywood starlet Marilyn Monroe, who was associated with Kennedy is still remembered today for her sexuality and powerful charisma, for she had both Mars and Jupiter in the 8th house.

Analysis of John F. Kennedy's Birth Chart

7th h. 32	8th h. 24	9th h. 24	10th h. 29
♓	♂ 25:43 Bha ☿ 27:53 Kri ♈	♃ 00:20 Kri ☉ 15:08 Roh ♀ 24:02 Mrg ♉	♇ 10:33 Ard ☋ 18:32 Ard ♊
6th h. 38 ♅℞ 01:00 Dha ♒	John F. Sr. Kennedy Tue 05-29-1917 15:00:00 Brookline USA	Timezone: 5 DST: 0 Latitude: 42N19'54 Longitude: 71W07'18 Ayanamsha : -22:42:29 Lahiri	11th h. 24 ♄ 04:27 Pus ♆ 09:57 Pus ♋
5th h. 30 ♑			12th h. 22 ☽ 24:30 PPh ♌
☊ 18:32 PSh ♐	♏	♎	Asc 27:17 Cht ♍
4th h. 31	3rd h. 25	2nd h. 28	1st h. 30

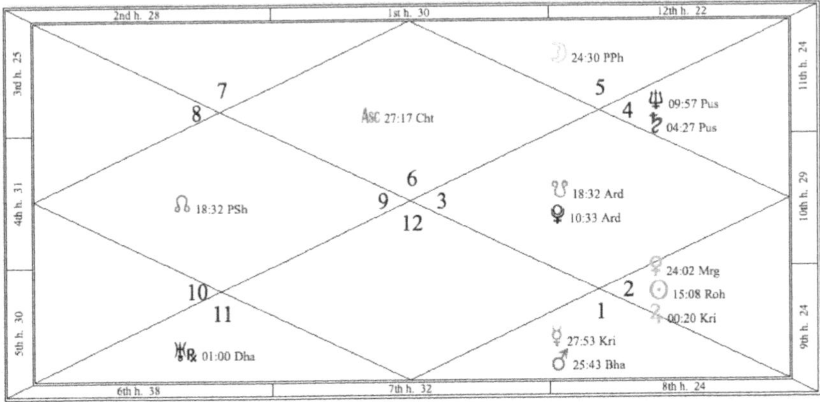

John F Kennedy has a Virgo ascendant but Mercury, ruler of his chart goes into the 8th house of death with a powerful Mars, which rules the 8th house. Both are in Aries. So the chart ruler in the 8th house with the ruler of the 8th house indicates a serious issue surrounding his life and death. Mars as the ruler of weapons and violence can indicate a sudden murder. Mercury is also the ruler of the 10th house, and its placement in the 8th house specifically depicts that he has a very dangerous job as the President. This 8th house of change and transformation indicates that he was involved in the massive reform of many pressing issues that changed the United States during these pivotal times. Ketu in the 10th also indicates the reform that he enacted along with the fact that Ketu's dispositor is Mercury in the 8th house.

On the brighter side, he has both Jupiter and Sun as the karakas for the 9th house, indicating an overwhelming and powerful father. Venus in the 9th house in Taurus indicates a wealthy father. These three planets in the 9th house are the key indicators of his powerful and controlling father. It was his father that encouraged and empowered him to run for President of the United States.

He has the same ascendant, Saturn and natal Moon as his father, indicating a distinct destiny with his father. He was born during his father's Saturn return. The fact that their Moons are exactly conjunct reveal the many ups and downs that they had together. The Moons for both are in their 12th houses. Political leaders frequently have planets in the 12th house since they deal with foreign affairs.

His navamsha ascendant is also Virgo and Mercury in this chart goes to the 4th house, which is known as the seat of power. It aspects the 10th house from the 4th house, and rules the 10th house, indicating a great deal of power and strategy involved in his position and career. Mars and the Moon in Scorpio in the 3rd house represent his drive, courage and ambition to achieve success. Rahu on the ascendant represents a life of fate and destiny.

D9 Navamsha (spouse)

♓ ☋ 7	♈ 8	♉ ☉ 9	♊ 10
♒ 6			♋ 11
♑ ♃ ♇ 5			♌ ♀ ♄ 12
♐ ☿ 4	♏ ☽ ♂ 3	♎ ♅℞ 2	♍ Asc ♆ ☊ 1

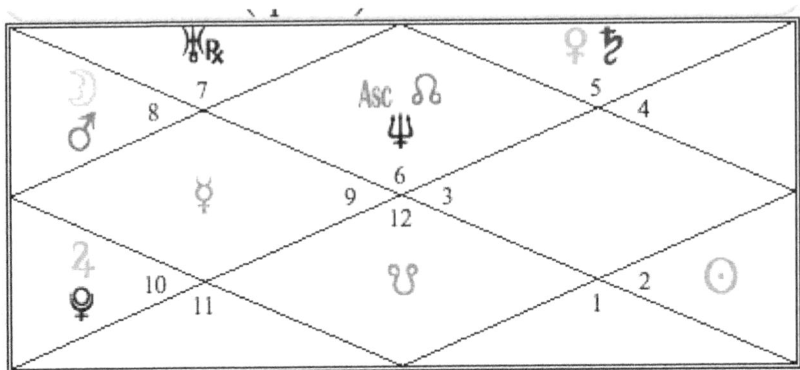

Other divisional charts will be taken into account as we process the events in his life.

The death of his brother, Joseph and sister, Kathleen came through the tragedy of airplane crashes. Joseph died August 12, 1944 and Kathleen May 13, 1948.

At the time of Joseph's death he was in the beginning of the Rahu maha dasha. Rahu is in 4th house in his birth chart. It aspects Mars, the karaka for siblings (brothers) in the 8th house. Mars also rules his 3rd house of siblings.

☊ - ☊	Sat	08-28-1943
☊ - ♃	Fri	05-10-1946
☊ - ♄	Sun	10-03-1948
☊ - ☿	Fri	08-10-1951
☊ - ☋	Fri	02-26-1954
☊ - ♀	Thu	03-17-1955
☊ - ☉	Sun	03-16-1958
☊ - ☽	Sun	02-08-1959
☊ - ♂	Tue	08-09-1960
♃ - ♃	Mon	08-28-1961

Looking at the Dreshkana chart for siblings, it is all the more revealed as Rahu is with the Moon in the 12th house of loss. The Moon also rules the 3rd house of siblings.

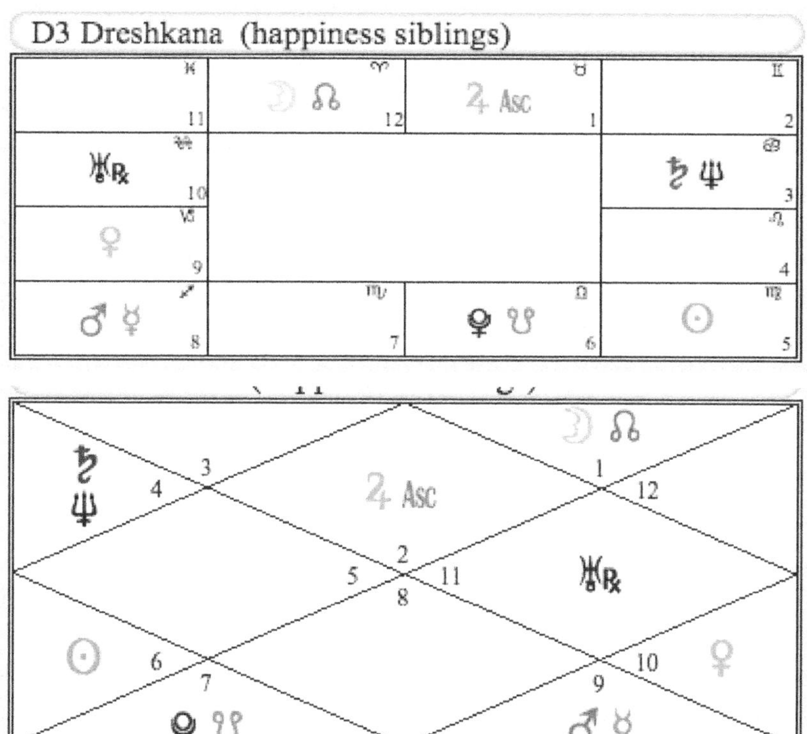

The transits for that day further predict this sad event, as transiting Rahu exactly hits natal Saturn in Cancer in his 11th house. The 11th house is the house of the eldest sibling. Joseph was the eldest sibling. The dispositor of Saturn is the Moon located in the 12th house of loss. This indicates the great sadness he felt during this time. Rahu is the most important transiting planet while he is in the Rahu Maha dasha and the Rahu Bhukti.

Transiting Mars was directly conjunct his natal Moon, ruler of the 11th house of the eldest sibling. Mars indicates a sudden, violent death. Remember he has Mars, karaka of siblings and ruler of the 3rd house of siblings in the 8th house. Mars also rules the 8th house, so this indicates the sudden, violent death of siblings.

On the day his sister Kathleen died May 13, 1948, he was in the Rahu maha dasha and the Jupiter bhukti. Counting from Rahu, Jupiter goes to the 6th house. This can indicate accidents. In the Dreshkana chart, Rahu is in the 12th house in Aries. Mars, the dispositor of Rahu is in the 8th house and is the karaka of siblings. Jupiter is in the 1st house but it rules the 8th house with Taurus ascendant.

Adding the transits for that day transiting Rahu was directly on natal Mars, karaka for siblings and ruler of the 3rd house of siblings. Rahu was also aspecting the natal Moon in the 12th house sighting the suffering for the mother and father, since the Moon is in Leo and the Sun, as the dispositor of the Moon is placed in the 9th house of the father. Jupiter was in Sagittarius aspecting Rahu in the 4th house, indicating the disruption for the mother and family. Transiting Saturn was at 23 degrees of Cancer, aspecting the ascendant (3rd house aspect) and natal Saturn, and closely aspecting natal Mars by its 10th house aspect. Mars is very specific as the indicator of siblings. So natal Mars was being hit simultaneously by transiting Rahu and Saturn.

On the day of his election as President of the United States there are indicators of great success in his chart. He was sworn in on January 20, 1961. He was at the end of Rahu's cycle, the Rahu maha dasha and the Mars bhukti. Rahu is intense but in the 4th house it represents the seat of power, and Mars is all-powerful in its own sign. Mars in the 8th house represents control and power but has dangerous connotations as well. Elected Presidents many times are on the verge of a changing maha dasha since there is a definite life change with the newly elected position in life. He began his Jupiter Maha dasha less than a year after he was elected.

Interestingly, Jupiter throughout many of the divisional charts is not as powerful as expected. I have to believe it is because his newly elected position represented the demise of his life. In his birth chart natal Jupiter is powerfully placed in the 9th house of father and law. He was known for his fight in foreign policies and fighting for civil rights. These are all 9th house matters, initiating and changing laws. But it is weak by only being 0 degrees into the sign of Taurus. As the dispositor of Rahu it indicates power, but essentially the opportunities came from the father. He had made the comment that he was drafted for this position in life.

Jupiter is nicely placed in the navamshas in the 5th house of leadership and authority, but it is debilitated in Capricorn. It is also debilitated in the Dashamsha chart for career and success and is in the 12th house. The 12th house again, pertains to foreign affairs.

D10 Dashamsha (great successes)

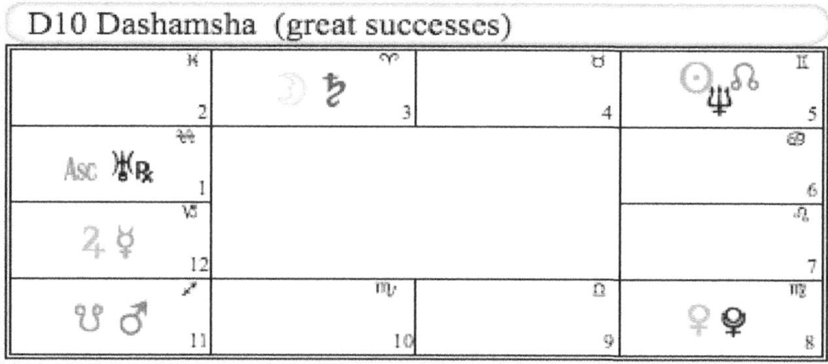

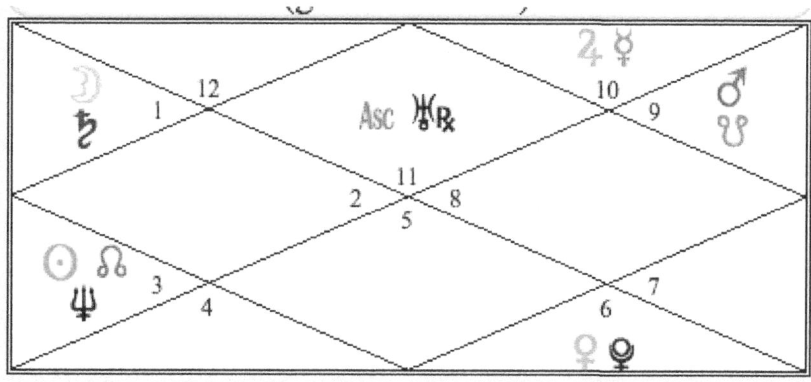

12th h. 27	1st h. 32	2nd h. 25	3rd h. 29
♓	Asc 20:13 Bha ♈	♉	♂Rx 08:26 Ard ♊
11th h. 24: ☽ 29:58 PBh ♀ 23:50 PBh ☋ 13:23 Sat ♒	Inauguration Day Fri 01-20-1961 12:00:00 Washington, District of Columbia USA Timezone: 5 DST: 0 Latitude: 38N53'42 Longitude: 77W02'11 Ayanamsha : -23:18:42 Lahiri		4th h. 32: ♋
10th h. 23: ☿ 16:44 Shr ☉ 07:06 USh ♑			5th h. 22: ♅Rx 01:24 Mag ☊ 13:23 PPh ♇Rx 14:23 PPh ♌
♄ 28:36 USh ♃ 25:21 PSh ♐	♏	♆ 17:52 Swa ♎	♍
9th h. 29	8th h. 30	7th h. 33	6th h. 31

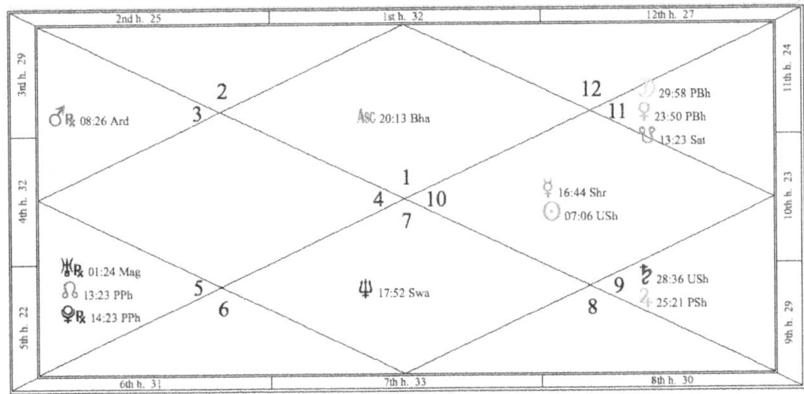

The transits must be analyzed on the inauguration day to understand his achievement as the most powerful man in the world. The inauguration of John F. Kennedy as the 35th President of the United States was held on Friday, January 20, 1961. Transiting Rahu was 13 degrees of Leo, activating his natal Moon in the 12th house. Rahu was aspecting both his Mars and Mercury in the 8th house, and his natal Rahu in the 4th house. So Rahu was actually activating a grand trine in his natal Chart between his natal Moon, Rahu, and Mars/Mercury. Most significantly, the transiting Jupiter /Saturn conjunction was very important in terms of his win and future. Jupiter was 25 degrees and Saturn was 28 of Sagittarius. Transiting Jupiter was exactly trine his natal Moon and conjunct natal Rahu (maha dasha ruler), casting a trine to his natal Mars and Mercury. So Jupiter was also activating his natal grand trine between Moon, Rahu and Mars/Mercury. Furthermore, transiting Mars (bhukti ruler) is in his 10th house at 8 degrees Gemini activating his natal Rahu and Ketu axis. This confirms his win as the President of the United States through the transiting planets.

But then the unspeakable happened on November 22, 1963 when Lee Harvey Oswald in Dallas, Texas assassinated him.

Let's see how this fated destiny came about. He was in a Jupiter maha dasha and a Saturn Bhukti. Jupiter in the 9th house and Saturn in the 11th house does not look very ominous.

♃ - ♃	Mon	08-28-1961
♃ - ♄	Wed	10-16-1963
♃ - ☿	Thu	04-28-1966
♃ - ☋	Sat	08-03-1968
♃ - ♀	Thu	07-10-1969
♃ - ☉	Fri	03-10-1972
♃ - ☽	Wed	12-27-1972
♃ - ♂	Sun	04-28-1974
♃ - ☊	Fri	04-04-1975
♄ - ♄	Sat	08-27-1977

In the navamsha, Saturn is in the 12th house and Jupiter is in the 5th house, but Saturn is situated 6 placements from Jupiter in the navamsha. This still isn't grave enough to predict this horrific event. But when the Trimshamsha D-30 chart of misfortunes is viewed this event becomes clear. In this chart, the Moon is in the 8th house with Rahu and Ketu. The dispositor of the lunar nodes (Rahu/Ketu) is Mercury, which is in the 12th house with Mars, ruler of the 6th house. But as he was in Jupiter and Saturn dashas, both Jupiter and Saturn are in the 7th house, the maraka house.

D30 Trimshamsha (misfortunes)

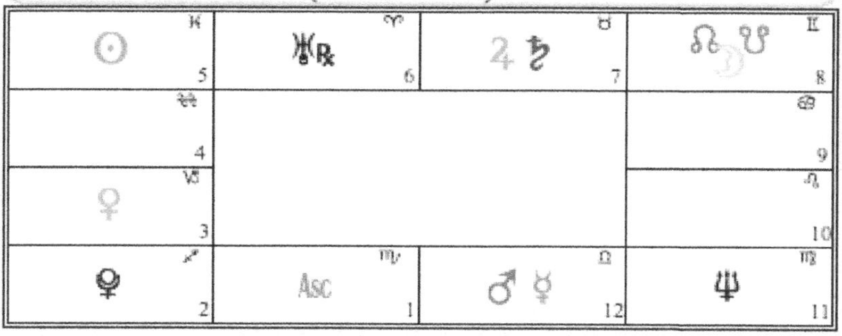

☉ ♓ 5	♅℞ ♈ 6	♃ ♄ ♉ 7	☊ ☋ ☽ ♊ 8
♒ 4			♋ 9
♀ ♑ 3			♌ 10
♇ ♐ 2	Asc ♏ 1	♂ ☿ ♎ 12	♆ ♍ 11

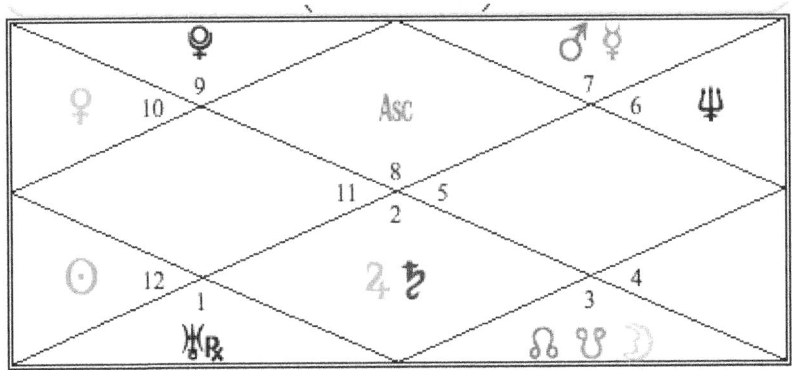

But as always the transits are truly what determine a prediction. The most significant transiting planet at the time of the assassination was transiting Rahu at 18 degrees of Gemini and Ketu was 18 degrees of Sagittarius, which means that transiting Rahu was conjunct natal Ketu in the 10th house, and transiting Ketu was conjunct natal Rahu in the 4th house. This was the exact aspect that predicted this fated event, for the lunar nodes reveal our fate and destiny. Symbolically his Ketu is in the nakshatra Ardra, which is a symbol for a teardrop. This event instigated many tears and sadness worldwide. Transiting Ketu was also aspecting natal Mars, Mercury and the Moon.

Remember that where Rahu and Ketu are transiting is where the eclipses are occurring within the year. The solar and lunar eclipses in his 10th house represent major changes in the career. Don't forget that the 10th house represents public and social standing, and transiting Ketu here represents major shifts and changes within his social status and public recognition.

Transiting Mars was 27 degrees Scorpio in his 3rd house (8th from the 8th) aspecting his 9th house planets - Jupiter, Sun and Venus. But it was also aspecting by an 8th house aspect his natal Ketu, where transiting Rahu was standing. Transiting Mars was square his natal Moon in Leo in his 12th house. This is a major aspect 10/4 relationship aspecting his career and the seat of power.

Interestingly transiting Mars at 27 degrees was aspecting natal Mercury exactly by a 6/8 relationship. This is not a full aspect used in Vedic astrology, but the placements of planets by exact degree must be recognized, for their effects are notable even though it doesn't fall under specific aspects. This is using the spatial relationships. Take into account when transiting planets are the same degree as the natal planets and see the number of houses counted from the transiting planet to the natal planet; and then count back around to the transiting planet. This is how we see these spatial relationships. They definitely indicate a prediction of an event, especially the 6/8 or 8/6 relationship in terms of accidents and death.

Transiting Saturn was in the 11th house aspecting his natal Saturn, but the 11th house is also the 12th house from the Moon.

This was a most significant world event that affected not only him personally but the world globally. This is foreseen through the 10th house of the public or masses of people. Ketu is seen as loss and the nakshatra Ardra (teardrop). Transiting Rahu, indicator of destiny brought this into the realization of the destiny of humanity.

Chapter 3

Robert Kennedy

Robert Kennedy (Bobby) has the makings of a life full of a certain destiny and fate. Bobby has an Aries ascendant and Mars in his 7th house with Saturn in Libra. The 7th house is the house of partnerships and his brother certainly set him up in politics during his Presidency, for he appointed him Attorney General. His father is also represented as powerful and commanding with Bobby's Venus and Jupiter in the 9th house of the father.

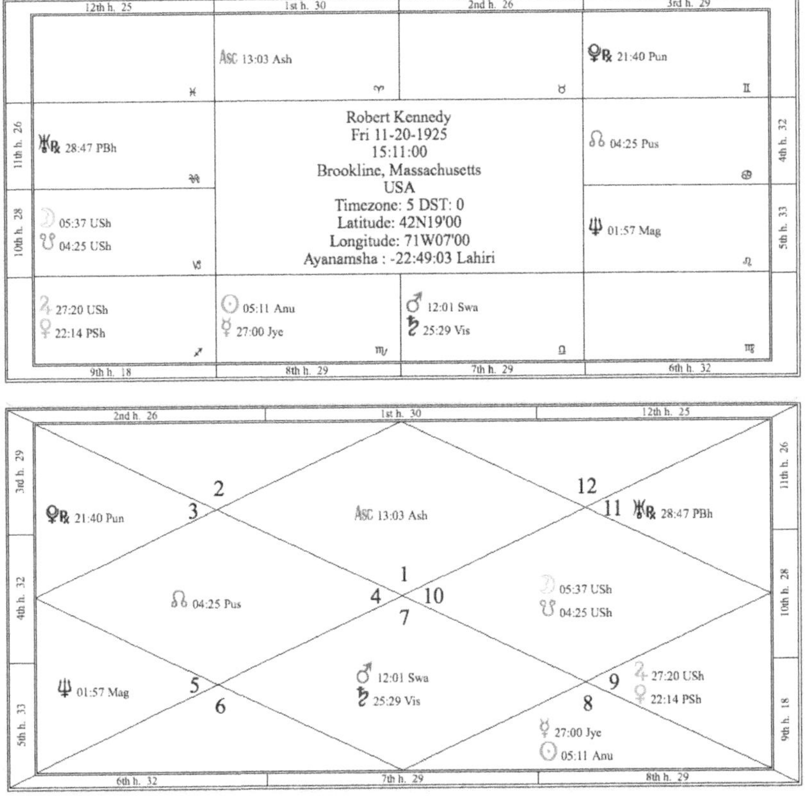

His destiny is clearly seen by the Moon and Ketu in the 10th house of fame and career. He, like his brother both had Ketu in the 10th house; and here the destiny seems etched in stone. Saturn rules the 10th house, and joins Mars in the 7th house, further indicating his career position given by his brother. Mars is the karaka for siblings. John and Joseph Kennedy were his older brothers, which is seen from Saturn as the ruler of the 11th house (older siblings), with Mars ruler of the 8th house of death. Moreover, Mercury as ruler of the 3rd house (generally all siblings) occupies the 8th house of death.

♃ - ♃	Thu	11-08-1962
♃ - ♄	Sun	12-27-1964
♃ - ☿	Mon	07-10-1967
♃ - ☋	Wed	10-15-1969
♃ - ♀	Mon	09-21-1970
♃ - ☉	Tue	05-22-1973
♃ - ☽	Sun	03-10-1974
♃ - ♂	Thu	07-10-1975
♃ - ☊	Tue	06-15-1976
♄ - ♄	Wed	11-08-1978

On the day his brother John F Kennedy was killed, he had just started the Jupiter maha dasha. Jupiter is in the 9th house. But looking at its placement in the navamsha it is placed in the 6th house, and in the Dreshkana chart (siblings) it is in the 1st and rules the 8th house. This isn't enough to predict the death of a brother, but let's now look at the transits to get the full picture.

D9 Navamsha (spouse)

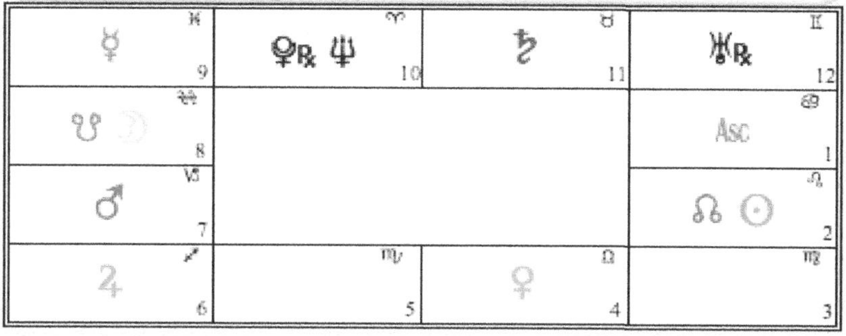

♓ ☿ 9	♈ ♇R ♆ 10	♉ ♄ 11	♊ ♅R 12
♒ ☋ ☽ 8			♋ Asc 1
♑ ♂ 7			♌ ☊ ☉ 2
♐ ♃ 6	♏ 5	♎ ♀ 4	♍ 3

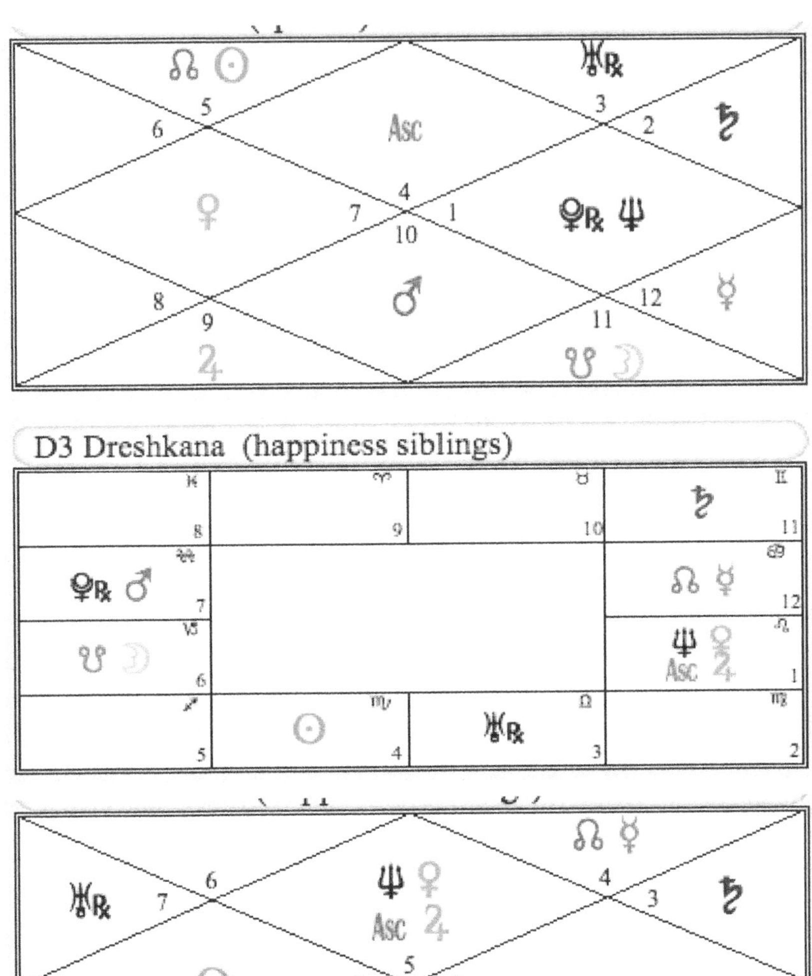

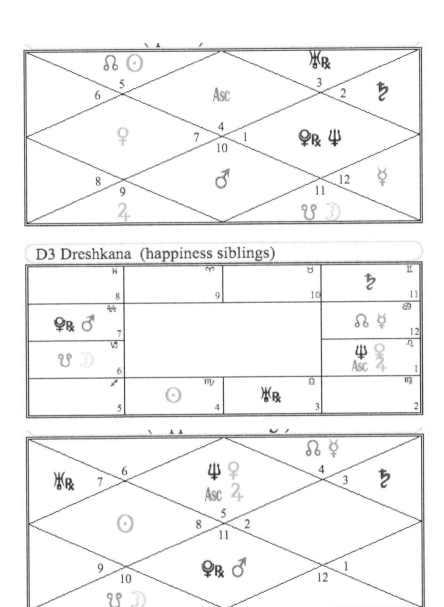

Transiting Jupiter was in the 12th house at 16 degrees of Pisces aspecting (trine) the 8th house and the Sun, Mercury and Rahu in the 4th house. But transiting Rahu and Ketu are in the 3rd and 9th houses. Rahu is in the 3rd house of brothers and sisters and Ketu is conjunct Jupiter and Venus. Transiting Ketu in the 9th also indicates loss for the father as well as himself. Rahu is aspecting Mars and Saturn in the 7th house. Mars is the karaka for brothers and it rules the 8th house of death.

Transiting Saturn was at 23 degrees of Capricorn in the 11th house of the older sibling, and aspected the ascendant, the 8th house, and the natal Sun and Mercury. But here is the real clincher: on this day, while transiting Saturn aspected natal Mercury ruler of the 3rd house of siblings, transiting Mars at 27 degrees Scorpio exactly conjoined natal Mercury in the 8th house, ruler of the 3rd house of siblings.

On the day he was shot June 6, 1968 he was campaigning late at night in Los Angeles for the presidency. During this time he was in the Jupiter maha dasha and the Mercury Bhukti.

Most importantly, his natal Mercury (bhukti) is in the 8th house and is almost exactly opposed by transiting Mars in the 2nd house at 26 degrees Taurus. He was shot with a gun - Mars rules weapons. His brother was shot when transiting Mars exactly conjoined his natal Mercury! Both transiting Saturn and Rahu are in his 12th house of loss and secret enemies. Transiting Rahu is aspecting his natal Mercury, and as transiting Saturn conjuncts transiting Rahu, Rahu carries the energy of Saturn as it sends its aspects.

Chapter 4

Jacqueline Kennedy Onassis

The Kennedy dynasty was revered as the kings of America, as the marriage between Jacqueline and John Kennedy mesmerized the people of America. The era they were in the White House is often referred to affectionately as Camelot. Jackie was noted for her elegant style and spent enormous amounts of money decorating the White House, as well as wearing stunning designer clothes. She set the styles and trends for America during her reign. She was only 31 years old when she became the first lady. And she was the most photographed woman in the world till her death.

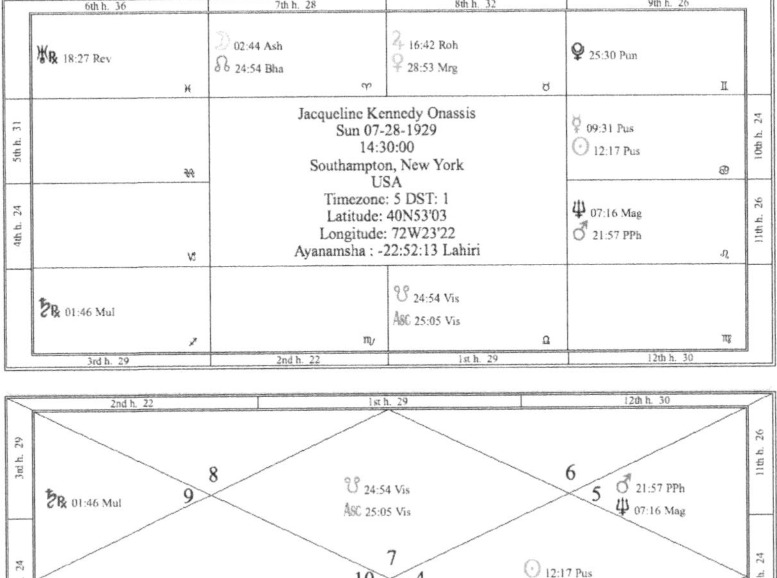

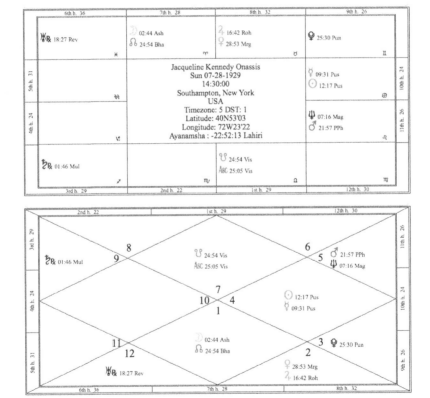

Jacqueline's birth chart is very revealing of her fate and destiny. Her ascendant was Libra with Ketu exactly on her ascendant degree. Ketu on the ascendant made her very elusive and mysterious. In Libra, it also gave her a slender stature and grace. But it should not be denied that Ketu is the karaka of loss, and directly on the ascendant it can be a potent indicator of a life of tragedy and loss. Venus, the ruler of her chart is in the 8th house of power, control, charisma and death. It is combined with Jupiter, ruler of the 6th house of enemies and difficulty. But the most specific aspect in her chart is her natal Moon and Rahu conjunct in the 7th house of marriage partners. The Moon as the ruler of the 10th house of career and fame points to the husband as the focal point that brought her to the public eye. Rahu is the indicator of destiny, and her husband, who became President of the United States. He certainly did bring her into the limelight.

She began the Moon maha dasha right at the onset of becoming the First Lady. This is amazing since her Moon is in the 7th house of marriage. The Moon with Rahu really explains the trend that her life took from that point on, a life of fate and destiny due to her marriage.

☽ - ☊	Sat	07-21-1962
☽ - ♃	Mon	01-20-1964
☽ - ♄	Fri	05-21-1965
☽ - ☿	Wed	12-21-1966
☽ - ☋	Tue	05-21-1968
☽ - ♀	Fri	12-20-1968
☽ - ☉	Fri	08-21-1970
♂ - ♂	Fri	02-19-1971
♂ - ☊	Mon	07-19-1971
♂ - ♃	Sat	08-05-1972

On the day of the assassination of President Kennedy Jacqueline was in a Moon maha dasha and a Rahu bhukti. Of course these are the two planets that confirm this life of destiny. Transiting Rahu and Ketu were in her 9th and 3rd houses, Ketu 18 degrees of Sagittarius is aspecting her 7th house and natal Moon and Rahu, and Mars in the 11th house ruler of the 7th house. Furthermore, transiting Mars was 27 degrees Scorpio aspecting natal Jupiter and natal Venus exactly. Venus is the ruler of her chart and is in the 8th house of death. This was a horrific death defying experience as she climbed onto the back of the car as it speed along, with her husband profusely bleeding all over her. And the world has seen filmed clips of this nightmare - this tragic event - over and over.

Transiting Saturn is in the 4th house of security at 23 degrees of Capricorn, and aspects the Sun and Mercury in the 10th house. Saturn is aspecting the ascendant degree and the Sun, which depletes the life force, and Saturn of course indicates death and endings.

The day of the assassination of her husband her life changed dramatically for she feared for her life and her children. She knew the police or secret service were not enough to keep her and her children safe. She had suspicions of the deeper implications of a deep-seated conspiracy. She no longer trusted the government, and felt the need to escape the United States. She quickly found solace in the Greek super power Aristotle Onassis. He was one of the richest men in the world, owning the biggest shipping Industry in Greece. She became the most photographed woman in the world, but all she wanted was to hide. Aristotle assured her protection by setting her up on an Island he owned, Skorpios. To live on a Greek Island away from the United States gave her peace of mind and a sense of safety.

She married Aristotle Onassis October 20, 1968. She was in a Moon maha dasha and a Ketu Bhukti. With natal Ketu in the 1st house, the 7th house from the Moon marriage is predicted. And the transiting planets describe the evolving story fully, as transiting Jupiter and Ketu are Virgo in the 12th house, indicating travels and residence in foreign counties. Upon close inspection transiting Saturn is at 28 degrees Pisces exactly aspecting her natal Venus, and transiting Rahu is at 16 degrees Pisces, the same degree as her natal Jupiter, which is conjunct Venus in the 8th house. This marriage consequently brought great discord in her life, battling Aristotle's daughter Christina over an inheritance. But in the end she was awarded over 20 million dollars and more than $200,000 a year - plus her children received money as well. She promised Christina that she would keep the Onassis' name permanently. So the 8th house gave her money through marriage (2nd from the 7th house), but through a long drawn out conflict. This was months after Bobby's assassination so Jackie intended to stay away from the United States. Her affair with Aristotle was going on while transiting Rahu was in her 7th house and transiting Jupiter was in Leo aspecting her 7th house. Rahu transiting the 7th house brings relationships into the life, and furthermore Rahu represents foreigners.

Transits: Marriage of Jacqueline Kennedy to Aristotle Onassis

4th h. 24	5th h. 24	6th h. 32	7th h. 30
♄℞ 28:15 Rev ☊ 16:12 UBh ♓	♈	♉	♊
3rd h. 30 ♒	Marriage of Jacqueline Kennedy to Aristotle Onassis Sun 10-20-1968 12:00:00 Athens Greece		8th h. 38 ♋
2nd h. 29 ♑	Timezone: -2 DST: 0 Latitude: 37N59'00 Longitude: 23E44'00 Ayanamsha : -23:25:13 Lahiri		9th h. 27 ♂ 24:25 PPh ♌
Asc 09:14 Mul ♐	♆ 01:46 Vis ♀ 05:35 Anu ♏	☉ 03:39 Cht ♎	♇ 00:28 UPh ♃ 01:41 UPh ♅ 07:54 UPh ☽ 13:35 Has ☋ 16:12 Has ☿℞ 23:55 Cht ♍
1st h. 24	12th h. 25	11th h. 25	10th h. 29

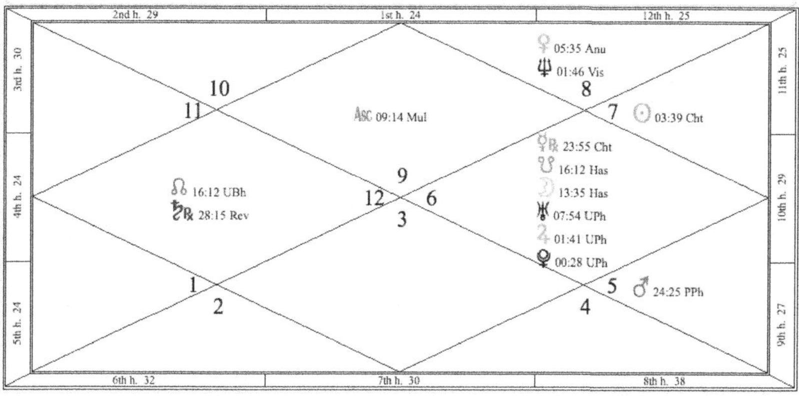

Chapter 5

John Kennedy Jr.

John Kennedy Jr. had a fate all of his own, being the son of President Kennedy. He was born in November the month his father was elected President of the United States. But he was only 3 years old when his father was assassinated. His chart indicates a life of fate and destiny for Rahu is the exact degree of the ascendant. He was born into the Mars maha dasha, but he just entered the Rahu maha dasha at the time of his father's death. Transiting Rahu was at 18 degrees of Gemini in his 11th house. It was conjunct natal Mars, ruler of the 9th house of the father. The opposing node Ketu was conjunct Saturn and Jupiter, but precisely conjoined Venus. Venus rules the 10th house - another house used to view the father - and indicates our reputation and fame. One of the most famous photographs was of three-year-old John saluting his father at his funeral.

He was extraordinarily handsome, and was forced to become a lawyer. It was expected by his family that he go into politics, but this was not his destiny, nor his interest. He failed the lawyer's bar exam twice, finally passing it the third time. He eventually followed in his mother's footsteps with writing and publishing. His ultimate success came when he published his famed magazine "George." His talent for writing is revealed through his natal chart. The 3rd and 5th houses are the houses for writing and creativity. He has Mercury in the 3rd house, and Jupiter, Venus and Saturn in the 5th house. The 5th house is indicated as the house of writing and creativity because it is the 3rd house from the 3rd house.

8th h. 28	9th h. 29	10th h. 27	11th h. 30
♓	♈	♉	♂ ℞ 25:12 Pun ♊
7th h. 24 ☋ 18:27 Sat ☽ 04:06 Dha ♒	John Kennedy Jr. Fri 11-25-1960 00:22:00 WASHINGTON, District of Columbia USA Timezone: 5 DST: 0 Latitude: 38N53'42 Longitude: 77W02'12 Ayanamsha : -23:18:33 Lahiri		12th h. 30 ♋
6th h. 22 ♑			1st h. 32 ♅ 02:28 Mag ♇ 14:45 PPh ☊ 18:27 PPh Asc 18:39 PPh ♌
♄ 22:14 PSh ♀ 18:35 PSh ♃ 12:30 Mul ♐	☉ 09:38 Anu ♏	♆ 16:26 Swa ☿ 19:55 Swa ♎	♍
5th h. 28	4th h. 23	3rd h. 34	2nd h. 30

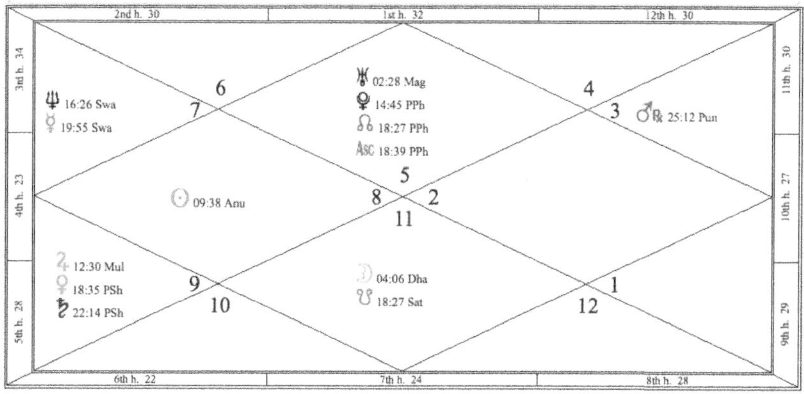

Venus rules his 3rd house (Libra) and is placed in the 5th house. This further connects the 3rd house to the 5th house. Venus is with Jupiter, magnifying his talent and opportunities. Saturn here gives discipline to produce his work. Mercury conjunct Neptune indicates a unique talent in writing.

But it all came to an end on July 16, 1999. He died in a fateful plane crash, as he was flying to Martha's Vineyard to a wedding in his own airplane with his wife and her sister . They were all killed.

He was in a Saturn maha dasha and a Mercury bhukti. In his birth chart Saturn is in the 5th house, but rules the 6th house of accidents and the 7th house, which is a maraka house. Mercury is in the 3rd house, which is a house of travel. It is with Neptune, which can cause problems with judgment. Neptune rules deception and not seeing clearly. Mercury is another maraka planet by its rulership of the 2nd house. So both Saturn and Mercury are maraka planets.

♄ - ☿	Fri	04-02-1999
♄ - ☋	Mon	12-10-2001
♄ - ♀	Sun	01-19-2003
♄ - ☉	Mon	03-20-2006
♄ - ☽	Fri	03-02-2007
♄ - ♂	Wed	10-01-2008
♄ - ☊	Tue	11-10-2009
♄ - ♃	Sat	09-15-2012
☿ - ☿	Mon	03-30-2015
☿ - ☋	Fri	08-25-2017

In the navamsha, Saturn is in the 2nd house and Mercury is in the 7th house, both maraka houses. Counting from Saturn to Mercury they are in a 6/8 relationship.

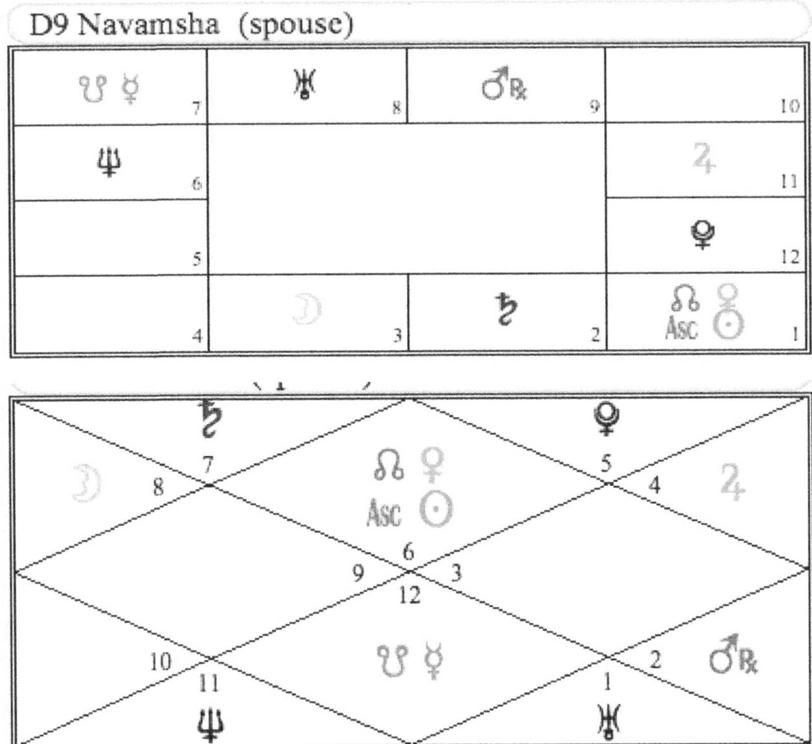

These are minor indications using the dashas from the birth chart and navamsha. To finalize a prediction the transits need to be added to this picture. The transits of the dasha rulers and the natal planets of the dasha rulers are the focus. Transiting Saturn (dasha ruler) was 21 degrees of Aries in the 9th house of travel, fully aspecting natal Mercury (bhukti ruler) in the 3rd house of travel. Additionally, both planets are marakas for his chart. Adding transiting Mars to this picture, Mars was 10 degrees Libra approaching his natal Mercury. Another aspect to watch is the square of Rahu and Ketu. There is a point where Rahu and Ketu have a midpoint that creates a transiting cross across a chart. Rahu and Ketu were at 19 degrees Cancer and Capricorn. Rahu was in Cancer in the 12th house and Ketu in the 6th house in Capricorn. They are exactly square natal Mercury, the point that is also aspected by both Saturn and Mars. So natal Mercury in the 3rd house of travel (also a maraka) is totally afflicted by malefics, Saturn, Mars, Rahu and Ketu, and it is the focal point, being the bhukti ruler.

Notice that Mercury is debilitated with Ketu in the 7th house in the navamsha chart. This can be an indicator of loss in marriage. Because of poor choices he was the cause of his wife and her sister's deaths. But was it destiny? Looking at the birth chart he has Moon with Ketu in the 7th house and the Moon rules the 12th house of loss. It seems it is his destiny!

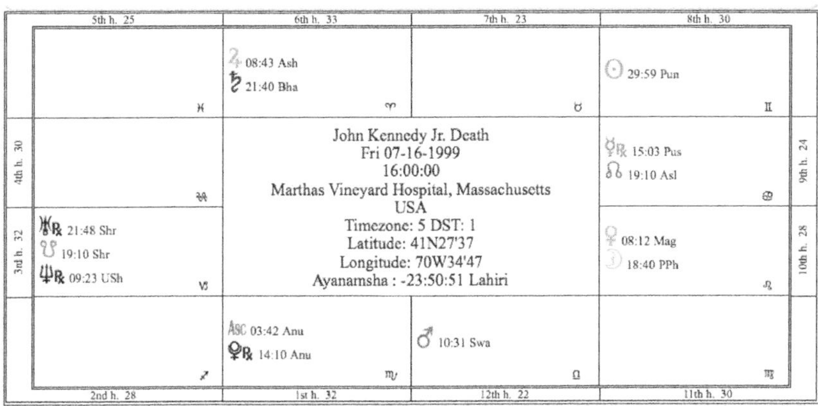

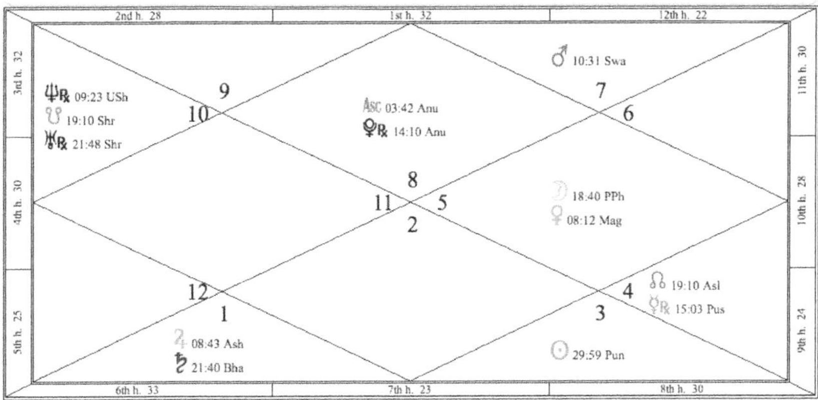

Chapter 6
Caroline Kennedy

The only Kennedy at this point who still remains is Caroline Kennedy. How does her chart reveal the many tragedies throughout life? There must be specific planetary configurations depicting her difficulties dealing with these great losses around her family.

5th h. 23	6th h. 32	7th h. 26	8th h. 27
♓	☋ 16:58 Bha ♈	♉	♊
4th h. 30 ♒	Caroline Kennedy Wed 11-27-1957 08:15:00 New York, New York USA Timezone: 5 DST: 0 Latitude: 40N42'51 Longitude: 74W00'22 Ayanamsha : -23:16:19 Lahiri		♅℞ 18:20 Asl ♋ 9th h. 29
3rd h. 25 ☽ 22:39 Shr ♑			♇ 09:02 Mag ♌ 10th h. 37
♀ 28:36 USh ☿ 00:04 Mul ♐	☉ 11:46 Anu ♄ 22:08 Jyc Asc 26:59 Jyc ♏	♆ 10:14 Swa ☊ 16:58 Swa ♂ 19:16 Swa ♎	♃ 29:48 Cht ♍
2nd h. 19	1st h. 30	12th h. 25	11th h. 34

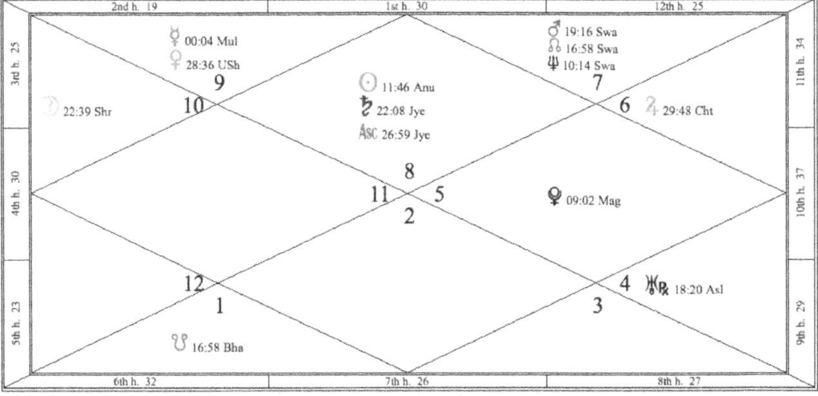

Caroline has a Scorpio ascendant, and Mars as ruler of her chart occupies the 12th house of loss and is conjunct Rahu, which magnifies the loss. Neptune combined here indicates the mystery and uncertainty of not knowing the reasons and causes for the problems and conspiracies. She has Saturn conjunct the Sun, representing loss around the father since the Sun is the karaka of the father, plus the dispositor of the Sun and Saturn is Mars in the 12th house (loss) conjunct Rahu. Saturn close to the ascendant represents a serious disposition and maturity beyond their years. This is also an indication of a life of hardship and sadness.

Financially she will always be compensated royally. Jupiter is the ruler of the 2nd house of money and is in the 11th house of great gains and wealth, additionally Venus and Mercury (natal benefics) are in Sagittarius in the 2nd house. They are both disposited by Jupiter. Jupiter in Virgo and Mercury in Sagittarius give Jupiter and Mercury mutual reception. They exchange signs of rulership. This exchange between the 2nd and 11th house rulers will bring great wealth. She inherited millions from her family. Her Moon in the 3rd house as ruler of the 9th house gave her a close relationship with her baby brother. But Uranus is opposed indicating uncertainty and accidents. The Moon is the karaka of the mother and as ruler of the 9th house represents the father as well. Her Moon is significant as a key to the sudden events, and emotional ups and downs for her mother and father. The Moon in Capricorn is powerfully aspected by Saturn, Mars, Jupiter and Uranus. The Moon as an indicator of emotions and the mother certainly produces a life of change and uncertainty.

The navamsha reveals an even deeper element to her life. Her ascendant is Pisces, and Mars and Rahu are in the 1st house. Her famous father is represented by Mars as the ruler of the 9th house in the 1st house with Rahu, but the Sun as karaka of the father is debilitated, and occupies the 8th house of death.

D9 Navamsha (spouse)

♓ ☊ Asc ♂ 1	♈ ☿ 2	♉ 3	♊ ♇ 4
♒ 12			♋ ☽ 5
♑ ♆ ♄ 11			♌ 6
♐ ♅℞ ♀ 10	♏ 9	♎ ☉ 8	♍ ☋ ♃ 7

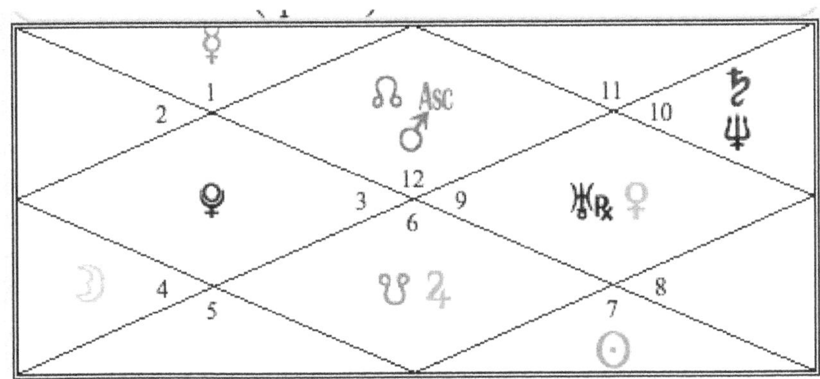

The Dwadashamsha chart D-12 is the chart that reflects the parents. In this chart Virgo is the ascendant and Mars, as ruler of the 8th house of death is in the 9th house of the father. Mars is the planet of weapons and violence. Additionally, it aspects Venus by opposition, ruler of the 9th house. The Moon as karaka of the mother is with Ketu indicator of loss. The Moon and Ketu are in the 2nd house indicating loss in her early life. The 2nd house indicates early life experiences. Rahu in the 8th house indicates death but gains through inheritance.

D12 Dwadashamsha (parents)

☉ ♓ 7	☊ ♈ 8	♂ ♉ 9	♊ 10
♆ ♅Rx ♒ 6			♄ ♋ 11
♑ 5			♃ ♌ 12
☿ ♐ 4	♀ ♇ ♏ 3	☽ ☋ ♎ 2	Asc ♍ 1

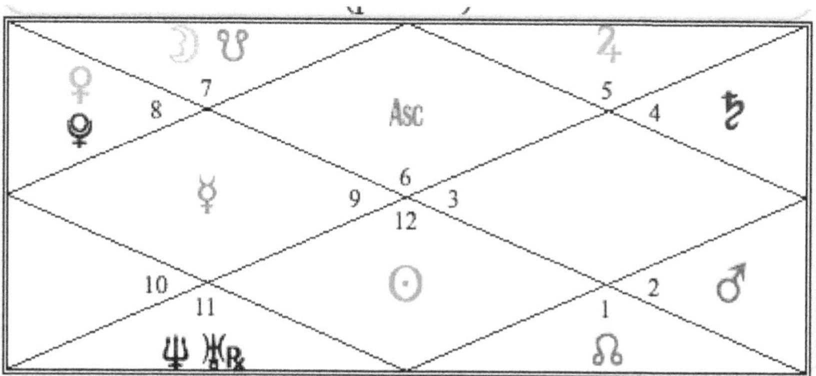

To further understand her life and the tragic loss of her brother, the Dreshkana chart D-3 for siblings must be assessed. This chart could not be clearer, as the Mars and Rahu conjunction are in the 8th house (death). Mars is the karaka for brothers and it is with Rahu and Neptune in the 8th house, indicating secrets. Plus the Moon is in the 3rd house of younger siblings, and Saturn, Mars and Jupiter are aspecting the Moon and 3rd house. Mercury as ruler of the 3rd house is in the 6th house of accidents, and is aspected by Ketu. Aside from her relationship with her brother, her mother lost 3 children - one miscarriage, one still born and one died 2 days after birth this was after John in 1963. So of course, the chart for siblings is a difficult one.

Now to understand when the potential for these events are to occur we must add the transits. Let's view the death of her father, her mother, and her brother. And as an added life event let's view her marriage and births of her children to understand how to make life predictions.

At the time of the death of her father November 22, 1963 she was in a Mars maha dasha and a Venus Bhukti. Mars is deadly in her chart, being in the 12th house with Rahu. It is the planet that really depicts her entire life of trauma. Venus looks benign on the surface, but a closer look reveals a deeper problem. Venus is in the 2nd house aspected by Mercury, ruler of the 8th house; and Ketu aspects from the 6th house of accidents.

♂ - ♀	Thu	04-25-1963
♂ - ☉	Wed	06-24-1964
♂ - ☽	Fri	10-30-1964
☊ - ☊	Mon	05-31-1965
☊ - ♃	Sun	02-11-1968
☊ - ♄	Tue	07-07-1970
☊ - ☿	Sun	05-13-1973
☊ - ☋	Sun	11-30-1975
☊ - ♀	Fri	12-17-1976
☊ - ☉	Tue	12-18-1979

In the navamsha chart, Venus is in the 10th house of social standing but is conjunct Uranus, dealing with sudden, unexpected events, and rules the 8th house of death.

The Dreshkana chart D-3 can be referred to as a chart of happiness. Here the truth is revealed as both Mars and Venus aspect each other by opposition and are conjunct Rahu and Ketu. Venus is with Ketu and Pluto, opposed Mars with Rahu and Neptune. The outer planets add a dimension relevant to this scenario. Pluto represents power and controlling forces, and Neptune means there is a conspiracy and deception around the assassination of her father. Furthermore Mars, Rahu and Neptune are in the 8th house of death.

D3 Dreshkana (happiness siblings)

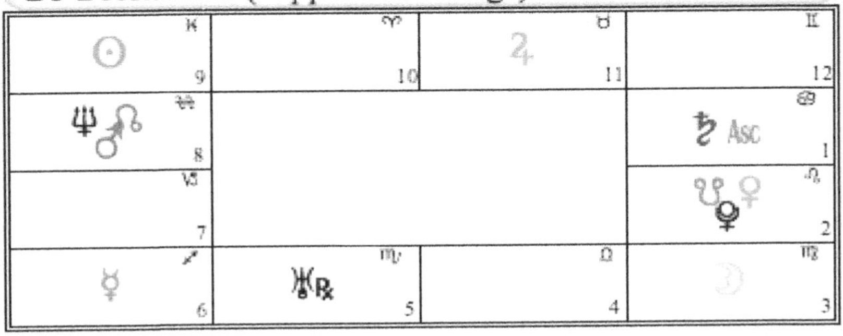

☉ ♓ 9	♈ 10	♃ ♉ 11	♊ 12
♆ ☊ ♂ ♒ 8			♄ Asc ♋ 1
♑ 7			☋ ♀ ♇ ♌ 2
☿ ♐ 6	♅ ℞ ♏ 5	♎ 4	☽ ♍ 3

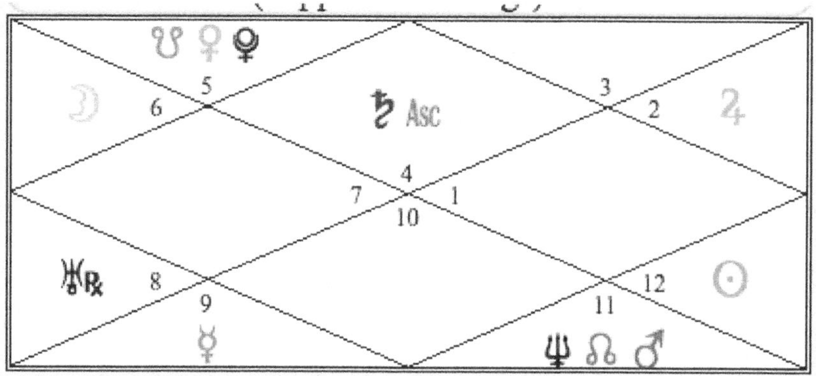

The Dwadasamsha chart D-12 is the chart of the parents, and again Mars and Venus aspect each other by opposition. Mars is in the 9th house of the father and rules the 8th house of death. Venus is with Pluto in the 3rd house but it is in Scorpio, and Mars is in Taurus meaning they are in mutual reception - connecting them. Mars, again is deadly as the ruler of the 8th and 3rd house.

The transits are the key for timing. On November 22, 1963, Mars (dasha ruler) was 27 degrees Scorpio exactly conjunct her natal Saturn in the 1st house. Saturn rules the 3rd and 4th house. The 4th house is the mother and sense of security, so this area of life is threatened. But Saturn in Scorpio means Mars is the dispositor of Saturn, and its placement in the 12th house of secret enemies with dangerous Rahu indicates the timing of this attack.

The natal Moon must be profoundly aspected since it is the planet that rules the 9th house of the father and is the karaka of the mother. Remember that it is powerfully aspected in the natal chart by Mars, Saturn, Jupiter and Uranus. Amazingly transiting Saturn was exactly conjunct her natal Moon. Furthermore, Ketu was in Sagittarius aspecting her natal Venus, the Bhukti ruler - and rules the 12th house.

The next tragedy involved the assassination of her uncle Bobby Kennedy on June 5, 1968. During this time she was in a Rahu maha dasha and a Jupiter Bhukti. Natal Rahu is in the 12th house with Mars. This will bring out danger and secret enemies. She was also living in a foreign country (Greece) with her mother at this time. As she was in Jupiter's Bhukti, natal Jupiter is in the 11th house, which is the 3rd house from the 9th meaning her father's brother. Transiting Saturn was exactly opposed natal Jupiter at 29 degrees Pisces. Additionally transiting Rahu was also in Pisces and Ketu in Virgo aspecting natal Jupiter at 23 degrees. Transiting Mars was at 25 degrees Taurus, exactly aspecting her ascendant and her natal Saturn. Saturn is the karaka of uncles. Adding the exact aspects of outer planets, Pluto at 26 degrees of Leo was squaring her ascendant degree, and Uranus at 1 degree Virgo was squaring natal Mercury. Mercury is sometimes associated with aunts and uncles.

She is married to Edwin Schlossberg. Edwin and Caroline met in December 1981 in New York City at the Metropolitan Museum of Art. They married on July 19, 1986.

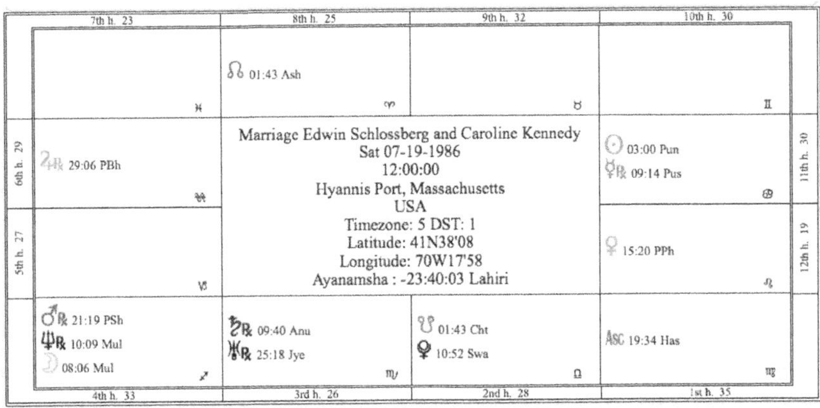

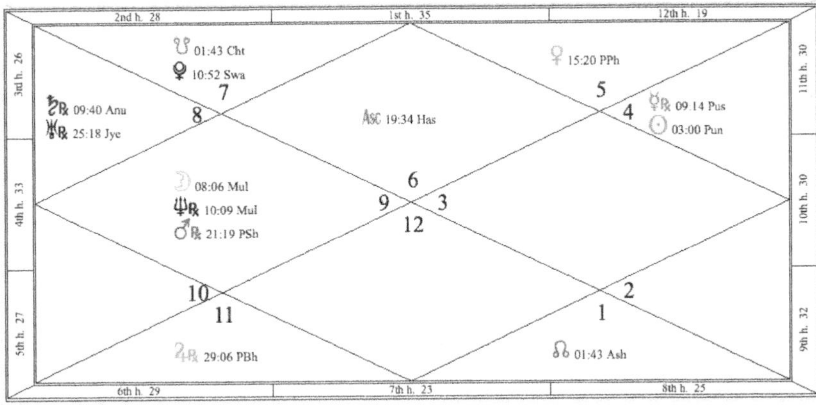

♃ - ♄	Thu	07-18-1985
♃ - ☿	Sat	01-30-1988
♃ - ☋	Mon	05-07-1990
♃ - ♀	Sat	04-13-1991
♃ - ☉	Sun	12-12-1993
♃ - ☽	Fri	09-30-1994
♃ - ♂	Tue	01-30-1996
♃ - ☊	Sun	01-05-1997
♄ - ♄	Mon	05-31-1999
♄ - ☿	Mon	06-03-2002

She was in Jupiter a maha dasha and a Saturn bhukti when they married. Both her Jupiter and Saturn aspect her 7th house of marriage in her birth chart. Jupiter is in the 7th house in the navamsha chart and Jupiter aspects Saturn in this chart.

But the transits were strongest when she met Edwin in December 1981 when transiting Ketu was conjunct her natal Venus, ruler of her 7th house. She was in a Rahu Maha Dasha and a Moon Bhukti, and her Moon is in the 5th house of love in the navamsha, and Rahu was in the 1st house.

She had her 3 children in her Jupiter maha dasha. This is a common occurrence (when a woman is of childbearing years) that they give birth to their children in Jupiter's maha dasha, since Jupiter is the karaka of children. Rose was born June 25, 1988, Tatiana-Celia was born May 5, 1990, and John was born January 19, 1993.

Her mother died May 19, 1994 from a battle with Cancer. Caroline was in a Jupiter maha dasha and a Sun Bhukti. Natal Jupiter is in the 11th house, which is the 8th house from the 4th house (death of mother) and Saturn is the ruler of the 4th house.

9th h. 29	10th h. 29	11th h. 32	12th h. 23
♓	♂ 02:59 Ash ♈	☋ 00:00 Kri ☉ 04:39 Kri ☿ 24:13 Mrg ♉	♀ 04:32 Mrg ♊
8th h. 31: ♄ 17:39 Sat ♒			1st h. 28: Asc 29:16 Asl ♋
7th h. 26: ♅ ℞ 02:25 USh ♑			2nd h. 26: ☽ 19:07 PPh ♌
♆ ℞ 29:24 USh ♐	☊ 00:00 Vis ♇ ℞ 02:51 Vis ♏	♃ ℞ 13:38 Swa ♎	♍
6th h. 28	5th h. 22	4th h. 33	3rd h. 30

Death of Jacqueline Kennedy Onassis
Thu 05-19-1994
12:00:00
Manhattan, New York
USA
Timezone: 5 DST: 1
Latitude: 40N47'00
Longitude: 73W57'58
Ayanamsha : -23:46:56 Lahiri

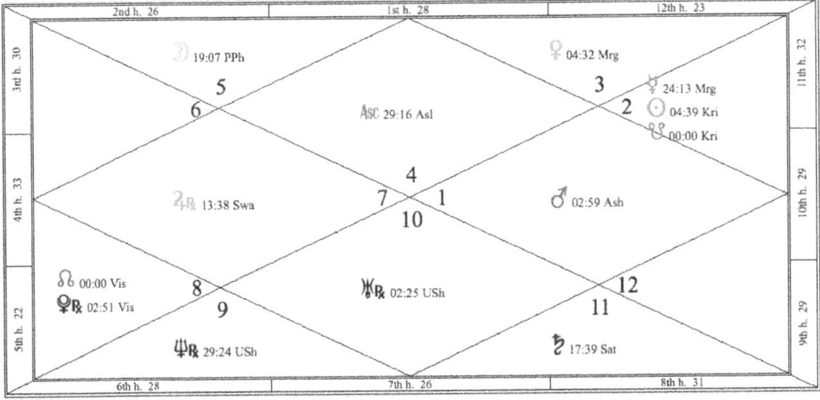

In the Dwadasamsha chart Jupiter, ruler of the 4th house is in the 12th house. Saturn is in the 11th house, again the 8th from the 4th house.

Transiting Saturn was at 17 degrees Aquarius in her 4th house of the mother and is fully aspecting natal Saturn, the ruler of the 4th house. It is aspecting natal Ketu in the 6th house of struggles. Transiting Jupiter was in the 12th house of hospitals and endings, aspecting her natal Rahu and Mars, and aspecting the 4th house of the mother.

The death of her brother was one the most difficult losses of all, for they were extremely close. He was a lifeline to her past and all the treacherous experiences that they endured together.

On July 16, 1999 her beloved brother John was killed in a plane crash. She was in the beginning of her Saturn maha dasha. In her Dreshkana chart Saturn is in the 1st house. Saturn is the dispositor of Mars and Rahu in the 8th house in this chart.

But again, the transits are the true signals of a serious problem. Transiting Saturn was at 21 degrees of Aries in her 6th house, fully aspecting her Rahu and Mars in the 12th house of loss, and Mars is the karaka for brothers. Additionally, transiting Mars was in the 12th house at 10 degrees Libra, aspecting natal Mars and Rahu and aspecting her natal Moon. Transiting Rahu and Ketu are in Cancer and Capricorn, and Ketu the indicator for loss is at 19 degrees Capricorn almost exactly conjunct her natal Moon in the 3rd house of siblings. Again her natal Moon is the focus of great loss and sadness.

Chapter 7

Edward Kennedy

The Kennedy that was apart of the most scandal and endured as much loss as Caroline was the baby brother in the Kennedy clan, Edward Kennedy (Teddy) was involved in the wrongful death of Mary Jo Kopechne, as he abandoned her in an overturned car while he was in a drunken stupor. This incident plagued his entire life with disgrace. He was never able to achieve a successful run for President.

4th h. 24	5th h. 26	6th h. 32	7th h. 29
♅ 23:55 Rev ♀ 18:39 Rev ☊ 03:20 UBh ♓	♈	♉	♇℞ 27:22 Pun ♊
3rd h. 26 ☉ 09:37 Sat ☿ 05:53 Dha ♂ 04:55 Dha ♒	Edward Kennedy Mon 02-22-1932 03:58:00 Dorchester, Massachusetts USA		8th h. 24 ♃℞ 22:49 Asl ♋
2nd h. 26 ♄ 06:54 USh ♑	Timezone: 5 DST: 0 Latitude: 42N17'50 Longitude: 71W04'28 Ayanamsha : -22:54:36 Lahiri		9th h. 22 ☽ 13:30 PPh ♆℞ 13:49 PPh ♌
Asc 17:54 PSh ♐ 1st h. 36	♏ 12th h. 32	♎ 11th h. 33	☋ 03:20 UPh ♍ 10th h. 27

2nd h. 26 | 1st h. 36 | 12th h. 32
3rd h. 26 | 11th h. 33
4th h. 24 | 10th h. 27
5th h. 26 | 9th h. 22
6th h. 32 | 7th h. 29 | 8th h. 24

9 — Asc 17:54 PSh
10 — ♄ 06:54 USh
11 — ♂ 04:55 Dha, ☿ 05:53 Dha, ☉ 09:37 Sat
12 — ☊ 03:20 UBh, ♀ 18:39 Rev, ♅ 23:55 Rev
1
2
3 — ♇℞ 27:22 Pun
4 — ♃℞ 22:49 Asl
5 — ♆℞ 13:49 PPh, ☽ 13:30 PPh
6 — ☋ 03:20 UPh
7
8

Let's analyze his chart in terms of his life and events.

Ted has a Sagittarius ascendant, and Jupiter ruler of his chart occupies the 8th house of death, charisma, scandal, and disgrace. His Jupiter is powerful (being exalted) but is retrograde. Many times an exalted planet is weakened when retrograde, but his promise is deflated as his Jupiter is debilitated in his navamsha. A planet's position in the navamsha reveals the outcome of the planet's positions in the birth chart. Planets that are exalted in the birth chart and become debilitated in the navamsha lose their strength later in life, but if a planet is debilitated in the birth chart and is exalted in the navamsha the reverse occurs, and they rise to power later in life.

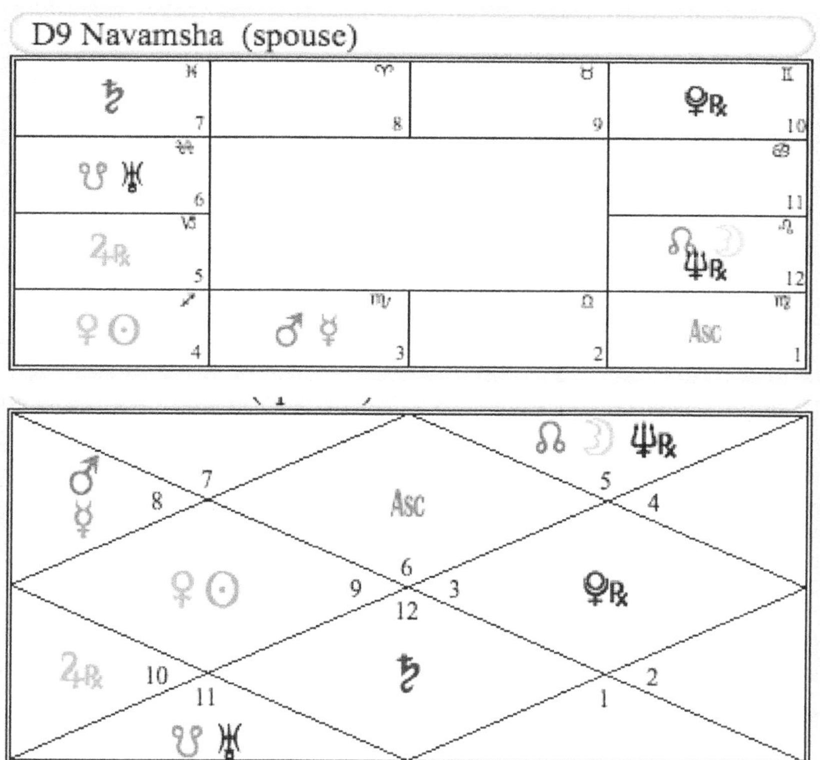

Looking at his 9th house of father, Edward Kennedy's father apparently put his energies into the older brothers and didn't have much hope for Teddy. In his 9th house he has the Moon, ruler of the 8th house conjunct Neptune. Neptune indicates a father who was dishonest and corrupt, but it can also allude to his father's dealings in the film industry. Neptune rules cameras and film. His father had indiscrete affairs with the Hollywood starlets such as Gloria Swanson. The lack of his success must have played out due to his difficult relationship with his father. It appears that his father felt that he was a disgrace to the family.

Ironically, Ted also has Ketu in his 10th house just as did his political brothers John and Bobby. The career was a part of his karma for good and bad throughout his life. In the seat of power sits exalted Venus and Rahu in the 4th house. Venus as ruler of the 6th house of health and conjunct Rahu can confer addictions. He battled alcoholism his entire life. Neptune with the natal Moon can lead to this conclusion as well, since Neptune can indicate alcohol or drugs, for it rules escapism.

But the most interesting house of all is his 3rd house (siblings) where he has Mars (karaka for siblings) with Mercury and the Sun. These three planets indicate sibling rivalry and a strong competitive nature. But since he was the youngest of the family the 3rd house of the youngest is the most powerful, indicating he is the youngest. The 11th house of older siblings is indicative of his brother's fate. Venus rules the 11th house and is between Uranus and Rahu, indicating sudden unexpected karmic events. Venus is exalted, indicating the power of these siblings, but with great loss.

Mercury rules the 10th house of careers and is in the 3rd house of siblings, meaning his brothers were the ones who inspired and gave him his opportunities. But Mercury being hemmed in between two malefics caused him to have problems with his career and problems in marriage, because Mercury rules both the 10th house of career and the 7th house of marriage.

He has Chandra Mangala yoga with Mars and Moon mutually aspecting each other through opposition. This breeds great business success. He was a congressman for Massachusetts. But Mars 7th from the Moon will cause great difficulties in marriage.

Let's see how the tragedies of his life can be predicted through our predictive uses of the dashas, transits and divisional charts.

The death of his siblings is revealed through his Dreshkana chart. The 11th house of older siblings has Mars ruler of the 8th house in this house along with the Sun and Mercury. The Sun represents their power but Mercury rules the 6th house representing difficulties and accidents. Pluto here indicates power and conspiracy. Mercury also rules the 3rd house indicator of all siblings.

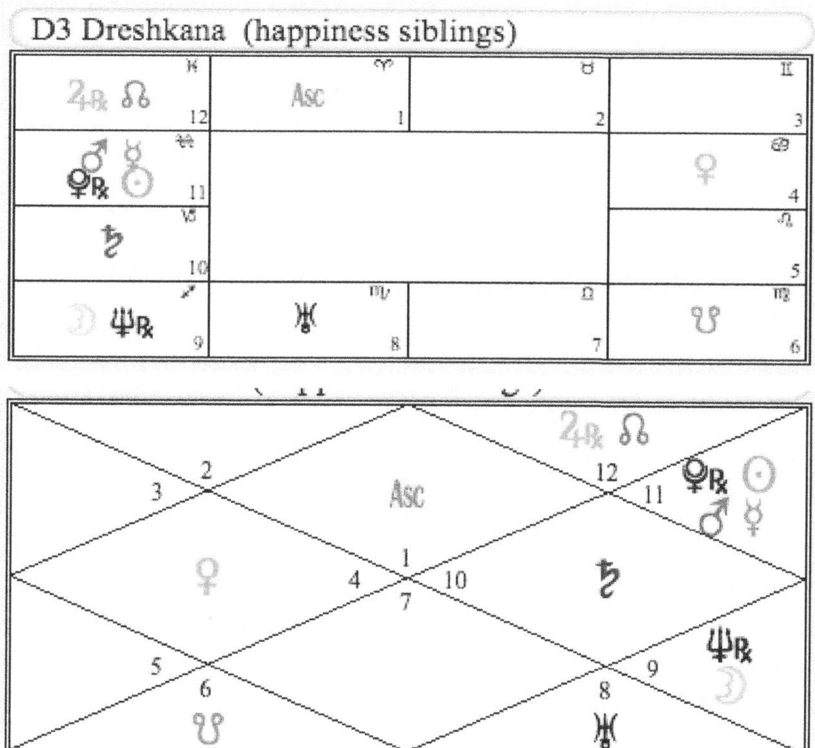

At the time of his oldest brother's death August 12, 1944 he was only12 years old. He was in Venus maha dasha, Jupiter bhukti. Venus is in the 4th house in all three charts birth, navamsha and the Dreshkana charts. This means his focus was around family matters. In his birth chart Venus rules the oldest sibling and is in the 4th house with Rahu and Uranus indicating an unexpected sudden event. Uranus can indicate accidents. His Jupiter is in the 8th house in the birth chart, and with Rahu in the 12th house of loss in the Dreshkana chart.

Period	Day	Date
♀ - ♃	Sat	01-17-1942
♀ - ♄	Sun	09-17-1944
♀ - ☿	Mon	11-17-1947
♀ - ☋	Sun	09-17-1950
☉ - ☉	Sat	11-17-1951
☉ - ☽	Thu	03-06-1952
☉ - ♂	Thu	09-04-1952
☉ - ☊	Sat	01-10-1953
☉ - ♃	Sat	12-05-1953
☉ - ♄	Thu	09-23-1954

The transits pinpoint this event as transiting Saturn was at 13 degrees Gemini exactly aspecting his natal Moon in the 9th house of father, indicating the deep loss the father felt, and the Moon as the karaka of the mother represents her loss too. But most importantly the Moon also rules the 8th house of death. Transiting Rahu was in the 8th house at 4 degrees Cancer activating the death potential, and Ketu was conjunct natal Saturn ruler of the 3rd house of siblings. Transiting Mars was 26 degrees Leo aspecting the natal Moon and the 3rd house with natal Mars, Mercury and Sun. Also, transiting Mars aspects the 4th house and the planets, Rahu, Venus, and Uranus with its 8th house deadly aspect. Venus is the dasha ruler and it rules the 11th house of the oldest sibling.

How did the sister's plane crash affect him? Kathleen was killed May 13, 1948. He was in Venus maha dasha and Mercury bhukti. Mercury is in the 3rd house of siblings conjunct Mars and the Moon aspects by opposition and rules the 8th house of death.

In the Dreshkana chart, Mercury (ruler of the 3rd house) is in the 11th house with Mars and Pluto. The 3rd and 11th houses are the houses of siblings.

Transits again nail the event, as transiting Mars was 4 degrees Leo, exactly opposed to natal Mars in the 3rd house of siblings, and Mars is the karaka of siblings. And transiting Saturn was at 23 degrees of Cancer, dead on exactly conjunct his natal Jupiter in the 8th house of death. Transiting Rahu was 20 degrees of Aries and Ketu was 20 Libra. Ketu was in the 11th house of older siblings, representing this loss. From the 11th house, Ketu aspected the 3rd house of siblings and aspected natal Mars (karaka of siblings), Mercury and Sun. And Rahu cast an aspect to the natal Moon, ruler of the 8th house.

At the time of the tragic assassination of his brother, President John Kennedy on November 22, 1963, he was in a Moon maha dasha and a Mercury bhukti. Both Mercury and the Moon aspect each other by opposition in the birth chart. Mercury is in the 3rd house of siblings and the Moon brings its 8th house rulership to Mercury.

☽ - ☿	Tue	09-17-1963
☽ - ☋	Tue	02-16-1965
☽ - ♀	Fri	09-17-1965
☽ - ☉	Thu	05-18-1967
♂ - ♂	Fri	11-17-1967
♂ - ☊	Sun	04-14-1968
♂ - ♃	Sat	05-03-1969
♂ - ♄	Thu	04-09-1970
♂ - ☿	Tue	05-18-1971
♂ - ☋	Mon	05-15-1972

His Mercury is in the 3rd house again in the navamsha chart. Mercury is with Mars, ruler of the 8th house of death and murder. The Moon is in the 12th house of loss with Rahu and Neptune, a loss that is surrounded by conspiracy, deception and hidden enemies.

In the Dreshkana chart the Moon is still with Neptune, but Mercury is in the 11th house of older siblings and it is with Mars, again ruler of the 8th house of death.

The transits are imperative in this event. Rahu and Ketu at 18 degrees of Gemini and Sagittarius affect this chart deeply as Ketu is exactly on his ascendant degree. And the midpoint creating a grand cross activated his natal Venus at 18 degrees of Pisces. Venus rules the 11th house of the older siblings. And again, incredibly, look at transiting Saturn at 23 degrees Capricorn - it exactly opposed his natal Jupiter in the 8th house of death. On the day his sister was killed transiting Saturn was exactly conjunct this degree. So this is around 15 years later since Saturn takes 28-30 years to go through the entire zodiac of a chart.

Neptune seems to be a key ingredient in the effect of these events since the lives of the Kennedys are surrounded by mystery, conspiracy and scandal. Look at transiting Neptune as it is at 22 degrees Libra in his 11th house, and exactly squares his natal Jupiter in the 8th house of death, and transiting Saturn is in opposition to natal Jupiter. That confirms the darkness and hidden secrets that surround this event.

Unbelievably, Ted was in a near fatal plane crash June 19, 1964, just seven months after his brother's assassination. Transiting Uranus was exactly conjunct his natal Moon in the 9th house of travel and the Moon rules the 8th house of death. He barely survived, but two others he was traveling with died. Transiting Mars was 8 degrees of Taurus and transiting Saturn was 11 degrees Aquarius, close to the natal Sun and opposed to the natal Moon. The natal Moon was involved in a T square with transiting Uranus, Mars and Saturn. This is definitely the indication of a dangerous accident. He is lucky to have survived.

It appears that someone wanted the Kennedys dead.

Transits: Teddy Kennedy Survived Airplane Crash

8th h. 35	9th h. 28	10th h. 25	11th h. 25
♓	♃ 22:22 Bha ♈	♂ 08:11 Kri ☿ 25:47 Mrg ♉	☉ 05:00 Mrg ♀℞ 05:27 Mrg ☊ 08:43 Ard ♊
7th h. 31 ♄℞ 11:39 Sat ♒	Survived Airplane Crash Fri 06-19-1964 12:00:00 Springfield, Massachusetts USA		**12th h. 23** ♋
6th h. 30 ♑	Timezone: 5 DST: 1 Latitude: 42N06'05 Longitude: 72W35'23 Ayanamsha : -23:21:21 Lahiri		**1st h. 30** ♅ 13:09 Mag ♇ 18:25 PPh ASC 25:09 PPh ♌
☋ 08:43 Mul ♐	♏	☽ 06:13 Cht ♆℞ 22:03 Vis ♎	♍
5th h. 27	4th h. 28	3rd h. 28	2nd h. 27

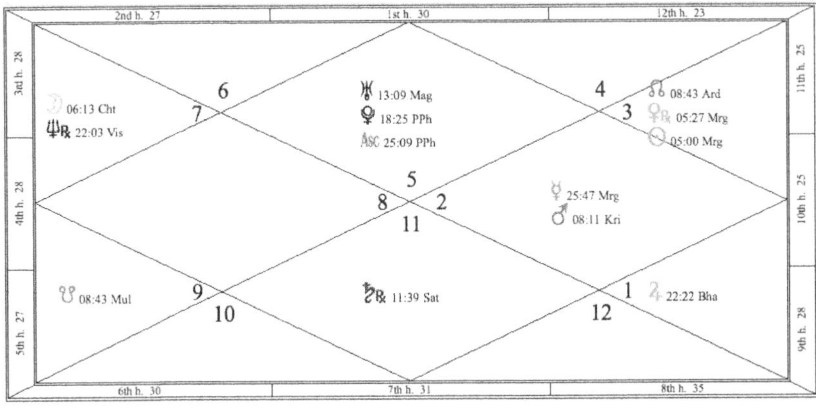

The assassination of his brother Bobby June 5, 1968 concerns another tragic event. How is his chart activated during this painful event? He was in a Mars maha dasha and a Rahu bhukti. Mars as the karaka of brothers is afflicted in all the divisional charts. But now that he is in this dasha it becomes more of a focus, and activates tragic events. Rahu is in the 12th house in both the navamsha chart and the Dreshkana chart.

On that horrific tragic day transiting Mars was in the 6th house at 25 degrees Taurus, aspecting the natal Moon in the 9th house ruler of the 8th house of death. It was aspecting the ascendant degree by its deadly 8th house aspect. But it was the transit of Rahu and Ketu that truly affected him severely at this time, for transiting Rahu was 23 degrees Pisces aspecting natal Venus, ruler of the 11th house of older siblings. Notice Rahu exactly aspected his natal Jupiter in the 8th house of death. Ultimately, his natal Jupiter seems to always be aspected at times of death.

Watch as his own demise can be predicted, by looking at aspects to his natal Jupiter. Exalted Jupiter here is an indicator of many deaths in a lifetime. Since his Jupiter disposits to his Moon in the 9th house, you may say that the family destiny was set in place due to the devious acts and karmas from the father. The Kennedy curse (as it has been named) originated with the father. This is revealed through the power and understanding of Neptune. Neptune is closely tied to his Moon. Neptune can indicate lies and deceit. The most disgraceful act concerning the young girl that downed in his car at Chappaquiddick was the ruination of his future and his career.

Lastly, transiting Saturn at 28 degrees Pisces is in the 4th house. This indicates the many deaths around his family and how it affected his mother. Then again, transiting Saturn conjunct natal Uranus in the 4th house affects the masses and his reputation. With natal Ketu in his 10th house he realized that he was next in line to run for the President of the United States, but the scandal brought him disgrace and humiliation.

Transits: Scandal at Chappaquiddick

1st h. 27	2nd h. 30	3rd h. 28	4th h. 32
Asc 08:44 UBh ♓	♄ 14:34 Bha ♈	♀ 19:42 Roh ♉	☿ 28:44 Pun ♊
12th h. 30: ☊ 29:02 PBh ♒	Scandal at Chappaquiddick Fri 07-18-1969 23:00:00 Chappaquiddick, Massachusetts USA Timezone: 5 DST: 1 Latitude: 41N23'14 Longitude: 70W30'16 Ayanamsha : -23:25:57 Lahiri		5th h. 25: ☉ 02:50 Pun ♋
11th h. 32: ♑			6th h. 33: ☽ 22:57 PPh ☋ 29:02 UPh ♇ 29:32 UPh ♌
♐	♆℞ 02:36 Vis ♂ 09:04 Anu ♏	♎	♃ 07:03 UPh ♅ 07:11 UPh ♍
10th h. 26	9th h. 23	8th h. 26	7th h. 25

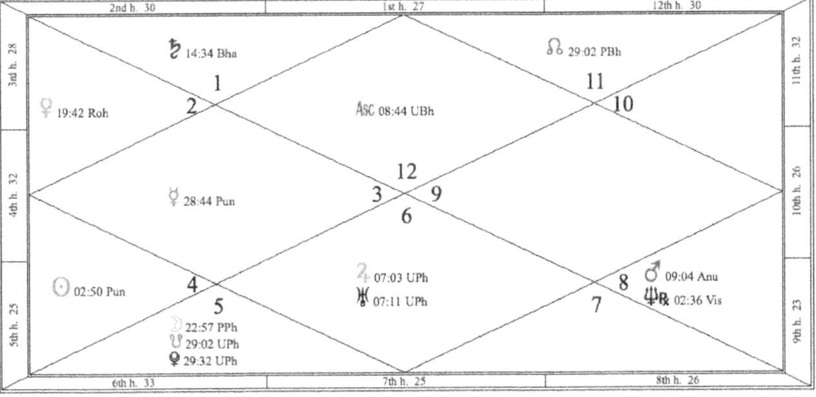

Ted's life took a turn for the worse with the scandal that occurred at Chappaquiddick on July 18, 1969. After a party in Martha's Vineyard, Ted left intoxicated with a young woman and overturned his car in the water. The young woman Mary Jo Kopechne died that night after Ted abandoned his car - she was found dead the next day. But he went home without reporting the accident until the next day after her body was found. The apparent lack of remorse and responsibility in the girl's death destroyed his future political career. Ted finally plead guilty in a serious court case concerning this incident. Five months later, on November 18, 1969 his father died. In 1980 he ran for President against incumbent President Carter and lost the run as the Democratic nominee. This was definitely due to the disgrace he experienced from this scandalous affair and incident at Chappaquiddick. This is the karma of natal Jupiter in the 8th house exalted but retrograde, and the Moon as the dispositor exactly conjunct Neptune. The 8th house has to do with disgrace, scandals and humiliation.

At the time of this disgraceful incident and his father's death he was in a Mars maha dasha and a Jupiter bhukti. Natal Mars is in the 3rd house and natal Jupiter is in the 8th house of disgrace and dishonor. Counting from Mars to Jupiter they are in a 6/8 relationship, which gives the effects of the 6th and 8th house. This was a horrible accident involving death and disgrace.

Jupiter is debilitated in the navamsha, and Mars is in the 9th house of father in the Dwadashamsha D-12 (parents).

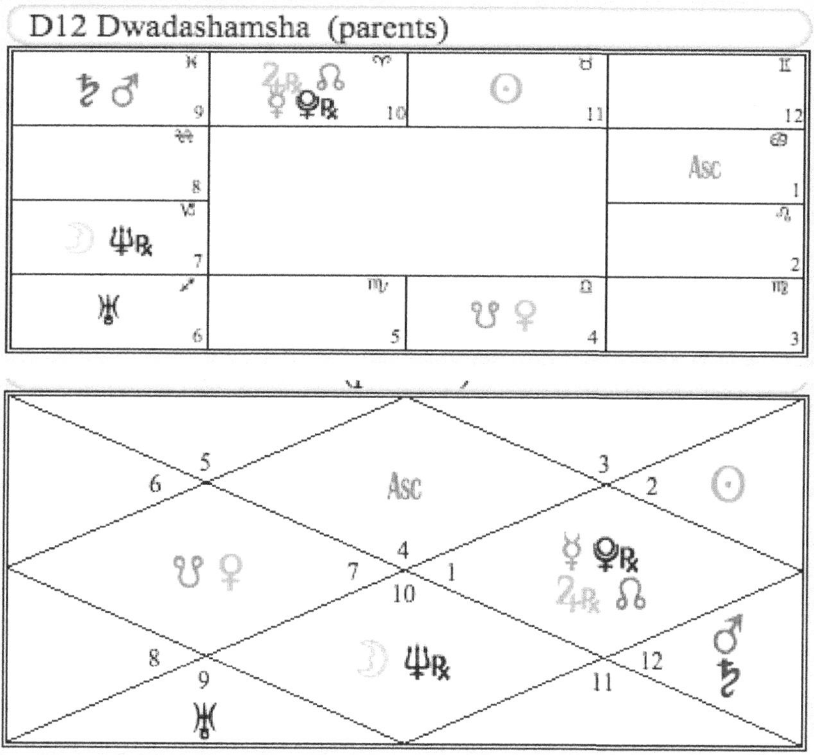

The transiting planets reveal the ultimate destiny of this disgraceful event. Notice that transiting Mars was at 9 degrees of Scorpio in the 12th house, exactly aspecting the natal Sun. The Sun is the soul and spirit of the chart, plus the Sun rules the 9th house of the father, and is the karaka of the father. This event lead to the demise of his father. Transiting Rahu and Ketu had just shifted signs; Ketu is 29 degrees of

Leo and Rahu is 29 degrees of Aquarius. But as the Moon's nodes begin to transit through Leo and Aquarius, Ketu is in the 9th house of law and justice. Ketu is conjunct the natal Moon (ruler of the 8th house) and Neptune (deception). And Rahu moves to conjunct his natal Sun, Mercury and Mars in the 3rd house. During this time the trail ruins any future aspirations he had for the Presidency.

In 1980 he tried to make his Presidential run, he was in a Rahu maha dasha and a Saturn Bhukti, but with both transiting Saturn and Rahu in Leo he was in a very difficult transit, for his natal Moon is in Leo. This is the depth of Sadhi Sati, when transiting Saturn is close to the natal Moon. His Moon, as the ruler of the 8th house brings disgrace, plus it is exactly conjunct natal Neptune. This indicates the disappointment and loss he experienced at the time.

☊ - ♄	Sun	12-23-1979
☊ - ☿	Fri	10-29-1982
☊ - ☋	Sat	05-18-1985
☊ - ♀	Thu	06-05-1986
☊ - ☉	Mon	06-05-1989
☊ - ☽	Mon	04-30-1990
☊ - ♂	Wed	10-30-1991
♃ - ♃	Mon	11-16-1992
♃ - ♄	Wed	01-04-1995
♃ - ☿	Fri	07-18-1997

On May 17, 2008 Ted had a seizure, which led to the discovery that he had brain cancer. His health declined from that point until his death on August 25, 2009. At the time of his seizure he was at the end of his Jupiter dasha. He was in a Jupiter maha dasha and a Rahu bhukti. His natal Jupiter is in the 8th house of death, which was a time he had to face his own demise. Natal Rahu is in the 4th house, which is sometimes viewed as the end of life.

♃ - ☊	Fri	06-23-2006
♄ - ♄	Sun	11-16-2008
♄ - ☿	Sun	11-20-2011
♄ - ☋	Wed	07-30-2014
♄ - ♀	Tue	09-08-2015
♄ - ☉	Wed	11-07-2018
♄ - ☽	Sun	10-20-2019
♄ - ♂	Thu	05-20-2021
♄ - ☊	Wed	06-29-2022
♄ - ♃	Mon	05-05-2025

In the navamsha chart, Jupiter is debilitated and Rahu is in the 12th house, but most importantly they are in an 8/6 relationship from each other, indicating a very difficult time in his life.

At the time of his death he had just entered into his Saturn maha dasha. It seems that his Jupiter dasha would have predicted his death, since it is placed in the 8th house of death, but Saturn is most definitely the indicator of death since it is in the 2nd house and rules the 2nd house. Death is most often predicted when in the dashas of maraka planets. Maraka planets are the planets placed in the maraka houses, or rulers of the maraka houses (the 2nd and 7th houses). His Saturn is also placed in the 7th house in his navamsha.

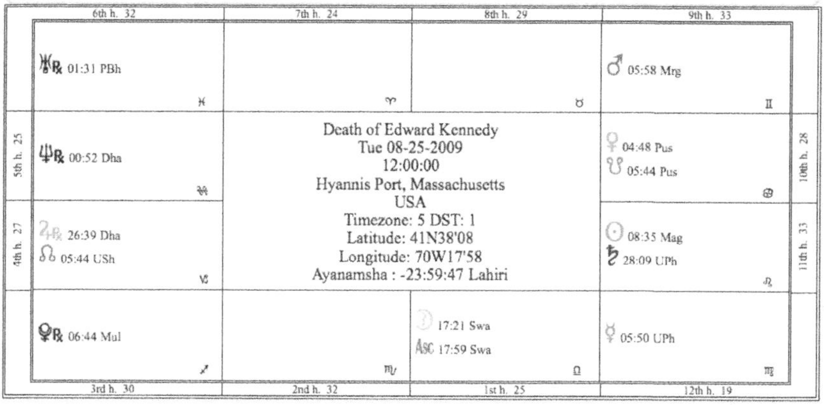

6th h. 32	7th h. 24	8th h. 29	9th h. 33
♅℞ 01:31 PBh ♓	♈	♉	♂ 05:58 Mrg ♊
5th h. 25: ♆℞ 00:52 Dha ♒	Death of Edward Kennedy Tue 08-25-2009 12:00:00 Hyannis Port, Massachusetts USA		10th h. 28: ♀ 04:48 Pus ☋ 05:44 Pus ♋
4th h. 27: ♃℞ 26:39 Dha ☊ 05:44 USh ♑	Timezone: 5 DST: 1 Latitude: 41N38'08 Longitude: 70W17'58 Ayanamsha : -23:59:47 Lahiri		11th h. 33: ☉ 08:35 Mag ♄ 28:09 UPh ♌
♇℞ 06:44 Mul ♐	♏	☽ 17:21 Swa Asc 17:59 Swa ♎	☿ 05:50 UPh ♍
3rd h. 30	2nd h. 32	1st h. 25	12th h. 19

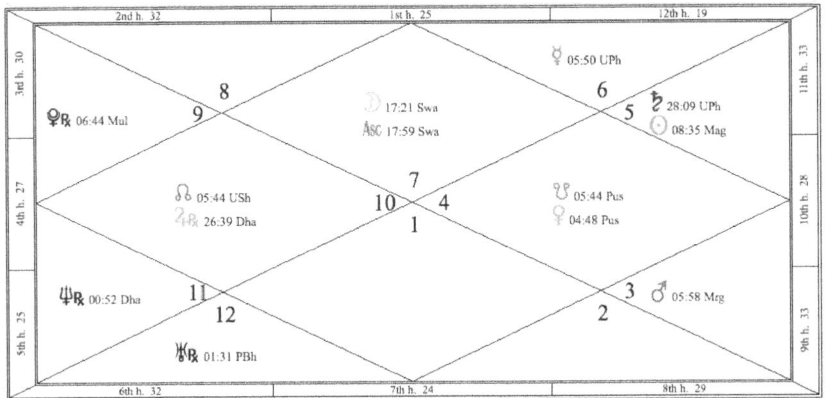

On the day of his death, August 25, 2009 transiting Saturn was 28 degrees of Leo, still in the sign of his Moon (Sadhi Sati). Transiting Jupiter was 26 degrees of Capricorn, aspecting natal Jupiter in the 8th house. Transiting Ketu was 5 degrees of Cancer in his 8th house, but transiting Rahu was directly conjunct his Saturn (maha dasha ruler) in his 2nd house (maraka house). Last but not least, transiting Mars was 5-6 degrees Gemini, which is aspecting natal Saturn exactly! This is precision in prediction.

With the amazing fate and destiny of the Kennedy family - American Royalty - after analyzing their charts, you wonder if we do or do not have free will. And you have to wonder if there was indeed a curse on their family. I believe their curse is merely their karmas, and that they were brought together to play out the karmas and destinies of their souls, or soul groups. Their charts were all configured together to bring about the destiny and the timing of these events played precisely as predicted. The Kennedys have taught us great and meaningful lessons about life, and yes, they were instrumental in my initiation into the art of astrology that began when I was eight years old in 1963.

GLOSSARY

Lagna = Ascendant, the sign rising on the eastern horizon at the time of birth. This determines the 1st house in a birth chart.

Kendras = Angles of the chart, houses 1, 4, 7 and 10. These houses are considered most powerful.

Bhavas = Houses, There are 12 houses in a chart that determine different life experiences and people. The houses are set up in accordance to the sign rising on the eastern horizon.

Bhavat bhavam = "from house to house" This is when a house is repeated in number. For example, 3rd from the 3rd (5th house), 4 from the 4th (7th house) or 5th from the 5th (9th house). The repetition of the numerical number indicates a similar basic core meaning.

Gochara = Transits, the movement of the planets in the heavens

Dasha = planetary cycles, this system of prediction is based on the nakshatras used in Vedic astrology. The natal Moon's nakshatra determines the cycles of a lifetime. There are 9 cycles that equate to 120 years.

Maha dasha = grand cycle, the grand cycle of a dasha lasts for the duration of the planetary cycle, but there are sub cycles within the grand cycle that determine events.

Bhukti cycle = sub-cycle – Within the grand cycle the bhukti is the next level or 2nd cycle, and is the most significant pertaining to events, and is viewed in relationship to the grand cycle.

Antara Dasha = a sub cycle within the grand cycle, it is the 3rd level down

Vargas = Divisional Charts, these charts are a mathematical division of the signs that represent a certain specific aspect of life.

Rashi chart (D-1) = original birth chart, all the divisional charts are derived from this chart.

Dreshkana chart (D-3) = divides the 30-degree sign into 3 parts of 10 degrees each. This chart concerns siblings, life force and courage. Also spelled as Drekkana.

Charturtamsha chart (D-4) = divides the 30-degree sign into 4 parts of 7.30 degrees each. This chart concerns wealth and gains from fixed assets such as real estate. Also spelled as Chaturthamsa.

Trimshamsha chart (D-30) = divides the 30-degree sign through a unique calculation into 5 parts of approximately 6 degrees each. This chart indicates misfortunes such as accidents. Also spelled as Trimsamsa.

Saptamsha chart (D-7) = divides the 30-degree sign into seven parts of 4.17 degrees each. This chart indicates children. Also spelled as Saptamsa.

Navamsha chart (D-9) = divides the 30-degree sign into nine parts of 3:20 degrees each. This is the most important chart and is always compared to the birth chart. It is called the fruit of the tree because it determines the results of life. It determines the second part of life and is also viewed as the marriage partner.

Dashamsha chart (D-10) = divides the 30 degree sign into 10 parts of 3 degrees each. This determines the career and social standing in life. Also spelled as Dasamsa.

Dwadashamsha chart (D-12) = divides the 30-degree sign into twelve parts of 2:30 degrees each It is the chart of the parents. Also spelled as Dwadasamsa.

Shodhashamsha chart (D-16) divides the 30-degree sign into 16 parts of 1:52'30" each, it is the chart of conveyances, which determines vehicles and cars. Also spelled as Shodasamsa.

Sadhi Sati = the seven and a half year period of the transit of Saturn in the sign before, sign of, and sign after the natal Moon. It is usually determined to indicate a difficult time in life. Also spelled as Sadhe Sati.

Chandra Lagna = The chart as viewed when the Moon is used as the ascendant. Transits from the Moon determine events in life as much as the birth ascendant.

Karaka= means indicator, as some planets rule specific things and people

Stirra Karakas = Stirra means fixed therefore there are specific things certain planets rule, such as Sun is father and the Moon is the mother.

Precession of the Equinoxes: The wobble of the earth that changes the reference point of the beginning of the zodiac. It takes around 26 thousand years to complete a cycle through all 12 signs. The precession cycles backwards through the zodiac.

Stationary planet= a planet that in the process of changing directions to retrograde or direct that appears to stand still. A planet becomes more intense while stationary.

Retrograde= When a planet appears to travel backwards through relation and speed from to the Earth. Planetary energy and what the planet represents changes during this time.

Dispositor= the planet that rules the sign a planet is in is the dispositor. Example: Venus in Aries, Mars is the dispositor of Venus, because Mars rules Aries, dispositors give the core essence or soul of a planet.

Eclipses = when the Sun and Moon align with the Moon's nodes (Rahu and Ketu). Eclipses occur during the New Moon (Solar Eclipse) when the Sun and Moon are conjunct with Rahu or Ketu or a Full Moon (Lunar Eclipse) when the Sun and Moon are in opposition with Rahu and Ketu. Eclipses seasons occur twice a year with Solar and Lunar eclipses occurring 2 weeks apart.

Drishti= aspects, specific degrees between the planets, there certain degree orbs between the planets that create events. Ex. Conjunction-0 degrees, Square-90 degrees or Opposition-180 degrees.

Shastastaka= literary means 6 and 8, which gives the effects of the 6th house and the 8th house. This is when 2 planets are placed 6 and 8 signs from one another. It is a very difficult aspect concerning accidents, difficulties and sometimes death or endings.

Yod= a configuration of 3 planets where one planet forms a quincunx (150 degrees) from 2 other planets. Within this configuration these 2 planets are in a sextile (60 degrees) from each other. This combination brings change through necessity and difficulty.

T-Square= involves 3 planets, all in hard aspect to each other, 2 are square (90 degrees) and the 3rd is in opposition (180 degrees). This combination creates obstacles that bring big change.

Grand Cross= involves 4 planets with 2 oppositions (180 degrees) and 4 planets forming a square (90 degrees). This combination causes great change and enormous stress due to the hard aspects of 4 planets simultaneously. This combination will involve planets in either cardinal, fixed or mutable signs, denoting a quality of energy involved.

Movable or Cardinal signs= Aries, Cancer, Libra and Capricorn – Extreme Action producing Events, Change, shifts of energy

Fixed or Stirra signs= Taurus, Leo, Scorpio, and Aquarius-unchangeable, constant and focused and concentrated energy

Mutable or Dual signs= Gemini, Virgo, Sagittarius, and Pisces-changeable, unpredictable, and uncertain shifts in energy.

Nakshatras= 27 divisions of the zodiac each 13 degrees 20 minutes. Their meanings are tied specifically to the fixed stars and mythology of these areas of the zodiac. They have planetary rulers, which determine the dashas, the predictive tool of Vedic astrology.

Rahu= north node of the Moon, where the Moon crosses the ecliptic (path of the Sun around Earth) ascending or moving upward. Indicates increase and gains with obsessions and sudden events that cause reversals.

Ketu= south node of the Moon, where the Moon crosses the ecliptic (path of the Sun around Earth) descending or moving downward. Indicates loss and sudden events that cause reversals.

References

All references to world events and the Kennedys came from Wikipedia and Biography.com

Other astrological references came from books by Joni Patry

Eastern Astrology for Western Minds

Astrology the Divine Order of the Universe

How to Make Money Using Astrology

Joni Patry Contact Information

joni@galacticcenter.org

www.Galacticcenter.org

YouTube: GetAstrologicNow

Facebook: Joni Patry Vedic Astrologer

Twitter: @jonipatry

Joni Patry

To read the stars is to read the messages of the Universe. Everything is in the stars, past, present and future. This gives the most powerful realization of who and what we are. This wisdom can transform humanity. Open and receive this most magnificent gift of the Universe, the gift of Astrology.

Joni Patry

Joni Patry is one of the most recognized teachers and Vedic astrologers in America. She was a faculty member for ACVA, CVA and Instructor for online certification programs, published many books, journals and appeared on national and international television shows. As the keynote speaker for international conferences, she has a Japanese website, writes for Saptarishi in India, Faces in Turkey and the Galactic Center. She specializes in Prediction, with books and websites for world, sports, and financial prediction.

Index

B

C

D

E

F

G

H

I

J

K

L

M

N

O

P

Q

R

S

T

U

V

Notes

Made in the USA
Coppell, TX
15 January 2021

48243801R00142